Advance Praise for
Trump, the Administrative Presidency, and Federalism

"This is an important, timely, and informative book. Three respected policy experts examine what the Trump administration has wrought during its first three years. While most discussions of the Trump presidency have focused on his often-outrageous rhetoric, to what extent has this administration affected public policy? We know that its legislative record is minimal, but what about the use of executive authority by the president himself and his appointees? This detailed look at a variety of policy arenas provides answers to these crucial questions."

—R. Shep Melnick,
*Thomas P. O'Neill, Jr., Professor of
American Politics, Boston College*

"In this timely and important book, the authors bring expertise in their respective fields of healthcare, the environment, and education to bear on the subject of the administrative presidency and federalism with an unusual degree of nuance, insight, and sophistication. It deserves to be read widely and will inform both the academic and policymaking communities."

—Timothy J. Conlan,
*University Professor Emeritus of Policy and
Government, George Mason University*

Trump, the Administrative Presidency, and Federalism

FRANK J. THOMPSON

KENNETH K. WONG

BARRY G. RABE

BROOKINGS INSTITUTION PRESS
Washington, D.C.

Copyright © 2020
THE BROOKINGS INSTITUTION
1775 Massachusetts Avenue, N.W.
Washington, D.C. 20036
www.brookings.edu

The Brookings Institution is a private nonprofit organization devoted to research, education, and publication on important issues of domestic and foreign policy. Its principal purpose is to bring the highest quality independent research and analysis to bear on current and emerging policy problems. Interpretations or conclusions in Brookings publications should be understood to be solely those of the authors.

Library of Congress Control Number: 2020938087
ISBN 9780815738190 (pbk)
ISBN 9780815738206 (ebook)

9 8 7 6 5 4 3 2 1

Typeset in Sabon LT

Composition by Elliott Beard

Dedicated to our present and former students,
and to a future student, David E. Green

Contents

Preface

This book seeks to illuminate the nature and efficacy of the Trump administrative presidency and how the forces of federalism shaped it in three important policy spheres: health insurance, as represented by the Affordable Care Act; climate change; and education. From the outset, we envisioned that the book would probe the first three years of the Trump administration. While covering his full first term might have been tidier analytically, we saw several advantages in having the volume published during an election year. With the invaluable support of the staff of the Brookings Institution Press, we pretty much stayed on schedule. In early March 2020, we finished reviewing the copyedited manuscript and sent it back to Brookings. We set the manuscript aside and anticipated waiting for the page proofs to review. Then the socio-economic and governance context of the book radically changed.

Beginning in mid-March, the COVID-19 pandemic exacted a dreadful toll on the United States and the world that in certain respects surpassed that of the great influenza pandemic of 1918. The coronavirus spread rapidly to hundreds of thousands of Americans, and the death toll from it mounted relentlessly. Many hospitals and other healthcare providers lacked basic supplies and could scarcely, if at all, cope with the demand for treatment. Meanwhile, as gubernatorial stay-at-home orders proliferated and vast multitudes practiced social distancing, the economy plummeted. The ranks of the unemployed soared, and experts predicted that GDP would shrink sharply in 2020. In response, a heretofore gridlocked Congress rapidly passed and President Trump promptly signed three major bills to ameliorate the health and economic damage wrought by COVID-19. While promoting a range of worthy objectives, this legislation promised to add trillions of dollars to the national debt and presented numerous implementation challenges. Meanwhile, the Trump administration took an array of executive actions in response to the disease while jousting with governors over who should take the lead in dealing with the pandemic and who had ultimate authority to close or reopen the economy and society. Many of the patterns we identify in this book resurfaced in the gripping new governance challenges that the pandemic in its initial stages posed.

The story of COVID-19 and government's response to it was unfolding as we wrote this preface. We had no crystal ball to predict the outcome. For present purposes, however, we thought it worth briefly considering whether at this early stage the pandemic has caused the Trump administration to abandon or significantly alter the executive initiatives of its first three years in the policy spheres described in this book. By and large, the pattern we observe suggests otherwise.

Not surprisingly, the pandemic sparked the greatest federal concern around issues of health policy. Among other things, it fueled questions about the adequacy of insurance coverage in the U.S. healthcare system. As chapter 3 describes, the Trump administration in its first three years had systematically sought to sabotage a major pillar of that system: the Patient Protection and Affordable Care Act (ACA), or Obamacare. The administration had launched executive actions designed to reduce enrollments in Medicaid and the ACA insurance exchanges, as well as promoted lower cost alternatives to the health insurance coverage offered through the exchanges, products which, among other things, often provided skimpy benefits and no protection for those with preexisting conditions. With the coronavirus crisis, millions of Americans suddenly faced the prospect of losing their employer-based coverage and needing to enroll in coverage through the insurance exchanges or through Medicaid. In response, President Trump signed legislation that poured additional monies into the healthcare system. Among other things, the legislation temporarily increased the proportion of Medicaid costs (the match) subsidized by the federal government relative to the states. To receive the enhanced federal match, state Medicaid programs had to cover COVID-19 testing and treatments. They also had to refrain from making their Medicaid eligibility criteria more restrictive, from increasing any premiums, and from terminating coverage for those enrolled when the emergency commenced. These provisions applied from January 1, 2020, to the end of the quarter in which the public health emergency represented by the coronavirus ceased.

The Trump administration also initiated certain incremental executive actions to forestall, at least temporarily, declines in Medicaid enrollments. It approved a new set of waivers sought by the states to increase their flexibility in administering Medicaid. It withdrew a rule designed to tighten state eligibility processes which, if implemented, would almost surely increase the administrative burdens on Medicaid applicants. It also delayed implementation of a "public charge" rule designed to discourage noncitizen residents legally in the country from using Medicaid.

On balance, however, the Trump administration's actions did not represent a reversal of its efforts to undermine the ACA. Despite pleas from Democrats, insurance companies, and healthcare providers to open a special enrollment window on the federally operated exchanges to accommodate those newly in need of health insurance, the Trump administration declined. While supporting a mandate that insurance companies pay for COVID-19 testing and diagnosis free of charge, it exempted the short-term health plans it had sponsored in its effort to circumvent the ACA's coverage standards. Most fundamentally, and despite calls to reconsider its position in light of the pandemic, the Trump administration persisted in its efforts, as described in chapter 3, to have the Supreme Court effectively destroy the Affordable Care Act. The court was scheduled to hear the latest legal challenge to the law's constitutionality in the fall of 2020. While promising to offer a better alternative to Obamacare, President Trump continued to offer no plan for doing so.

The pandemic did much less to roil federal policy developments in the climate and education arenas. Chapter 4 describes the search-and-destroy strategy that the Trump administration employed to reverse Obama-era initiatives to reduce greenhouse gases linked to climate change. The onset of the pandemic yielded no appreciable change in this strategy. Most notably, the Trump administration pushed ahead with efforts to promulgate new vehicle emission standards. These were far more modest than what the Obama administration had established or what California had sought through a long-standing waiver authority that had been reversed by the Trump administration. The administration also pressed the courts to provide timely and favorable decisions on legal challenges to other rules it had pursued to weaken climate regulations, despite the pandemic. Federal stimulus legislation largely bypassed the entire energy sector, although President Trump actively explored international and domestic options for propping up industries devoted to the production and refinement of oil and natural gas while ignoring economic challenges faced by renewable energy producers.

The pandemic also had little impact on Trump administration initiatives in education, as described in chapter 5. To be sure, the spread of the coronavirus profoundly reshaped the delivery of K–12 and higher education. Most classroom instruction across the country ceased, with faculty, students, and parents struggling to convert to various modes of remote learning while working from home. But decisions on closing educational institutions and shifting to distance learning primarily came from state policymakers and local school boards rather than from the federal government. Consistent with its general commitment to reducing federal involvement in education, the Trump administration was more a spectator than a participant as these developments unfolded. It did not, for instance, move rapidly to address disparities in broadband access and instructional quality in virtual instruction. However, a modest exception to this pattern occurred in the case of federal student loans. As discussed in chapter 5, the Trump administration had pursued several executive initiatives that adversely affected the interests of these borrowers. Faced with the pandemic, the Trump administration made an effort to accommodate this group by suspending their need to make loan payments for at least sixty days.

Acknowledgments

We have benefitted greatly from the assistance of others in writing this book. Two anonymous readers for the Brookings Institution carefully reviewed the initial submitted draft and offered perceptive, detailed suggestions. They greatly improved this book. Other readers also offered insightful comments along the way, including David Mechanic and Alan Monheit in the case of the Affordable Care Act, Norman Vig and Michael Kraft regarding climate policy, and John Dinan and Elizabeth Mann Levesque concerning education.

Each of us also benefitted from the strong support provided from our respective universities. At Rutgers, two doctoral students, Cynthia Golembeski and Apoorva Gupta, greatly assisted our efforts to track and fathom the evolution of the Affordable Care Act under the Trump administration. For his part, Bram Poquette unfailingly came to the rescue when asked for technical assistance in preparing the manuscript. Charles Menifield, dean of the School of Public Affairs and Administration at Rutgers-Newark, and Joel Cantor, director of the Rutgers Center for State Health Policy in New Brunswick, also supported the scholarly research that underpins this book in myriad ways.

At Brown, graduate students in the Urban Education Policy Program inspired a sharper focus on equity, diversity, innovation, and accountability in analyzing education policy. For their part, Henry Gaylord and

Asher Lehrer-Small provided invaluable research assistance. The writing of this book also benefitted strongly from the supportive interdisciplinary research milieu facilitated by the dean of faculty at Brown, the Annenberg Institute, the Taubman Center for American Politics and Policy, and the university's Department of Education.

At Michigan, graduate student Hannah Smith provided extensive research support and thoughtfully commented on multiple versions of the manuscript. Students Noah Rothstein and Annika Hoffmann contributed valuable research input on methane policy. So too students from two undergraduate classes and one graduate course offered useful insights in response to presentations of portions of this book during the 2019–2020 academic year. We also thank Thomas Cook, Sharon Disney, Bill Kelly, Theo Tangalakis, and Eric VanDeventer of the Gerald R. Ford School of Public Policy for their timely technical and administrative support throughout the project, including during the early months of the pandemic, as well as Bonnie Roberts and Tom Ivacko of the Center for Local, State, and Urban Policy for facilitating an authors' workshop during a key point of this project.

The staff of the Brookings Institution Press also provided strong assistance in the creation of this book. Once we submitted the initial manuscript, they obtained two detailed, insightful reviews within a month. They also achieved the highest standards of efficiency in the production process, once we submitted the revised draft. Our special thanks to Bill Finan, the press's director, who offered valuable advice from beginning to end, and Cecilia González, who more immediately managed the production process.

Finally, we thank our spouses—Benna Brodsky, Michelle Wong, and Dana Runestad—for their insights, support, good humor, grounding, and, above all, patience as we became increasingly (and at times singularly) preoccupied with completing this book.

While a constellation of individuals helped make this book a lot better than it would have otherwise been, we alone remain responsible for any errors of fact and interpretation in the current version.

ONE

Policy Transformation through Executive Branch Action

In early June 2018, the Justice Department announced it would not defend key provisions of the Patient Protection and Affordable Care Act (ACA, or Obamacare) from a suit seeking to overturn the law in a federal district court. Specifically, the Trump administration refused to back provisions of the health reform law that guaranteed Americans with preexisting conditions, such as high blood pressure, diabetes, or cancer, access to insurance at premiums comparable to those paid by healthier people. Democrats in Congress denounced the Trump administration for failing to defend the law, as the Obama administration had done. And Republican Senate Majority Leader Mitch McConnell asserted: "Everybody I know in the Senate—everybody—is in favor of maintaining coverage for preexisting conditions."[1] Nine months later, before a federal court of appeals, the Trump administration changed its position to argue, despite opposition from the Attorney General, that the entire ACA was unconstitutional.[2]

"What a glorious mess," thundered Representative John Dingell upon learning in 2007 that the Supreme Court had assigned federal responsibility for climate change to the Environmental Protection Agency (EPA) through a case brought by coastal states. "The only way in which that can be properly addressed is by seeing to it that the Congress goes in and cuts down the thicket so we can achieve an intelligent policy."[3] But Congresses have repeatedly failed to adopt policy on climate change since it reached the national agenda in the 1980s. President George W. Bush deflected that Supreme Court pressure, but successor Barack Obama swiftly embraced the same 2007 decision, ordering aggressive reinterpretation of multiple provisions of the 1990 Clean Air Act amendments. Donald Trump prioritized repeal, reversal, or delayed implementation of every major climate policy initiative advanced by his predecessor through executive action. He boasted in 2018 that he had begun to eviscerate all the climate policy steps of his predecessor, noting in one prominent case: "Did you see what I did to that? Boom. Gone."[4] The policy reality was far more complicated, however, and the glorious mess endures.

———————

In April 2017, Trump signed an executive order declaring: "It shall be the policy of the executive branch to protect and preserve State and local control over the curriculum, program of instruction, administration, and personnel of educational institutions, schools, and school systems, consistent with applicable law."[5] According to a senior official in the U.S. Department of Education, the executive order aimed to eliminate "top-down mandates that take away autonomy and limit the options available to educators, administrators, and parents."[6] More specifically, the executive order authorized Secretary of Education Betsy DeVos to conduct a comprehensive review of any federal regulatory and administrative rules that undermined state and local educational decisions and practices. According to an executive order supporter, the review would include "Dear Colleague letters, interpretive memoranda, policy statements, manuals, circulars, memoranda, pamphlets, bulletins, advisories, technical assistance, and grants of applications for waivers."[7] While President Barack Obama extensively used a spectrum of executive tools to expand federal involvement to address inequality in K–12 education, Trump shifted in the opposite direction.

———————

These three vignettes ostensibly have disparate policy foci, but they uniformly illustrate a salient feature of American governance—the degree to which executive branch action profoundly shapes policy. The last ninety years have witnessed a major transformation of American governance. Within the separation-of-powers system, a significant shift in discretion toward the executive branch has occurred—toward what many supporters of President Trump have called the "deep state." Congress has frequently lacked the capacity and will to write statutes that specifically shape the design and implementation of large, complex public programs. It has often explicitly delegated vast authority to the bureaucracy to make major decisions about these programs. Moreover, growing partisan polarization over the last four decades has interacted with highly competitive elections and the resulting "permanent campaign" to fuel congressional dysfunction. Manifestations of this dysfunction include a growing proportion of congressional staff devoted to party communications rather than the substance of legislation, a rise in the number of partisan message votes on bills that stand no chance of passage, and, more generally, congressional gridlock in the face of pressing policy problems.[8] Recent Congresses have struggled mightily to adopt new legislation in many areas of domestic policy.[9] Moreover, when programs run into troubles that undermine their effectiveness, Congress finds it nearly impossible to pass legislative amendments that repair them and get their implementation back on track.[10] Policy learning and maintenance become enfeebled. In the face of congressional dysfunction, pressures on the executive branch to step into the breach and shape policy have intensified.[11]

This development has raised important questions of democratic accountability. Some scholars underscore that it signals the growing power of a professional bureaucratic complex within the government. Writing a half century ago, Frederick C. Mosher[12] depicted the traditional distinction between policy and administration as a "myth" and noted the rise of "the professional state" whereby "in government, the professions are the conveyer belts between knowledge and theory on the one hand and public purpose on the other" (p. 103). In Mosher's view, various professional groups had staked out their turfs within an array of government agencies. They had become an "elite corps with substantial control over the operations of the agency" and "significant influence on agency policies" (p. 110). While acknowledging that political appointees in the executive branch might check the power of these professionals, he noted that many of them shared the educational backgrounds and outlooks of the career service (pp. 171–72). Sensing the risk of experts being "on top rather than on tap" in administrative agencies, Mosher expressed hope that professional education in universities and more generally might instill an ethos or mindset that would make "the professions safe for democracy" (pp. 213–14, 219).

More recent scholarly literature, however, calls into question Mosher's thesis concerning professional dominance. This research documents that the shift of major decisions to the executive branch has marched in lockstep with the surging importance of the administrative, or unilateral, presidency. The commitment and capacity of the White House and top political executives to shape who benefits from federal programs without changes in law, other forms of congressional approval, or the support of professionals within agencies has come under the microscope.

This book seeks to illuminate the dynamics of the administrative presidency under Donald Trump in three critically important policy arenas: health care, climate change, and education. In each of these spheres, the arrival of the Trump administration represented a *hostile takeover*[13] where highly salient White House policy goals departed sharply from the more "liberal" ideologies[14] and objectives of key agencies and actions taken by the prior presidential administration to realize them.[15] In all three domains, executive action in myriad forms loomed front and center in the Trump administration's efforts to reverse course. By focusing on the Trump administrative presidency in selected policy arenas, we address five major research questions. First, what were the goals of the Trump administration in these arenas during its initial period in office? Second, to what degree and in what ways (for example, tools and strategies employed) did the White House and Trump appointees strive to achieve their objectives via administrative processes? Third, to what extent did their administrative strategy succeed or fail in promoting these objectives, and are any accomplishments likely to prove durable? Fourth, what are the likely implications of executive actions for the achievement of key program outputs and outcomes in a given policy sphere (for example, health insurance coverage, greenhouse gas emission reduction, and student achievement)? Fifth, how do the cases advance understanding of the potential and limits of the administrative presidency as a vehicle for promoting or undermining democratic accountability in American governance?

This chapter provides the provenance for addressing these questions. We open by reviewing the growing literature on the administrative presidency. This research has cast considerable light on this phenomenon but has, until recently, neglected the implications of federalism when state and local governments serve as implementing agents of the national government. The chapter then turns to the particular characteristics of the Trump administration—the political context it faced as well as the values, knowledge, and executive skills the new president brought (or did not bring) to the position.

The Administrative Presidency Reexamined

Decisive unilateral actions by presidents date back to the early days of the republic. Thomas Jefferson's Louisiana Purchase and Abraham Lincoln's Emancipation Proclamation are but two in a sea of examples from American history. The executive actions presidents employ to shape domestic policy have become especially pertinent since the inception of what political scientists Sidney Milkis and Nicholas Jacobs term the "executive-centered administrative state" under Franklin D. Roosevelt in the 1930s and 1940s. In reviewing this historical development, they portray the period from the end of World War II to the late 1960s as a period where partisan concerns played a relatively modest role in shaping the administrative presidency. Since that time, however, and coincidental with a growing research focus on the administrative presidency, political polarization has "encouraged the White House to deploy executive power in the service of partisan objectives." They spotlight the presidency of Richard Nixon as a catalyst for this development, but identify Ronald Reagan as the pathbreaker in "exploiting administrative power for . . . partisan objectives."[16]

In his seminal work establishing the concept of the "administrative presidency" as an important research focus, political scientist Richard Nathan also underscored the significance of the Reagan presidency.[17] He portrayed Reagan as vastly more effective than Nixon in using executive branch tools to accomplish major policy objectives. Following in Nathan's wake, other scholars also pointed to Reagan as ushering in a "sea change"[18] in the emergence of an aggressive, partisan, finely tuned administrative presidency. As Robert Durant observes: "Upon assuming the presidency, Ronald Reagan relentlessly applied an administrative strategy in pursuit of his policy goals in a fashion and to an extent unprecedented in terms of its strategic significance, scope, and philosophical zeal."[19] Reagan embraced a spectrum of tools to promote his administrative presidency: a centralized mechanism for clearing (or rejecting) administrative rules, reorganizations, budget reallocations, and agency rulemaking. Above all, he used his appointment authority to staff agencies with officials personally loyal to him as well as deeply committed to his ideological and policy agenda.[20] More recent work has focused on how presidents pursue their objectives through executive orders, proclamations, directives, memoranda, signing statements, and the like. Political scientist William Howell finds such unilateral actions to be "the distinguishing mark of the modern presidency."[21]

Subsequent presidents built on the Reagan model to pursue their own vigorous, multifaceted versions of the administrative presidency. To be sure, Reagan's immediate successor, George H. W. Bush, toned down the politicization of the bureaucracy and made commitment to "movement" conservatism less central to the appointment process.[22] But the Clinton, second Bush, and Obama administrations aggressively employed executive actions to pursue their policy goals. While promoting objectives consonant with the values of much of the career bureaucracy, Bill Clinton moved to strengthen the role of the president in directing administrative agencies. According to Elena Kagan, "presidential control of administration, in critical respects, expanded dramatically during the Clinton years, making the regulatory activity of the executive branch agencies more and more an extension of the President's own policy and political agenda."[23] Clinton's strategy directly intersected with the legal question of whether congressional delegations of authority to an agency head were buffered from direct control by the president. Clinton strongly rejected this view. As Kagan notes, his "principal innovation in the effort to influence administrative action lay in initiating a regular practice . . . of issuing formal directives to executive branch officials regarding the exercise of their statutory discretion." By so doing, Clinton made administrative action "his own, in a way no other modern President had done."[24]

As we will subsequently discuss, Clinton also proved to be a pacesetter in the context of presidential federalism, expanding the use of program waivers as a tool of the administrative presidency. Prior to Clinton, the federal government had used demonstration waivers to the states sparingly and mostly to probe research questions generated by state implementation of welfare, Medicaid, and related social programs. The number and range of approved waivers under Clinton increased dramatically.[25] They became much less concerned with testing research hypotheses and much more focused on giving states the opportunity to expand policies that resonated with the Clinton administration's program priorities. The second Bush, Obama, and Trump administrations continued to use waivers in this expansive, programmatic fashion.

Upon assuming office in 2001, George W. Bush launched a muscular approach to the administrative presidency. His administration pursued a coordinated personnel selection process that resembled, and may well have eclipsed, that of the Reagan administration in its sophistication and emphasis on personal and ideological fealty to the president. The Bush transition team, for instance, created a more comprehensive database on applicants for presidential appointments than any incoming administration had ever assembled.[26] Bush followed past presidents in using the White House review of agency regulatory proposals to further his goals. He also actively employed executive orders and other directives. In January 2001, for example, he issued an executive order that established the White House Office of Faith-Based and Community Initiatives. This action sought to expand the role of religious organizations in government programs, among other things opening the door to federal funding of their activities. The Bush administration followed up by requiring pertinent agencies to audit procurement and other practices to identify factors that discouraged faith-based organizations from receiving federal grants to deliver social services.[27] Additionally, President Bush (with strong support from Vice President Richard Cheney) embraced unitary executive theory, repeatedly referring to it in signing statements. This legal doctrine departs massively from conventional practice in arguing that the president has sole responsibility for what occurs within the executive branch. It holds, for instance, that the president has the authority to remove commissioners in independent regulatory agencies for political reasons. More generally, it seeks to constrain congressional authority to limit presidential control over administrative agencies.[28]

The Obama administration has also drawn scholarly attention for its aggressive use of executive action to achieve policy and partisan goals. While claiming to have issued fewer executive orders than other presidents, Obama employed other administrative means to accomplish his ends. In the view of two observers, he "developed more creative tactics that framed administrative partisanship as more routine and less visible" and "brought informal but policy consequential tactics to a new level."[29] Continuing in the tradition of Bill Clinton, Obama issued numerous presidential memoranda to agency heads. These and related documents (for example, statutory findings, guidance materials) prompted these officials to make important policy changes.[30] In February 2011, for instance, the president determined that a 1996 statute prohibiting the federal government from recognizing same-sex marriages was unconstitutional, and he directed the Justice Department not to defend the law in court. In June 2012, the president provided guidance documents to the Department of Homeland Security that established Deferred Action for Childhood Arrivals (DACA), which shielded certain undocumented residents who had been brought to the United States prior to age sixteen from deportation. Obama, to a greater degree than his predecessors, also used the appointment of "policy czars" based in the White House to accomplish his presidential aims.[31] His administration issued numerous waivers to free states and their schools from the requirements of No Child Left Behind legislation passed under President George W. Bush. In these and countless other ways, the Obama administration pursued executive initiatives to further its policy and partisan goals.

The muscular, multifaceted versions of the administrative presidency that have emerged over the last four decades stem not only from the forces that have vitiated Congress in the policy process. They also reflect increasingly elevated public expectations about what a president should achieve. More than any other actor in the political system, the public holds the president responsible for developments in government, the economy, and broader society. Numerous media outlets aggressively cover the president in a twenty-four-hour news cycle, reinforcing the public's focus on him and stoking debate about his performance. As Elena Kagan has observed, "For the President not to lose control of the debate about him, he must grab the public stage and make the news himself" to "demonstrate action, leadership, and accomplishment."[32] With legislative achievements hard to come by, executive action becomes more alluring. In turn, a kind of one-way ratchet effect becomes more probable—the more presidents take control, the more the public (both liberal and conservative) expect them to do so. Partisans claim executive overreach when the opposing party controls the White House. But they fully expect presidents of their own party to adopt an aggressive approach to executive branch action.[33]

Presidential Federalism and Executive Action

This book also seeks to enhance understanding of the administrative presidency in the context of intergovernmental programs rooted in federalism. What does it mean for states to implement federal policies over an extended period in which those policies are whipsawed by shifting presidential federalism preferences and strategies rather than legislation? The national government relies on the states and localities to implement either partially or fully its policies in an array of areas—education, health care, housing, income support, environmental protection, transportation, and more. Early research on the administrative presidency paid scant attention to the special challenges presented by intergovernmental programs. More recently, however, studies have increasingly analyzed the ways presidents leave their mark on these programs through executive action. For instance, a growing body of research suggests that to improve their electoral prospects, presidents (often more than members of Congress) shape federal grant allocations to particular states.[34] More central to this book, presidents also seek to advance their policy preferences through executive action. For example, several studies have highlighted a pattern of "executive federalism" where presidential administrations negotiate with governors and, at times, state legislators to reshape and transform intergovernmental programs via the administrative process. They have stressed the dramatic importance of program waivers as a tool of the administrative presidency in education,[35] health care,[36] and other policy spheres.[37] As noted earlier, Bill Clinton did much to fuel this trend, and subsequent presidents have followed in his footsteps.

Presidential initiatives through waivers and other means often persuade states to be enablers of White House policy goals. Typically, some states welcome these actions, whereas others recoil at the prospect. They may even assemble roadblocks to the administrative presidency, substituting for a diminished Congress as a check on executive branch power. For instance, the environmental priorities of President George W. Bush precipitated a "collision between the administrative presidency and state experimentation."[38] More generally, states may decline to participate in a federal grant program or refrain from submitting waiver requests that are consistent with themes the White House is promoting. State officials may drag their feet or otherwise undermine the achievement of presidential priorities in their implementation of federal policies. They may also pass laws that impede the implementation of federally administered programs.[39]

In addition to governors and legislators, state attorneys general have since the mid-1990s loomed especially large in challenging executive branch actions and congressional legislation.[40] Elected to office on a partisan basis in forty-three states, attorneys general often act independently of other state policymakers to file suits in the federal courts. At times, they collide with their governors and can be elected from different political parties. As befits a period of intense partisan polarization, attorneys general have organized themselves by political party, with the Republican Attorneys General Association, formed in 1999, and its Democratic counterpart, formed in 2002. In addition to fundraising, these associations play pivotal roles in devising and coordinating legal strategies to advance their partisan agendas. At times, presidential initiatives benefit from the broad, bipartisan support of state attorneys general.[41] Frequently, however, presidents can count on the vigorous support from attorneys general from their own party and strong opposition from those of the other. The associations of attorneys general often work closely with private interest groups that share their ideological perspective in pursuing litigation (for example, business associations in the case of Republicans and liberal advocacy groups in the case of Democrats). Forging alliances with private groups often bolsters the financial capacity of state attorneys general from both parties to hire prominent private lawyers to direct their lawsuits.

Moreover, two trends in federal jurisprudence have enhanced the leverage of these officials. First, the federal judiciary has granted states "special solicitude" in determining whether they have standing to bring suits, which makes it easier for state attorneys general to access the courts. Second, state attorneys general have gained leverage from the increased willingness of federal district court judges to issue sweeping injunctions that block executive actions nationwide rather than in more limited domains.[42] This development further increases the number of potential veto points for presidential initiatives in the American system of fragmented governance.

A Focus on Implementation under Hostile Takeover

Viewed broadly, research on the administrative presidency has devoted considerable attention to such tools as political appointments and executive orders. It has offered broad characterizations of executive branch strategies pursued by various presidents. Fewer studies, however, have focused on the implementation of presidential initiatives—their dynamics; whether they, in fact, advance White House goals; and the resulting implications for public policy.

Robert Durant's study of the Bureau of Land Management in the Interior Department under President Reagan illuminates the potential contribution of such implementation studies.[43] Durant describes how Reagan's appointees worked diligently to reduce regulation of public lands, foster economic development on them, and enhance local control. Drawing on evidence from New Mexico, he examines the politics that played out as these administrators sought to accomplish White House goals in four cases, involving rangeland management, land exchanges to facilitate urban development, water projects, and coal mining on public lands. His meticulous analysis of the cases leads Durant to conclude that Reagan appointees made "some progress towards the President's goals in each" (p. 251) but that gains were often modest and, in the case of coal leasing, "Lilliputian" (p. 193). Further progress in advancing a theory of the administrative presidency partly depends on adding to the pool of in-depth implementation studies akin to Durant's. This book's comparative analysis of the Trump administration's hostile takeover of the federal bureaucracy in the health, climate, and education arenas contributes to that research objective.

In pursuing this objective, two caveats deserve note. First, our focus on the policy implications of a hostile takeover contrasts sharply with another body of implementation research on the administrative presidency. Various scholars have underscored that unilateral actions such as executive orders or other presidential decisions leave open the question of whether they will be implemented in ways that comply with a president's preferences.[44] They have presented cases that demonstrate the limits to presidential influence. Often, these accounts focus on executive orders or actions that are not publicly salient, are of low priority to a presidential administration, reflect more incremental policy shifts, and may be initiated later in a presidential term.[45] In contrast, hostile takeovers involve high priority, politically salient presidential efforts to reorient a major policy. They tend to be signature actions of a president upon taking office. As such, the causal dynamics shaping the implementation fortunes of a hostile takeover are likely to differ appreciably from those of less prioritized and visible presidential actions involving more incremental policy adjustments.

Second, given our focus on the first three years of the Trump administration, we can only partly address the issue of durability; that is, whether the policy shifts his administration galvanized will endure beyond one term.[46] Still, our research illuminates discussions of the administrative presidency and policy durability. We explicitly consider the degree to which the Trump administration succeeded or failed in undermining Obama's policies in our three spheres. We also engage in informed assessment of the extent to which Trump's executive actions seem likely to be resistant to sharp reversal by subsequent presidential administrations.

The Administrative Presidency of Donald Trump

The dynamics of an administrative presidency partly depend on the partisan context a president faces. Three key partisan characteristics marked the first term of the Trump administration. First, Republicans controlled the presidency and both houses of Congress (for the first time since 2006) during the critically important first two years of Trump's hostile takeover. This not only heightened prospects that Trump's legislative proposals might win approval, it also suggested that Congress would be less likely to check the exercise of executive authority via vigorous oversight. Unified Republican government gave Trump a partisan advantage that Ronald Reagan, George H. W. Bush, and (for part of his term) George W. Bush did not enjoy. After the 2018 midterm election, Democrats won control of the House of Representatives. This greatly increased House oversight of Trump's executive actions in our three policy arenas. But with Republicans firmly in control of the Senate and presidency, the Democrats stood virtually no chance of overriding Trump's administrative initiatives through legislation.

Second, Republicans dominated state governments. The party occupied thirty-three governorships and controlled both legislative chambers in thirty-two states during most of Trump's first two years. (Republicans held more state legislative seats than at any time since the 1930s.) Republicans controlled the governor's office and both legislative chambers in twenty-five states compared to just seven states for the Democrats. This enhanced prospects for Trump administration initiatives (for example, the promotion of work requirement waivers targeting Medicaid enrollees) that depended on state cooperation for their success. The federalism context became somewhat less politically hospitable to the Trump administrative presidency after the 2018 midterms. As 2019 dawned, the number of Republican governors had declined by about 20 percent, to twenty-seven. States where Republicans controlled both houses of the legislature stood at thirty, and the number where they controlled all three elective branches had dropped to twenty-two. Meanwhile, states under unified Democratic control had doubled, to fourteen. While this context was less favorable to Trump's executive initiatives, the administration could still count on a sympathetic hearing from policymakers in about half of the states.

Third, Republicans held the office of attorney general in twenty-seven states, compared to twenty-one for the Democrats (with two being nonpartisan) when Trump took office. After the 2018 election, this balance shifted, with Republicans holding twenty-four of these offices and Democrats twenty-five (one nonpartisan).[47] The precise numbers are not very important, however, since a dedicated minority of attorneys general can still do much to stymie executive initiatives in the courts. From the start, Democratic state attorneys general assumed the adversarial role their Republican counterparts had played during the Obama years.

The fortunes of an administrative presidency also depend on the knowledge, values, and skills of a chief executive. In this respect, the Trump administration raised questions of competence that prior presidencies had not. Transition planning under Trump was vastly less developed that those of his predecessors.[48] Moreover, an assortment of commentators noted Trump's general "disengagement" from the specifics of policy and management.[49] The turnover levels in the White House and in many departments created a sense of administrative chaos. For instance, one analysis of White House turnover among Trump's "A Team" of top-ranked staff greatly exceeded those of five predecessors, going back to Ronald Reagan.[50] Amplifying this theme, David Frum, a former speechwriter for President George W. Bush, noted how Trump's "unstable temperament: his self-pity, his tantrums, his blame shifting . . . created a snake pit working environment." So, too, did the president's uncoordinated social media tweets, emphasis on personal loyalty to the point of encouraging sycophancy, and short attention span reinforce low opinions of his managerial capacity and skills.[51] Others noted that Trump's real estate business had not necessitated that he deal with stockholders or a board of directors, experience that might have enhanced his understanding of how to deal with the myriad stakeholders in the U.S. system of fragmented governance.[52] In summing up evidence on President Trump's first year as a manager, a leading political scientist and his associates concluded that "while the president claims expertise as a manager . . . his approach had few of the visible hallmarks of a successful executive in business or government."[53]

Moreover, the glacial speed at which Trump moved to fill political appointments, a key tool of the administrative presidency, also drew attention. An incoming president has the authority to make about 4,000 political appointments to federal positions, with roughly 1,200 of them requiring Senate confirmation.[54] At times, the president made remarks that suggested limited appreciation for this tool as a means to impose his will on the bureaucracy. For instance, eight months into his presidency, Trump asserted, "I am not going to make a lot of these appointments that would normally be—you don't need them."[55] The White

House Personnel Office, which under Ronald Reagan and George W. Bush had won recognition for masterfully placing administrators loyal to the president throughout the bureaucracy, attracted media attention for incompetence under Trump.[56] The presidential personnel office employed fewer than forty people, compared to more than 100 for most presidential administrations.[57] By mid-2018, the Senate had confirmed appointments for about half of the 673 "key positions" that required its approval; the Trump administration had yet to submit nominees for 186 of these posts and generally lagged behind four prior presidents in filling these top jobs.[58] Top political appointees often found the slow pace of appointments to subcabinet positions particularly frustrating.[59] These developments threatened to thrust significant decisions into the hands of career civil servants who were unsympathetic to many Trump initiatives.

Could a chief executive with this panoply of deficits possibly mount an effective administrative presidency? Initial research on the Trump administration suggested that the answer is a resounding yes. General assessments of Trump's first year in office point to his executive actions (along with his judicial appointments) as a sphere of achievement.[60] For instance, two academic observers wrote that the "speed" with which Trump has undone Obama administration executive initiatives "is impressive." In their view, the initial period of the Trump administrative presidency shows that "the President's ability to control administration has become sufficiently powerful that erasing a prior Administration requires little more than determination—and perhaps a dash of ruthlessness."[61] These analyses suggest factors that have mitigated some of the president's leadership and managerial deficits. Of particular importance, Trump's approach to political appointments, for all its ostensible limitations, at times served his policy objectives. The role of Vice President Mike Pence proved pivotal in this regard. As one political scientist has observed, many of Trump's top-level political appointments in the departments were "names he got from Pence." The vice president "was exceptionally well-wired in established conservative circles, and his recommendations reflected that."[62] Hence, the top cabinet positions tended to be filled with loyal ideological conservatives who shared many of the president's (and, perhaps even more, the vice president's) policy inclinations.[63] With little specific direction from the White House, they diligently worked to reverse Obama administration initiatives in the policy arenas examined in this book.

The degree to which the Trump administration's executive actions have achieved strategic sophistication and efficacy resides, of course, at the heart of this book's focus. Subsequent chapters support the theme that Trump's administrative presidency has made some headway in achieving its policy goals in health care, climate policy, and education. They document how Trump has pushed the envelope of executive action to unprecedented levels in the annals of the administrative presidency. But our analysis also suggests the limits to executive action as a vehicle for policy transformation in these spheres. While considerable uncertainty shrouded the executive achievements of the Trump administration after its third year, the period provides a cautionary note about the president's ability to master policy implementation challenges associated with the administrative presidency.

Why Not Immigration Policy?

Each of the policy spheres examined in this book provides an excellent provenance for illuminating the dynamics and efficacy of the administrative presidency under the conditions of a hostile takeover where the forces of federalism loom large. But issues of external validity inevitably arise. Would similar dynamics and levels of presidential attainment apply in other politically salient domestic policy spheres where states and localities play a large implementation role? In considering this question, immigration policy stands front and center. Donald Trump's presidential campaign, above all, promised radical change in the country's approach to immigration. His administrative presidency has vigorously sought to seal the country's borders from those seeking illegal entry; to track, detain, and deport undocumented residents currently in the United States; and to deny public benefits to unauthorized residents.

Trump's unprecedented executive actions in the immigration arena undoubtedly deserve detailed analysis by students of the administrative presidency. Several practical reasons inhibited us from pursuing such inquiry for this book.[64] In addition, we concluded that the forces of federalism, while certainly present, were not as consistently manifested in the immigration sphere as in our three policy arenas.

To be sure, federalism left its mark on the Trump administration's efforts to locate, detain, and deport 10 million to 12 million undocumented immigrants residing in the United States. The Illegal Immigration Reform and Immigrant Responsibility Act of 1996 had invited local government collaboration with the federal Immigration and Customs Enforcement agency (ICE) in apprehending and detaining the undocumented. In response, many localities, typically in more conservative political areas, signed agreements to assist ICE. Meanwhile, other local officials declared their jurisdictions to be "sanctuary cities," where law enforcement would not assist in identifying and detaining the undocumented. To punish these jurisdictions, the federal government attempted to withhold grant funds from them. As of early 2020, different appellate courts had issued conflicting rulings on the legality of this initiative.[65] Meanwhile, the acting director of ICE pointed to sanctuary cities as part of the reason that arrests and deportations of unauthorized residents declined by 10 percent from federal fiscal year 2018 to 2019.[66]

The forces of federalism also have manifested themselves in the degree to which states and localities have put down the welcome mat for the undocumented by offering them public benefits. Among these benefits are in-state tuition rates for public higher education, state financial aid for students, access to drivers' licenses, and state-funded health care. In turn, other states and local governments, in addition to collaborating with ICE, have offered none of these benefits, instead requiring verifications for employment that hinder the unauthorized from obtaining jobs. As in our three policy arenas, partisan factors substantially predict state behavior. Blue states tend to be more accommodating to the undocumented and red states more aversive.[67]

The dynamics of federalism have, however, been less present in Trump administration efforts to keep migrants from entering the country. To be sure, state attorneys general filed suits against the travel bans that Trump imposed on citizens from certain countries upon taking office. But many of the administration's executive initiatives to halt the flow of migrants across the Mexican border have focused on the national bureaucracy, sidestepping states and localities. These initiatives have included such actions as the presidential proclamation of a national emergency enabling the diversion of funds from other federal agencies to the construction of a border wall. They also have featured a series of executive actions that have slowed the processing of political asylum claims and made it harder for migrants to enter the country while waiting for their claims to be processed. These actions left thousands of petitioners housed for extended periods in makeshift camps across the Mexican border.[68]

Trump executive actions to close off the border have, to a much greater degree than our three cases, featured foreign policy initiatives. The Trump administration has pursued various initiatives to pressure Central American countries and Mexico to impede the travel of migrants to the U.S.-Mexican border. For instance, it persuaded Mexico to deploy thousands of security forces to help detain migrants traveling through that country en route to the border. These actions have led to a sharp drop in the number of migrants trying to cross into the United States.[69]

In sum, the immigration policy arena under President Trump presents extremely fertile ground for the study of the administrative presidency under the conditions of a hostile takeover. It also partly illuminates the dynamics of federalism that comprise the heart of this book's analytic focus. But the forces of federalism do not as comprehensively permeate the immigration domain as they do the ACA, climate policy, and education arenas.

Overview

This chapter has highlighted a major trend in the American polity—the growing role of the executive branch in shaping who gets what, when, and how from the government. This development stoked concern that career professionals in the bureaucracy, what supporters of Donald Trump often term the "deep state," have come to wield democratically unaccountable power and influence. But a substantial body of evidence counters this vision, pointing to the rise of a muscular administrative presidency in shaping the exercise of administrative discretion. Concern about democratic governance here centers less on the career bureaucracy and more on whether presidents have gained excessive influence relative to Congress and the rule of law.

This study seeks to enhance understanding of the potential and limits of the administrative presidency as a vehicle for achieving a president's goals under conditions of a hostile takeover. It does so by examining the implementation dynamics and efficacy of the Trump administration's executive initiatives to reverse Obama-era policies in health care, climate change, and education.

The next chapter sets the policy stage for the Trump administrative presidency by examining the Obama-era policy legacy in each of our three spheres. In addition to legislative developments during these eight years, it briefly describes the often-aggressive executive actions the Obama administration pursued. Chapter 3 assesses the Trump administration's efforts to sabotage and, ultimately, destroy the signature legislative achievement of his predecessor—the ACA. President Trump pursued executive initiatives to vitiate this law even prior to the collapse of major congressional efforts to repeal it in 2017. The steps Trump took undermined the reform law's insurance exchanges, Medicaid expansion, and quality assurance provisions. Chapter 4 examines Trump administration initiatives to reverse Obama's policies that had sought to reduce greenhouse gases. It explores the administration's withdrawal from an international agreement to reduce greenhouse emissions (the Paris Agreement) as well as its aggressive efforts to reverse, weaken, or delay regulatory efforts addressing climate change across multiple sectors of the economy. These include far-reaching disruption of a unique intergovernmental partnership that had enabled California to be a pacesetter among states seeking to reduce vehicle emissions for more than half a century. Chapter 5 targets the Trump administration's efforts to reshape the federal government's role in education policy. The weakening of federal direction and oversight with respect to civil rights and the handling of sexual misconduct on campus comes under the microscope, as do efforts to expand school choice. Trump initiatives to undercut regulation of and otherwise encourage for-profit higher education institutions also receive attention.

Chapter 6 extracts lessons from a comparative analysis of the administrative presidency as hostile takeover in the three policy arenas. We compare similarities and differences in the objectives of the Trump administration in the three spheres, as well as the tools and strategies it employed to accomplish them. We also assay the degree to which the Trump administration accomplished its policy objectives, and strive to explain differences in the level of achievement. This discussion intersects with issues of the extent to which Obama-era policies proved durable in the face of efforts to undermine them. It also raises the broader issue of the extent to which the policies embody cost-effective, impactful ways to deal with pressing problems in our three spheres. A concluding section deals more explicitly with the implications of our findings for the fabric of American democracy. To what degree did the courts and the forces of federalism substitute for an ineffective Congress in checking actions of the Trump administration that threatened the separation-of-powers system and the rule of law?

TWO

THE OBAMA POLICY LEGACY

The book examines three important policy spheres, each with an intergovernmental dimension rooted in federalism, where the Trump administration held strong preferences that ran contrary to the more ideologically "liberal" missions and actions of pertinent agencies, especially as manifested under the Obama administration. In each case, the political appointees responsible for administering programs shared and even doubled down on President Trump's commitments to reverse policy directions. Hence, the cases provide an excellent foundation to advance our knowledge of the dynamics and efficacy of the administrative presidency under the conditions of a hostile takeover. To provide a baseline for establishing the ways and degree to which the Trump administration strove to reverse the policies of his predecessor, the next three sections briefly assay the Obama policy legacies in health, climate, and education.

The Affordable Care Act

Approved in late March 2010, the Patient Protection and Affordable Care Act was President Obama's signature achievement—the most significant legislative breakthrough in extending health insurance coverage since the passage of Medicare and Medicaid in 1965. The ten titles of the sprawling law addressed a cornucopia of topics, but three initiatives went to its heart. First, the law expanded Medicaid, which over the decades had become by far the largest grant program to the states, providing health insurance to well over 60 million low-income people. The Affordable Care Act (ACA) mandated that, with certain exceptions, Medicaid would cover all nonelderly, nondisabled people with incomes up to 138 percent of the poverty line. It called for the federal government to pay the entire cost for the newly eligible for three years starting in 2014. In 2017, this federal match would start to decline before leveling off at 90 percent in 2020. An estimated 16 million uninsured Americans would gain coverage this way.

Another 16 million were to obtain insurance via state-based exchanges (or marketplaces), the ACA's second major pillar. Individuals and small businesses (that is, those with up to fifty full-time-equivalent employees) would be able to purchase insurance from private companies participating on the exchanges.[1] People with incomes between 100 and 400 percent of the poverty line would receive federal subsidies to buy this insurance. Those with incomes below 250 percent of poverty would receive additional help. In return for not charging this cohort certain deductibles and copayments, insurance companies would receive cost-sharing reduction (CSR) payments from the federal government. The marketplaces rested on a governance strategy of partial preemption. The federal government would provide states with grants to plan and establish their own exchanges. But if a state declined to do so, federal officials would step in to create and operate one. Insurance carriers participating in the exchanges would have to offer "qualified health plans" that covered certain services and met other standards. To encourage insurance companies to participate and hold premiums down, the ACA adopted various risk-reduction mechanisms to ease the burden on carriers that attracted disproportionate numbers of less healthy, more expensive patients. Keeping the lid on premiums also necessitated that insurance companies have balanced risk pools with many healthy enrollees. To encourage such pools, the ACA imposed a tax penalty on individuals who failed to obtain insurance (the "individual mandate").

Federal regulation to enhance the quality of all insurance sold in the individual and small group markets (not just the exchanges) comprised the third major pillar of the ACA. Prior to 2010, the states held primary responsibility for regulating these insurance markets, and they varied considerably in their policies. (Large employers tended to self-insure and were subject to light federal regulation.) This regulatory context meant that many individuals had insurance that covered limited services and did not provide them with protection against bankruptcy in the event of severe, prolonged illness. Individuals with preexisting conditions also had difficulties obtaining and retaining affordable coverage.

To remedy these and other deficiencies, the ACA imposed an array of regulatory requirements. Among other things, it required insurers to cover ten essential health benefits (including mental health services). It also provided "guaranteed issue" to those with preexisting conditions, forbidding insurance companies from denying them coverage and from charging them appreciably more than other enrollees (community rating). The ACA also prohibited insurers from imposing annual or lifetime spending caps on health care for an enrollee, thereby reducing risks of medical bankruptcy. While seeking to upgrade the quality of insurance coverage, the law (subject to certain stipulations) grandfathered in insurance that people had prior to the ACA's passage. Individuals could keep coverage that did not meet ACA standards if carriers continued to offer it. Over time, however, the law envisioned that a shrinking proportion of Americans would have such substandard coverage.

The ACA won approval without a single Republican vote in the House and Senate. Its implementation quickly became a partisan battlefield. Undercutting the ACA's Medicaid expansion proved to be fertile ground for Republican opponents. Immediately after the ACA's passage, Republican state attorneys general banded together to file a suit in federal district court to have the law declared unconstitutional. Among other things, the suit claimed that the Medicaid expansion amounted to unlawful federal coercion of the states since jurisdictions that refused to comply risked having funding for their existing Medicaid programs cut. In June 2012, the Supreme Court, in *National Federation of Independent Business v. Sebelius*, sided with the Republican attorneys general and other plaintiffs. The court prohibited the federal government from defunding a state's current Medicaid program if it failed to join the ACA's Medicaid expansion. This made state participation voluntary, and most Republican-dominated states opted out.

In seeking to surmount Republican resistance, the White House initiated a bevy of incremental measures. For instance, it delayed implementation of certain statutory deadlines, such as the effective date for large employers to pay a penalty for failing to offer adequate insurance.[2] Other actions, however, loomed larger in importance, especially its use of demonstration waivers. Authorized under Section 1115 of the Social Security Act, these waivers have proliferated and profoundly shaped Medicaid over the last three decades.[3] About 80 percent of the states had

Section 1115 demonstration waivers either operating or pending when the Obama administration left office.

The interest of conservative policymakers in market-oriented Medicaid waivers gave the Obama administration an opening to negotiate participation in the ACA's expansion in some states.[4] The waivers these states obtained sought to push Medicaid more fully toward a model of health care that stressed private insurance, competition among providers, individual choice, consumer empowerment, and personal responsibility.

The market-oriented model emphasizes, in varying degrees, two broad themes.[5] One is individual choice and personal responsibility. This variant stresses that Medicaid enrollees will behave more "responsibly" if they have some "skin in the game" when making health care decisions, such as by paying premiums, having copays for services, or managing health savings accounts. It seeks to discourage "inappropriate" care by imposing greater cost sharing when enrollees rely on hospital emergency rooms for "non-urgent" services. It also uses economic incentives to reward enrollees if they engage in certain desired health care behaviors (for example, waiving premiums if they get an annual wellness exam) or other activities, such as employment training or work. Under Obama, Indiana, Michigan, and Montana received waivers emphasizing individual choice and personal responsibility as a condition for expanding Medicaid.

A second major theme of some market-oriented waivers is premium assistance. This approach involves the use of Medicaid monies to purchase coverage from private insurance companies on the ACA's newly created insurance exchanges.[6] The Obama administration approved waivers in Arkansas, Iowa, New Hampshire, and Pennsylvania[7] that stressed this kind of premium assistance.

In using market-oriented waivers as carrots for Medicaid expansion, the Obama administration did not grant all state requests. For instance, it resisted efforts by Republican governors in Arizona, Indiana, Kentucky, Ohio, and Pennsylvania to impose work requirements on Medicaid applicants. In other cases, the Obama administration rejected enrollee cost sharing that it considered excessive; it resisted state measures that would increase the administrative burdens of Medicaid enrollment processes.[8] The use of waivers as well as other policy dynamics led to slow but steady progress in increasing the number of Medicaid-expansion states. By the time the Trump administration took office, thirty-one states and the District of Columbia had expanded Medicaid.

The forces of partisan polarization also pervaded efforts to establish the ACA exchanges. Congressional supporters of the law had envisioned that the states would seize the opportunity to run the health insurance marketplaces under the system of partial preemption. But Republican policymakers in the states soon came to see operating the exchanges as an act of complicity in preserving a program that key party stakeholders vehemently opposed. In the face of these stiff partisan headwinds, the Obama administration, nonetheless, persevered in its efforts to entice some participation from ideologically resistant states. In this vein, it rejected the all-or-nothing approach to state participation envisioned by the ACA and established a "partnership" model after negotiations with the National Association of Insurance Commissioners (an intergovernmental lobby for these state officials). The partnerships typically called on the federal government to develop and manage the computer-based infrastructure (web portal) needed to enroll applicants on the exchanges. States, in turn, would perform some of the other functions, such as certifying and monitoring exchange insurance carriers.[9] Despite these conciliatory efforts, the task of implementing the exchanges fell fully to federal officials in twenty-eight states by the time Trump took office. Only sixteen states, mostly dominated by Democrats, ran their own exchanges (along with the District of Columbia); six other states had forged partnerships.[10]

While over 10 million people were enrolled in the marketplaces when President Obama left office, stakeholders from across the partisan spectrum sensed their fragility. Exchange vitality varied considerably among and within states.[11] Many insurance companies offering exchange plans had lost money due largely to higher than expected claims costs. This prompted some of them to raise premiums significantly, while others fled the exchanges, leaving consumers with few options and undercutting market competition. To some degree, exchange fragility reflected the intrinsic limits of the ACA as a viable policy hypothesis.

But implementation problems also stemmed from Republican efforts to undermine them. Specifically, the House of Representatives filed suit in November 2014 challenging the constitutional authority of the Obama administration to make CSR payments to insurers without an explicit congressional appropriation. These payments reimburse insurers for costs they incur in reducing deductibles, copayments, and other expenses for enrollees with incomes between 100 and 250 percent of the poverty level. In May 2016, a federal district judge sided with Congress but stayed her order to allow the Obama administration to appeal, which it did in October.[12] After the presidential election, Congress asked the appellate court to delay hearing the case so the Trump administration could decide whether to continue the appeal.

The ACA's regulatory provisions to upgrade the quality of health insurance did not fuel the partisan acrimony that engulfed implementation of Medicaid and the exchanges. Instead, a "quiet politics of bargaining and consent" prevailed as federal administrators negotiated implementation details with the National Association of Insurance Commissioners.[13] In many jurisdictions, state insurance commissioners could implement ACA reforms without legislative approval, thereby defusing partisan tensions.

While the ACA undoubtedly bolstered the quality of health insurance coverage, it did not establish universally observed standards. Two developments deserve note. First, state insurance commissioners negotiated concessions from federal officials that allowed them to shape quality standards in their jurisdictions. Implementation of the ACA's requirement that insurance cover ten essential health benefits (for example, ambulatory care, mental health services, prescription drugs) offers a case in point. The ACA delegated substantial discretion to the Secretary of Health and Human Services to define these benefits. The secretary could, for instance, decide whether certain high-cost drugs must be covered. While key Democrats in Congress wanted federal officials to be assertive in defining these benefits to assure that all Americans had ample coverage, the Obama administration substantially deferred to the states. State officials could, for instance, use their coverage requirements for certain employer-sponsored plans or for state government employees as benchmarks to define ACA benefits. Hence, the scope of coverage for each of the ten essential health benefits varied by state.

Second, many Americans continued to have "grandfathered" insurance that did not meet the ACA's quality standards. Reflecting President Obama's promise that "if you have insurance, you can keep it," the ACA had permitted people to keep lower-quality coverage obtained prior to the bill's passage if insurers continued to offer it. Subsequently, however, federal administrators issued a regulation that narrowed this exemption. Among other things, the rule asserted that if a carrier significantly altered an individual policy, such as by modifying deductibles or benefits, it would no longer be grandfathered.

In October 2013, a focusing event dramatized the implications of this rule. NBC ran a lead story reporting that "millions of Americans are getting or about to get cancellation letters for their health insurance under Obamacare . . . and the Obama administration has known that for at least three years."[14] Faced with a torrent of bad publicity, President Obama took executive action to go beyond a literal reading of the ACA by creating a new category of "grandmothered" noncompliant plans. This step allowed states to permit the people who had purchased insurance between March 2010 and October 2013 to retain these substandard policies until late 2017. Thirty-five states opted to permit noncompliant insurance products, and an estimated 1 million individuals had them at the time Obama left office.[15]

In sum, the Obama administration faced relentless, salient, intense opposition by Republican policymakers at the federal and state levels as it attempted to implement the ACA's Medicaid and exchange provisions. Only in the case of regulating insurance did patterns of cooperative federalism, with its attendant bargaining and negotiation between levels of government, readily emerge. Confronted with this implementation battlefield, the Obama administration employed a spectrum of executive tools and strategies to cut its losses and advance its goals. Along the way, the administration suffered some defeats, which meant that the ACA's expansion of high-quality insurance coverage would not be as great as originally projected. Still, the ACA had achieved much by the time the Trump administration took office. Above all, the U.S. population without health insurance had fallen to 8.8 percent, nearly half the uninsured rate at the time of the ACA's passage in 2010.[16]

The Quest for Climate Protection

Barack Obama spoke at considerably greater length about climate change in his second inaugural address than in his first. His January 2013 speech followed a successful 2012 re-election campaign in which little was said about the topic.[17] Beginning his second term with a significant electoral victory, he declared from the steps of the Capitol: "We will respond to the threat of climate change, knowing that the failure to do so would betray our children and future generations."[18] Obama would attempt to deliver on that promise without any expectation that the legislative branch would play a supportive role. This represented a reversal of his 2008 campaign plans to develop a broad climate strategy through comprehensive legislation that would place a price on carbon emissions, gain bipartisan congressional support, and produce durable policy. Instead, Obama would direct key federal departments and agencies to accelerate first-term administrative efforts while simultaneously launching major new second-term initiatives. In both cases, this involved far-reaching executive branch reinterpretation of air quality legislation adopted between 1967 and 1990 to pursue major greenhouse gas emission reductions from key economic sectors.

These efforts would legitimize American leadership in crafting the December 2015 Paris Agreement on climate change, a novel international pact involving more than 180 nations. Contrary to the ill-fated 1997 Kyoto Protocol and its plan to distribute binding emission-reduction pledges en route to an anticipated global carbon emissions trading regime, Paris asked individual nations to volunteer nonbinding targets, known as Nationally Determined Contributions, or NDCs. If all participating nations delivered on these pledges, the prospects of containing environmental and human health damage from climate change would increase. This decentralized and flexible international governance regime was deemed more politically feasible to secure and maintain political support from individual nations, potentially leading to cross-national or even global cooperation through such policy tools as carbon taxes or cap-and-trade.

Paris was also designed to accommodate the domestic political realities on climate change facing the 44th president.[19] Obama desperately wanted to influence and sign a major global climate accord but recognized that Senate prospects to ratify any conceivable deal during his second term were dim. Indeed, the Clinton-Gore administration never made a serious attempt to ratify Kyoto in the late 1990s, given broad Senate opposition, allowing the George W. Bush administration to formally spurn membership.[20] Paris allowed more flexible terms of entry far short of a formal treaty or binding emission-reduction commitments for participating nations.

For the United States, this made possible the option of an "executive agreement" rather than a treaty, whereby a national leader such as an American president could pledge fealty on behalf of the nation without securing any form of congressional assent. This flexibility enabled Obama to pledge that the United States would reduce its greenhouse gas emissions by 26 to 28 percent from 2005 to 2025 as its Paris contribution. Such a pledge could potentially be transformed into a treaty commitment with support from a future Congress, but Obama had no expectation that this type of legislative support was plausible during his tenure. Instead, his climate plan for the balance of his presidency after Paris featured an expanded administrative presidency approach reliant on aggressive reinterpretation of existing legislation that presumed a seamless handoff to a supportive Democratic 45th president in 2017 to assure durability.

The Hillary Clinton campaign had decided not to make climate change a major issue during the 2016 election and was unlikely to propose bold new climate legislation after an anticipated electoral victory. But her advisors began working quietly with the Obama team and scholarly experts well in advance of an anticipated transition to sustain the pursuit of Paris goals through implementation of recent executive actions. At the same time, they began to ponder additional administrative options to assure the accomplishment of the Paris targets or even to exceed them.

Such steps seemed plausible, given both the anticipated electoral outcomes and the fact that the American emission-reduction pledges through 2025 seemed within reach given emerging federal regulatory initiatives. American emissions reached record highs in 2005, making it a popular emissions baseline that offered maximum symbolic impact from any subsequent reductions. The combination of economic recession alongside expanded natural gas and renewable source electricity production as more carbon-friendly alternatives to coal fueled a 12 percent reduction in U.S. emissions between 2005 and 2015, the point at which Obama embraced Paris. A compilation of state and local government emission-reduction policies also contributed to this emissions decline, many of which were scheduled to expand their scope over time. The Obama administration contended that a combination of federal administrative steps could move the United States within striking distance of a 26 to 28 percent reduction by 2025. This assumed that neither a future president, Congress, nor federal judiciary would reverse these steps and that all fifty states would comply fully with new regulatory provisions.

Ironically, Obama anticipated during his 2008 campaign that he would sign comprehensive climate legislation in either 2009 or 2010, providing momentum for more ambitious reductions and a bolder international agreement. Both Obama and his Republican opponent John McCain had broadly supported as Senators federal legislation to cap national greenhouse gas emissions and establish a market-based strategy to reduce them steadily in a cost-effective way. This concurrence also extended into the 2008 campaign despite their differences on particulars, producing a seeming inevitability that some consequential climate legislation would emerge after Obama was elected with sizable Democratic majorities in both legislative chambers.

But any prospects for congressional engagement collapsed after the

House narrowly passed the American Clean Energy and Security Act (better known as Waxman-Markey for its cosponsors, California's Henry Waxman and Massachusetts' Ed Markey) in June 2009. This featured cap-and-trade alongside numerous other provisions designed to propel transition from fossil fuels toward renewables and energy efficiency. Even securing House passage was difficult, resulting in a bill that exceeded 1,400 pages and was loaded with incentives and exemptions to secure votes from reluctant legislators. Only eight Republicans supported the bill, which passed by seven votes, given forty-four Democratic defections.[21]

This relatively early step during the 111th Congress left considerable time for Senate action and the development of a final bill that Obama would eagerly sign. But climate change faced a crowded agenda, given other issues such as the economic recovery and major health care and banking sector reforms. In turn, fossil fuels retained particularly strong support in the Senate, since the majority of states produce some fossil fuels. The shale boom dramatically expanded production while fostering economic recovery in many states. The Senate never approached agreement on a companion bill, with final negotiations collapsing in mid-2010. No subsequent Congress came remotely close to adopting any climate, air quality, or energy legislation for the balance of the Obama presidency.

Nonetheless, Obama had prepared for a Plan B based on administrative actions well before the legislative collapse, most of which would be based on far-reaching executive reinterpretation of a hallmark 1990 environmental law.[22] This alternative approach could potentially complement anticipated legislation, be negotiated away if needed to broker a legislative deal with Congress, or guide national greenhouse gas emission reductions if Congress failed to act. These efforts began with an early set of first-term steps that reversed executive actions taken by his predecessor, George W. Bush, after a number of states had pressed the courts for federal climate action under the Clean Air Act (CAA).

Ironically, George H. W. Bush was the first president to endorse a major federal effort to address climate change, arguing as early as the 1988 presidential campaign that he intended to bring "the White House effect to the greenhouse effect." His climate efforts as president, however, were far more modest, and greenhouse gases were excluded from his signature environmental achievement, the 1990 CAA amendments. After a prolonged period of executive and legislative combat over clean air reforms that began in the early 1980s, Bush and a bipartisan majority in Congress brokered a major 1990 compromise that would represent the last subsequent reauthorization of that legislation.[23] It included major efforts to tighten regulatory standards on numerous air contaminants from industrial and transportation sources, including a historic effort to establish a national cap on sulfur dioxide emissions that would be lowered through an emissions trading program. The entire bill specifically avoided any direct reference to climate change or carbon dioxide, although methane releases could be addressed under certain provisions. However, the revised legislation included a number of mechanisms whereby the Environmental Protection Agency (EPA) could respond to evolving scientific understanding about human health risks from air contaminants, including those linked to fossil fuel production or use. It also allowed some opportunity for states with concerns about particular environmental risks to take unilateral efforts if a president was willing to give them authority to do so.

This was most notable in the case of transportation-related emissions. Congress in 1967 established provisions, maintained through 1970, 1977, and 1990 amendments, that expressly granted one state, California, unique regulatory powers, despite the fact that vehicles routinely cross state borders and manufacturers strongly preferred that any emissions control policy be nationally uniform in scope. This legislation provided California with the unusual authority to request federal waivers allowing it to take emission control steps beyond national standards that were reflective of its acute air quality problems, history of active policy long before federal engagement, and growing clout in the House of Representatives.[24] This waiver provision set three very clear criteria for the EPA to consider in review, constraining agency discretion in ways far beyond the more general waiver criteria operational in health care and education policy. This provided California with considerable leverage to fashion a state-specific strategy that would regularly prompt ultimate federal adoption of the same policy to sustain national consistency.

The legislation gave California clear and compelling measures to address in making their case for waivers, leading to nearly 120 approvals between 1968 and 2016. Every president granted at least one waiver during this period, and Ronald Reagan both submitted waiver requests as governor of California and approved them as president. The 1990 amendments protected provisions initiated in 1977, whereby any other state could embrace a California standard once it received an EPA waiver. This could create a "bandwagon effect," whereby one state's efforts would, ultimately, create a multi-state coalition that could prompt the EPA to embrace that coalition's position as national policy, preventing a geographically fragmented set of requirements for vehicle manufacturers. Over multiple decades, this "leveraged federalism" gave a small set of states with limited vehicle manufacturing activity considerable latitude to drive national reforms on how future vehicles would be produced.[25]

The George W. Bush administration, however, rejected state efforts to use the CAA to declare climate change a threat to their well-being and secure federal approval for setting greenhouse gas standards on new vehicles. This represented the first major rejection of a California waiver proposal, one that was linked to 2002 state legislation.[26] It led to protracted litigation and a historic 2007 U.S. Supreme Court decision (*Massachusetts et al. v. U.S. Environmental Protection Agency et al.*) that concluded states had legal standing to file suit and had advanced a credible claim that they were at risk from failures to address greenhouse gas emissions. The 1990 CAA amendments did not expressly address carbon dioxide, even though this was actively considered during years of debate in the 1980s over the proper scope of air quality policy. However, the legislation also provided considerable flexibility for the EPA to respond to emerging threats as scientific understanding evolved.

Speaking for a five-member majority in the case, Associate Justice John Paul Stevens acknowledged clear restrictions on state authority set forth in the Constitution. But he concluded that the agency's failure to regulate greenhouse gas emissions under the CAA presented a risk of harm to Massachusetts and other states that was both "actual" and "imminent." Stevens contended: "Under the clear terms of the Clean Air Act, EPA can avoid taking further action only if it determines that greenhouse gases do not contribute to climate change or it if provides some reasonable explanation as to why it cannot or will not exercise its discretion to determine whether they do."[27] In dissent, Chief Justice John Roberts argued that the majority had invented a "new theory of Article II standing for states" and was acting because it was "apparently dissatisfied with the pace of progress of this issue in the elected branches."[28] Associate Justice Antonin Scalia went farther, scolding the majority for inserting the court into policy decisions that belonged to the president and federal agencies.

This decision, however, did not prompt immediate executive branch compliance. The Bush administration refused to issue an "endangerment finding" in response to the ruling that could open the door to using the CAA as a climate-protection tool, raising the possibility of further litigation to resolve the issue of the federal role in climate change mitigation under this legislation. However, the incoming Obama administration wasted little time in taking such a step, issuing its endangerment finding prior to the 2009 House vote on climate legislation. As political scientist Norman Vig has noted: "Whereas the Bush administration had refused to act on the basis of the court decision, Obama saw it as an opportunity to carry out much of his climate change agenda through the executive branch."[29]

President Obama not only took executive steps to declare carbon dioxide worthy of coverage under the CAA, but within weeks embraced an endangerment finding to legitimize a far-reaching administrative extension of the legislation to cover vehicle emissions without seeking congressional approval. In a Rose Garden ceremony, the president embraced California's waiver and also approved the state's regulatory standards as federal policy, which would be implemented by merging the EPA's implementation of air quality standards with Department of Transportation implementation of fuel economy standards, given their considerable overlap when applying carbon calculations.

These units had never previously collaborated in this area, and the decades-old fuel economy program under the 1975 Energy Policy and Conservation Act prohibited state waivers or exceptions of any sort from federal preemption.[30] Nonetheless, this integrative step was necessary to blend these two separate initiatives into a unified effort to simultaneously tighten both tailpipe emission and fuel efficiency standards on newly manufactured vehicles, with the potential for reducing future greenhouse gas emissions through purchase of new vehicles. This step was bolstered by a pair of 2007 federal court decisions, including a particularly influential case in Vermont that concluded that "state law's purpose of assuring protection of public health and welfare under the Clean Air Act" were not preempted by any overlapping fuel economy standards.[31] Supportive governors were prominently featured during the White House ceremony, which occurred while the president held unique leverage over American-based vehicle manufacturers, given their desperate requests for massive bailout assistance.

This multiagency agreement was launched in April 2010, about the time cap-and-trade legislation entered its political death spiral. It required passenger cars, minivans, sport-utility vehicles, and other light trucks to meet combined tailpipe emission levels averaging 250 grams per mile of carbon dioxide for model year 2016, comparable to a 30 percent reduction in emissions from 2010 levels.[32] This equated to national fuel economy standards of thirty-four miles per gallon by 2016 that would increase steadily through 2025. The Obama administration aggressively pursued implementation and worked until its final days to accelerate formal approval of tighter reduction targets that would approach fifty-five miles per gallon by 2025, considerably boosting its ability to meet Paris mid-decade reduction pledges, assuming massive purchase of the more environmentally friendly vehicles.[33] This appeared to rest upon a solid constitutional foundation given the longstanding operation of the state emission waiver process for air quality without serious legal challenge. However, its merger without any congressional input with a fuel economy program that preempted any state role carried it into complex new political, administrative, and legal territory.

The Obama administration also pursued far-reaching reinterpretation of separate sections of the CAA, addressing electricity generation through its creation of the Clean Power Plan (CPP). This sector had already experienced significant emission reductions due to considerable energy source transition and various state policies. The electricity sector was likely heading toward net emission reduction greater than the 26 to 28 percent levels envisioned nationally under the Paris Agreement by 2025. However, the CPP was intended to ensure that it met and potentially exceeded those targets, thus representing a second key step toward honoring the international reduction pledge.

Whereas the vehicle emission initiative dominated the first Obama term, the CPP occupied center stage during the second. It reflected a massive EPA planning and outreach effort, beginning with a 2014 draft rule. After reviewing more than 4.3 million public comments and responding to numerous state appeals for tailored adjustments, the EPA released its final CPP rule in August 2015, modifying existing CAA provisions to require a 32 percent reduction of carbon electricity emissions from 2005 levels by 2030. The CPP relied on an established state implementation plan mechanism for utility air emissions whereby states would propose a strategy for federal approval but face potential imposition of a federal implementation plan if their offering was deemed inadequate. Each state received a specific emission-reduction requirement based on a complex set of federal formulas and projections tempered by political considerations. A number of states that had already taken major steps to reduce electricity sector emissions, commonly led by Democrats and located on opposite coasts, were given more modest reduction targets. They generally welcomed the CPP, pledging steadfast support.

But many other states were not enamored with this strategy, particularly after the issuance of the final rule. More than a dozen immediately filed suit, attempting to block the plan as an unconstitutional extension of presidential powers. This coalition expanded over time to include twenty-seven states, including many with strong legacies of either producing fossil fuels for use in electricity, using them extensively for power production, or both. In contrast, eighteen states formally endorsed the CPP. Opponents contended that the Obama administration vastly overreached its CAA authority. They challenged all dimensions of the CPP, motivated in part by the likelihood that in a number of states the required emission-reduction levels would not be achievable through technologies that could be used on regulated power plants. This raised the specter of either far-reaching plant retirements or the necessity of supplemental reductions "beyond the fence" of power plants.

The EPA noted that plants might consider far-reaching energy efficiency commitments and that states might develop single- or multi-state cap-and-trade programs, emphasizing that the latter would be most cost effective and was the option that the agency clearly preferred. The agency also announced federal implementation plans that would impose cap-and-trade on states that failed to submit an acceptable state plan.[34] In a remarkable reach of the Obama administrative presidency, cap-and-trade was resurrected as a primary regulatory tool to reduce greenhouse gas emissions despite sustained legislative opposition to take similar steps in recent Congresses.

State-propelled litigation produced a major court decision, albeit fundamentally different from the 2007 Supreme Court case that opened the way to the Obama transportation strategy. In the electricity case, the Supreme Court took the highly unusual step of issuing a stay in February 2016, less than one year before the 45th president would take office. The stay largely froze CPP implementation by the EPA and gave states legal room to abandon state implementation plan development pending a final court decision. Any chance to resolve the stay in the near term ended with the subsequent death of Associate Justice Antonin Scalia. This created a deadlock in court membership that would not be resolved until after the November 2016 elections and the appointment of a successor. This limited the EPA's ability to cement CPP provisions in place prior to the change of presidential leadership. Congressional efforts to block the CPP were thwarted when Obama twice vetoed disapproval resolutions under the Congressional Review Act.

Other Obama administration efforts to direct administrative powers toward an assault on greenhouse gases continued without court interruption, however. Methane has a particularly intensive warming impact during its first decades of release into the atmosphere and accounts for approximately 10 percent of U.S. and 15 percent of annual global greenhouse gas emissions. But its near-term intensity means that it is responsible for about one-quarter of all global warming that has occurred during the past century. Methane is produced from the energy, livestock, agricultural, and waste management sectors and has potential market value as a key component of natural gas. But its release, whether through venting or flaring at the point of oil and gas production and supply distribution, solid waste landfills, livestock, or various agricultural practices, has proven technically difficult to measure with precision and politically difficult to regulate with effectiveness in the United States and internationally.

The Obama administration took major administrative steps to reduce methane releases, particularly during its second term. This included such diverse agencies as the EPA and the Departments of Agriculture, Energy, and Interior, all of which undertook major regulatory reviews. For the EPA, this entailed development of new CAA regulations on releases from energy production and landfills, while the Interior focused on energy production on federally held lands. Obama attempted to build on these initial efforts through the creation of a North American methane partnership with the prime minister of Canada and the president of Mexico. This culminated in a 2016 summit and linked pledges to reduce oil and gas sector emissions 40 to 45 percent below 2012 levels by 2025. These were generally consistent with methane-reduction goals that Obama was preparing to pursue unilaterally in the United States, moving the nation closer to Paris reduction targets if sustained and fully implemented. Like Paris, it involved a presidential-executive agreement and, therefore, did not require congressional endorsement.

Enhancing the Federal Role in Education

Education is primarily the responsibility of states. State constitutions specify the role and responsibility of the state government in elementary and secondary schools and higher education. The Elementary and Secondary Education Act (ESEA) and the Higher Education Act (HEA) in the Great Society era of the 1960s marked the beginning of an increasingly prominent federal role to promote civil rights, schooling opportunity, research, and other investments in the quality and capacity of the education service delivery system. The two Bushes and Clinton continued the federal involvement in improving education. The Obama presidency clearly aimed at broadening the federal commitment in both K–12 and higher education.

Barack Obama was an active education president in elementary and secondary education. During his two terms, he granted waivers to over 90 percent of the states on meeting proficiency goals under the 2001 No Child Left Behind Act (NCLB); created multiple financial streams as incentives for states to adopt the Common Core of academic standards and to improve teacher quality; and guided states on intervention strategies to turn around the lowest performing schools. The Obama presidency actively used administrative power to address the nation's challenge of inequality in education.

When Barack Obama took the presidential oath for the first time, in January 2009, the state of American education was mixed despite eight years of NCLB implementation. This legislation, a signature legislative achievement of the George W. Bush presidency, had created tension in the intergovernmental policy system. As political scientist Paul Manna observed, there was a significant gap between the theory of accountability based on the federal intent and the practice of accountability at the state and local level.[35] The literature on the implementation of NCLB has suggested several key challenges in aligning the federal reform agenda with the complex intergovernmental system of education governance.[36]

First, federalism allows for varying degrees of policy specification in meeting federal expectations. Under NCLB, states defined their own set of proficiency standards and measures in meeting the federal Adequate Yearly Progress (AYP) requirements.[37] Consequently, state assessments varied (and continue to vary) widely in terms of the level of rigor, as indicated by the substantial gaps between student proficiencies on state tests and differences in performance on the National Assessment of Educational Progress (NAEP) among the states.

Second, political negotiations among key stakeholders within states tended to slow the pace of initial implementation of the NCLB, which came as no surprise to observers of ambitious policy implementation. Four out of five states were not ready to meet the federal requirement on placing highly qualified teachers in the classroom during the initial implementation period. The annual testing requirement, a core concept in the new accountability system, faced major resistance. Virginia, Connecticut, Utah, Michigan, and several other states registered their opposition with legislative and legal actions. In a 2011 study conducted by the Center for American Progress, state education commissioners pointed out that strong accountability and innovative practices were the exceptions in state education agencies.[38]

Third, the NCLB elevated the visibility of the racial and income gap in school performance. The extent to which districts or schools met the NCLB annual AYP proficiency goals was affected by the concentration of high needs students in the schools and districts. In their analysis of AYP in California, James Kim and Gail Sunderman found that the percentage of schools meeting AYP tended to decline as the number of subgroups (for example, based on race/ethnicity, socioeconomic status, limited English proficiency, and disabilities) in those schools rose.[39] While 78 percent of the schools with only one subgroup met the reading AYP in 2003, only 25 percent of the schools with six subgroups were able to do so. When the authors considered the AYP data in Virginia, they found that 85 percent of the schools that met both the state and federal proficiency standards had two or fewer subgroups. Only 15 percent of the schools that met the AYP had three of more subgroups.

Fourth, the Obama administration encountered a significant congressional impasse in the reauthorization of the next version of NCLB. The new legislation, the Every Student Succeeds Act (ESSA), was about eight years late and emerged near the end of the Obama presidency in 2015 with broad support across partisan lines. In response to congressional delays and the lack of substantial progress in educational equality under NCLB, President Obama extensively used administrative initiatives to address these policy and intergovernmental challenges. Fiscal incentives and waivers were used simultaneously as major federal strategies to improve K–12 education during much of the Obama presidency.

With respect to fiscal incentives, the Obama administration launched new competitive funding streams to promote education reform at the state and local levels. Under federal guidance, states and districts competed for Race to the Top grants as well as other federal funding, to "transform" their current policy and practices in educator accountability (such as teacher evaluation), charter schools, and turning around low-performing schools.

Building on the NCLB framework for "corrective actions," the Obama administration pushed for more direct district intervention in persistently low-performing schools. Education Secretary Arne Duncan issued guidance on several strategies to turn around the nation's lowest performing 5 percent of schools (approximately 5,000 schools), and the federal government committed $5 billion during 2010–2012 to support these efforts. Duncan's strategies tightened the approaches established under NCLB, allowing for fewer district options.

Equally important was Obama's strong guidance on local and state institutional reform through competitive grants such as the Race to the Top. Funded by the American Recovery and Reinvestment Act of 2009, this initiative departed from formula-based categorical allocations. Instead, the Obama administration invited states to submit their best ideas on system transformation and school innovation to the national competition for the Race to the Top. Delaware and Tennessee were selected as the first two awardees in the initial round of Race to the Top, in April 2010. The competition resulted in grant awards to a total of nineteen states and Washington, D.C.

With financial support from the federal government and grants from several nonprofit foundations (such as the Gates Foundation), 80 percent of states were incentivized to adopt the Common Core standards and assessment by early 2010. These Common Core standards were not federal mandates, although the national government used financial and deregulatory incentives to encourage state adoption. These standards and assessments were organized by two independent professional organizations—the Partnership for Assessment and Readiness for College and Careers (PARCC) and the Smarter Balance Assessment Consortium (SBAC).[40] With the Common Core, states aimed to compare themselves to their peers in terms of academic progress, creating economies of scale for technical assistance, streamlining teacher recruitment and support, and, most important, raising academic rigor to meet twenty-first-century expectations. At the same time, implementation of the Common Core was contentious in some states, specifically on topics such as teacher readiness, web-based assessment capability, and perceived federal intrusion into state and local academic affairs.

In addition to fiscal incentives, the Obama administration drew heavily on waivers to kindle education reform. In the absence of congressional action on legislation to replace NCLB, Education Secretary Duncan used waivers authorized under Section 9401 of NCLB as a bargaining chip with the states. In essence, he signaled to states that if they wanted to escape the unworkable mandates of NCLB, they had to accommodate the Obama administration's reform preferences (which the administration had been unable to get Congress to accept). Section 9401 gives the Secretary of Education the authority to "issue waivers of any statutory or regulatory requirement of the ESEA for a state educational agency

(SEA), LEA [local educational agency], Indian tribe, or school (through an LEA) that receives funds under an ESEA program and requests a waiver."[41] From the states' perspective, waivers tended to create new opportunities to regain programmatic control, but they also generated a certain sense of uncertainty, as many of the proposed ideas were untested.[42] In the first cycle of applications, in November 2011, eleven states formally sought alternative ways to implement their accountability systems in exchange for fulfilling a new set of federal requirements. By early August 2012, thirty-three states and the District of Columbia received federal approval for their NCLB waivers. By the summer of 2014, almost 90 percent of the states had these waivers.

From the Obama administration's perspective, waivers promised to address some of the key reform concerns at the state and local level.[43] In liberating states from the need to demonstrate improved proficiency for all students (as previously stipulated in NCLB's target of 100 percent proficiency by 2014), the federal government solicited political support from states toward adopting more rigorous and uniform standards for college and career readiness, a requirement most easily satisfied by adopting the Common Core standards and assessment. Waivers also created an incentive for states to implement teacher evaluation systems that used measurable student outcome data. Seeing the need to balance sanctions and support for low-performing schools, the Obama administration leveraged waivers to incentivize states to implement a comprehensive system of recognition, accountability, and support for all schools. In other words, the Obama administration saw a policy window in the absence of ESEA reauthorization to advance some of its reform priorities. Indeed, a survey of thirty-eight states conducted in the fall of 2012 suggested a generally favorable view. State respondents believed the waivers were designed to address problems associated with NCLB accountability; they were also positive about college- and career-ready standards for student learning and recognized the importance of moving toward new teacher evaluation systems.[44]

Waiver applications generally aligned with the priorities of the Obama administration.[45] For example, the post-NCLB Nevada system of accountability, which received federal approval in August 2012, planned to use student achievement growth and other measures to differentiate schools that needed particular support and intervention. Nevada's state superintendent of public instruction touted the significance of the waiver approval: "This next generation accountability system is a central lever in statewide efforts to substantially elevate student performance. This system was built through robust collaboration with key partners, together with whom we will re-engineer Nevada's educational system to realize true college and career readiness for all students."[46] In other words, waiver states expressed their intent to implement the Obama administration's reform agenda, such as adopting the Common Core standards.

However, the extent to which states actually carried out their proposed reform initiatives remained a key issue.[47] According to a sixteen-state study, practically every state met the requirements pertaining to the Obama reform areas of implementing college- and career-ready standards, assessments for all students, and data collection and use. In contrast, fewer of the sixteen states in the study sample met the waiver requirements on principal and teacher evaluations and implementing systemic strategies to improve the lowest performing schools. Not surprising, these expectations often required legislative and gubernatorial involvement in enacting more fundamental changes in current policies and practices. Teachers' union opposition to some of these reform issues also contributed to the lack of progress in half of the sample states. Partisan differences often fueled tensions. For example, Indiana, a state with strong Republican control, received pushback from its Superintendent of Public Instruction, Glenda Ritz. In Indiana, the Superintendent is an elected office, and Ritz, who is a Democrat, engaged in continued conflicts on education reform and teacher evaluation with then Governor Mike Pence, a Republican. In short, state politics shaped waiver implementation and the variation of implementation success across different reform areas.

The 2014 midterm election resulted in a Republican Senate majority, with the House Republicans maintaining their control as well. The Obama administration was ready to work with Republican Senator Lamar Alexander of Tennessee, Chair of the Senate Committee on Health, Education, Labor and Pensions (HELP), toward the passage of new federal education legislation. As the new chair of the HELP committee, Alexander promptly reintroduced a bill he had developed in the previous congressional session to lay a framework for the final legislation.

The 2015 ESSA signaled the reversal of a growing federal role. In response to states' concerns, the legislation placed constraints on federal overreach on the Common Core, student assessment, and teacher evaluation, among other issues.[48] At the same time, ESSA kept the federal requirements on annual testing of students in core subjects in grades three through eight as well as a high school grade, and annual report cards on achievement gaps. It signaled a strong commitment to early childhood education, community engagement, and innovative practices. More important, the act restored states' policymaking power on issues that had been overshadowed by administrative actions during the first seven years of the Obama presidency, including the choice of academic standards, criteria in identifying and intervening in low-performing schools, and flexibility in evaluating teaching effectiveness. In short, ESSA offered a policy framework for a new federal-state partnership in K–12 education. Later in the book, we will examine how the Trump administration has continued to push for greater state rights and local control within the boundary of this new policy framework.

A commitment to equity and the promotion of private sector engagement also characterized the Obama administrative presidency. Obama aimed to broaden federal leadership in two key areas. First, the Obama administration, like its predecessors since the Clinton presidency, strongly supported charter schools in educating students with high needs. Taking a proactive outlook on public-private partnerships, the Obama administration announced the ConnectED initiative to promote the implementation of digital learning in November 2014. The key components included: an expansion of broadband connectivity in isolated communities with 50-50 financial support from the private sector and the Federal Communications Commission; and digital learning and professional development resources supported by the private sector, including AT&T, Microsoft, Apple, Adobe, and Verizon, among others.

As part of the ConnectED initiative, the federal government promoted Future Ready Districts across the country. These Future Ready Districts, with pledges signed by the superintendent, aimed at fostering a culture of digital learning; accelerating progress toward universal access for all students to high quality, price-competitive devices and content; and mentoring districts on their transition to digital learning. By February 2015, over 1,600 districts had pledged to participate in the Future Ready network across fifty states and territories. These districts included not only public school districts but also charter schools and Roman Catholic schools. California had the largest number of Future Ready Districts (246), followed by Texas (109), Michigan (108), and Illinois (98).

Second, President Obama elevated the nation's attention to racial/ethnic, income, gender, and sexual orientation inequity in K–12. During the Obama years, the Office for Civil Rights in the Department of Education conducted extensive monitoring of civil rights violations related to gender discrimination (Title IX),[49] the rights of lesbian, gay, bisexual and transgender students (LGBTQ), as well as students with disabilities and other needs. At the K–12 level, interagency collaboration, led by Attorney General Eric Holder and Secretary of Education Duncan, leveraged federal resources and political will to address complex challenges that African American children and youth faced, including violence, an achievement gap, chronic absenteeism, and teacher quality.[50] A prominent example of Obama's commitment to educational equity was his effort to improve schools for Native Americans on reservations. Obama highlighted education as a key pillar in revitalizing Indian Country.[51] He instructed Secretary Duncan and Secretary of the Department of Interior Sally Jewell to formulate a comprehensive plan to support tribal self-governance over schools in the reservations, promote early access to integrated services, improve school leadership, and strengthen teacher recruitment and retention in Indian Country.[52]

In addition to initiatives aimed at K–12, Obama sought to address issues related to postsecondary education. While the Obama administration intervened in the core functions of the K–12 delivery system, as authorized by NCLB, its higher education strategies did not aim at changing curriculum standards, hiring practices of college instructors, or the academic mission of higher education programs. In higher education, President Obama focused on affordability, student rights, and accountability for the growing for-profit sector. The president's first major speech before a joint session of Congress in 2009 clearly signaled his readiness to take an active role in higher education. The American Council on Education praised the speech as "the strongest statement we heard about the importance of post-secondary education" from a president.[53] Obama declared his commitment to significantly increasing the percentage of high school graduates who would attain postsecondary credentials by 2020. His endorsement of this goal sprang from his view of economic necessity for the twenty-first-century global marketplace. Workers' skills for a wide range of jobs were projected to require postsecondary training and problem-solving knowledge.

The Obama administration's legislative agenda reflected this commitment. In assembling the economic stimulus and fiscal stabilization package for Congress in 2009, President Obama significantly increased funding for Pell grants and other programs for student support. The package extended Pell grants to 800,000 more students and increased maximum grant levels from approximately $4,730 to $5,500.[54] Obama subsequently promoted legislation that would make Pell grants an entitlement to any students meeting eligibility criteria (with lower family income being the prime factor) rather than a number determined by an annual appropriation from Congress. He also sought to index the grants for inflation to account for the erosion in their value that had occurred since the program's creation in 1972. Final legislation in 2010 authorized some inflation adjustment but did not make Pell grants an entitlement.[55]

The Obama administration also took executive action in several significant areas to advance its policy goals. Initiatives targeting for-profit postsecondary institutions, student borrowers, and campus handling of sexual misconduct loomed especially large. Most notably, with the use of Dear Colleague letters that far surpassed their use by prior presidents,[56] the administration strove to buttress the rights of students who alleged they had been sexually assaulted. As political scientist R. Shep Melnick has observed, a major shift in the federal enforcement of Title IX occurred when the Assistant Secretary of Education in 2011 issued new guidelines that broadly focused on institutional climate and practice rather than targeted investigations of alleged Title IX violations by individuals.[57] The new guidelines instructed colleges and universities to empower their Title IX office with a comprehensive set of monitoring, training, enforcement, and adjudicatory responsibilities, especially in cases of sexual harassment.[58] Universities responded to the more comprehensive guidelines by significantly expanding their administrative staffs to ensure compliance. For example, the compliance office at Yale grew to a staff of thirty.

So, too, the Obama administration struggled mightily and with modest success to reign in excesses of the for-profit postsecondary sector. In 1987, President Reagan's Secretary of Education William Bennett had articulated views that subsequently animated the Obama administration. Bennett denounced much of the for-profit postsecondary sector as "diploma mills designed to trick the poor into taking on federally backed debt, milk them for their loan money, and then wash them out or 'graduate' them ill-prepared to enter the job market and pay off their loans."[59] Despite Bennett's concern, the period from 1993 to 2010 witnessed a nearly ten-fold increase in for-profit enrollments to some 2 million students. Compared to those enrolled in private nonprofit or public colleges, a much higher percentage of students in the for-profits had federal loans (roughly 90 percent) and subsequently defaulted on them (close to a quarter). A much smaller proportion of them graduated within six years with a bachelor's degree.[60] Congressional investigations sporadically revealed that many for-profit institutions employed deceptive, high-pressure recruitment tactics to bolster their enrollments.

The ability of for-profits to fend off critics such as Bennett largely reflected their growing political muscle. Alone among institutions of higher education, for-profits can make campaign contributions. As their enrollments took off in the 1990s and early 2000s, they formed political action committees and funneled millions of dollars into campaigns. They not only developed a firm alliance with Republicans but also reached out to many Democrats. For instance, certain members of the Congressional Black Caucus have vigorously defended for-profit institutions on grounds that they enroll students from disadvantaged backgrounds.

In 1991, Congress had made piecemeal efforts to curb the excesses of the for-profit sector. Legislation signed by President George H. W. Bush imposed an 85/15 rule on for-profit trade school revenues, which meant that at least 15 percent of their revenues had to come from sources other than the federal loan program. The rule aimed to deter schools that depended almost solely on federal subsidies from operating. (In 1998, Congress deferred to the for-profits and reduced the ratio to 90/10.) To bolster educational quality, the 1991 legislation also enacted a 50/50 rule, which forbade the use of federal student aid at schools that enrolled more than half their students in correspondence (for example, online) courses. The legislation also made modest attempts to regulate the recruitment practices of for-profits.[61]

George H. W. Bush was the last Republican president to evince any interest in restraining for-profit postsecondary institutions. The administrative presidency of his son George W. Bush featured multiple efforts to deregulate this higher educational sector. The latter Bush appointed the former chief lobbyist for the Apollo group, which operates the massive for-profit University of Phoenix, to the role of Assistant Secretary for Postsecondary Education. She pursued several initiatives to water down the regulation of for-profits. For instance, the department softened penalties for institutions that heavily rewarded recruiters who enrolled higher numbers of students. When the Department of Education was presented with evidence of major recruitment abuses at the University of Phoenix, it levied only a modest fine compared to the well over $1 billion in revenues the university generated. A Republican-controlled Congress revoked the 50/50 rule in 2006.[62]

Concerned that students were incurring considerable debt for degrees that did little to advance their employment prospects and created a substantial drain on the federal treasury due to unpaid loans, the Obama administration undertook various initiatives to curb abuses by the for-profit postsecondary sector. Despite intense opposition from this sector, the Obama administration made some headway. Of particular note, it finalized a gainful employment administrative rule in 2014. This rule established measures for determining whether certain postsecondary institutions prepared students for employment that was sufficiently remunerative to enable them to pay off their federal loans. Failure to meet these standards could cause the institution to lose eligibility for the federal student loan program. In 2015, for example, Corinthian Colleges Inc., which at one time managed more than 100 campuses, was fined almost $30 million for falsifying employment information on their graduates.[63] Under Secretary of Education Ted Mitchell, who chaired an interagency task force on oversight of for-profit institutions, summed up the Corinthian case: "Their substantial misrepresentations evidence a blatant disregard not just for professional standards, but for students' futures. This is unacceptable, and we are holding them accountable."[64] Subsequently, Corinthian Colleges Inc. filed for bankruptcy protection.

Beyond the gainful employment regulation, the Obama administration also took steps to provide more procedural protections to student borrowers. The Higher Education Act of 1998 granted waivers to for-profit organizations to relax the enrollment cap for student borrowers of federal loans in online programs. Consequently, for-profit programs proliferated and saw enrollment increases. By fall 2012, there were about 1.8 million undergraduates and graduate students enrolled in education programs managed by for-profit organizations.[65] Over half of these students were in online programs. As a growing number of students experienced unemployment and encountered fraudulent lender practices, the Obama administration saw the need to protect student borrowers. The Borrower Defense to Repayment rule comprised one of its initiatives. This rule allowed student borrowers to request cancellation of their federal loans if the education programs they attended egregiously engaged in misinformation or fraudulent practices. A dramatic illustration of the effects of this rule in protecting student borrowers, which outlasted the Obama administration, involved the bankruptcy case of Corinthian Colleges Inc. The federal government estimated that over 300,000 former students of Corinthian were eligible for loan cancellation due to the organization's fraudulent practices.

Conclusion

This chapter has briefly described the substantial policy legacy of the Obama years in health care, climate, and education. This legacy featured major legislative breakthroughs in health care and education. The ACA won approval on a strict party line vote and ignited implementation battles as congressional Republicans and their fellow partisans at the state level attempted to derail the program. In contrast, ESSA emerged from a rare case of bipartisan compromise in a polarized era, although it was nearly a decade overdue in addressing needed updates. Climate policy was bereft of any significant statutory changes, with the early death of cap-and-trade legislation being particularly noteworthy.

The Obama years also featured a multidimensional, muscular approach to the administrative presidency in all three policy spheres. The president used an array of tools to promote his agenda, with waivers being especially prominent. In the case of the ACA, the Obama administration used market-oriented waivers to entice more conservative states to join the Medicaid expansion. In the case of climate policy, Obama aggressively reinterpreted the 1990 CAA amendments, developing a wide range of new regulations that were applied across multiple economic sectors. Most notably, he enthusiastically embraced a waiver for greenhouse gas emission reduction for California, using a process first etched into federal air quality legislation in 1967. This single state waiver was simultaneously established as national policy for reducing transportation sector emissions through a policy merger with federally preempted fuel economy standards achieved without new legislation. In education, top officials used waivers to overcome the rigidities of and state resistance to the No Child Left Behind legislation. The education arena also witnessed considerable executive action to promote civil rights for students and to curb the abuses of for-profit institutions of higher education. On balance, the Obama administration experienced considerable, though far from complete, success in promoting its policy objectives through both legislative and executive action.

The Trump administration took office with starkly different goals, especially in healthcare and climate, but in aspects of education policy as well. As the next three chapters attest, Trump soon launched numerous executive initiatives to reverse the course the Obama administration had charted.

THREE

THE ADMINISTRATIVE WAR ON
THE AFFORDABLE CARE ACT

In August 2018, officials from Baltimore, Chicago, Cincinnati, and Columbus (Ohio), along with two individual plaintiffs, filed suit in a federal district court claiming that President Trump had "turned to executive action alone to try to sabotage" the Affordable Care Act (ACA).[1] The suit claimed that Trump's actions violated the Administrative Procedure Act and the constitutional requirement that the president "take care that the laws be faithfully executed."[2] These city officials were far from alone in applying the term "sabotage" to the strategic posture of the Trump administration toward Obamacare. Scholarly work[3] has also used the term, as have congressional Democrats,[4] in criticizing the president. In this chapter, we argue that the term "sabotage" aptly characterized the preponderance of executive actions the Trump administration took toward the ACA.

What does sabotage mean in the context of the administrative presidency? Presidents, upon taking office, have priorities that typically trigger executive actions strengthening some programs while weakening others. In essence, they pick winners and losers. The losing programs often face reductions in resources, pressure to deemphasize certain goals, directives to alter their administrative approaches, and other measures that can undermine their effectiveness. In doing so, a presidential administration often pays lip service to the program, claiming it has been "modernized," made less burdensome, or otherwise improved.

In contrast, Webster's dictionary defines "sabotage" as efforts to foster deliberate "destruction and obstruction" of some target by opponents. It connotes a basic effort to "cause the failure of something."[5] In the context of the administrative presidency, sabotage goes beyond more common presidential initiatives to deemphasize certain agencies and programs. Instead, it reflects a commitment to program termination. Pursuing sabotage, President Trump openly denounced Obamacare as a failure. The president predicted that the ACA's insurance exchanges would explode, and his actions from the start sought to fulfill that prophecy. Subsequently, the Trump administration extended its sabotage initiatives beyond the exchanges to the entire ACA, including the Medicaid expansion. It did so by ordering the Justice Department not to defend the ACA's core provisions in an appellate court after a district court judge in Texas deemed the entire law unconstitutional. To an extraordinary, perhaps unprecedented, degree in the annals of the administrative presidency, executive actions toward the ACA raised doubts that the Trump administration was fulfilling the constitutional requirement to take care that the laws be faithfully executed.

This chapter opens by briefly assessing the largely abortive efforts of congressional Republicans to repeal and replace the ACA. While failing at major legislative change, tax legislation approved by Congress did remove one of the ACA's linchpins—the financial penalty associated with the mandate requiring Americans to obtain health insurance. The chapter then describes the strategies the Trump administration employed to sabotage the health insurance marketplaces. Core strategies included: the reduction of outreach and opportunities for enrollment, the slashing of federal subsidies to insurance companies, the construction of several off-ramps to lower-quality insurance that would siphon off healthier enrollees from the exchanges, and the failure to fully defend the ACA against a suit challenging its constitutionality brought by state Republican officials.

The chapter then explicates the Trump administration's efforts to reshape Medicaid, the second major pillar of the ACA's coverage expansion. Executive action here centered on the approval of demonstration waivers that imposed work requirements and other administrative burdens on enrollees. It also included efforts by the Department of Homeland Security to discourage legal immigrants from seeking Medicaid for themselves and their children. If fully implemented, these actions would likely depress Medicaid enrollments appreciably. The chapter's concluding section assesses the degree to which the Trump administrative presidency succeeded in vitiating the ACA during its initial period. Given unresolved court challenges brought by state officials and others, as well as additional state policy initiatives, uncertainty shrouds this assessment. On balance, however, the record appears mixed. The Trump administration has succeeded in unleashing termites to weaken the foundation of the ACA. But the exchanges and Medicaid have proven more resilient than many expected.

Barely and Partly Dodging a Congressional Bullet

From the time it took office in January 2017, the Trump administration pursued a range of executive initiatives to undercut the ACA. In those heady initial days, Republican policymakers fully expected that Congress would be the main vehicle for fulfilling their six-year signature commitment to repeal and replace Obamacare. The opening act in the congressional drama took place in the House of Representatives and led to the May passage of the American Health Care Act (AHCA) by a 217 to 213 vote.[6] The AHCA established a core theme that marked nearly all subsequent Republican proposals. The point was not just to replace Obamacare but also to retrench Medicaid, which had been a central element of President Lyndon Johnson's Great Society program in 1965. The AHCA proposed, as of 2020, to reduce the federal contribution, or match, for covering the Medicaid expansion cohort from 90 percent to the proportion that applied to other enrollees (from 50 to about 75 percent, depending on the state). Beyond this, the AHCA converted Medicaid from a fiscal entitlement where the federal government matched whatever a state spent to a "capitated" block grant with an upper limit on the federal subsidy.[7] The Congressional Budget Office (CBO) projected that the AHCA would reduce Medicaid spending by $834 billion and cause 14 million enrollees to lose coverage over ten years.[8]

The AHCA also contained myriad provisions related to the exchanges. It terminated cost-sharing reduction (CSR) payments to exchange insurance companies as of 2020 and reduced federal tax credits to individuals purchasing coverage. The law also eliminated the tax penalty for not having insurance, while allowing insurance companies to increase premiums for people who did not maintain continuous coverage. From a federalism perspective, it sought to reverse the thrust of the ACA, which had greatly increased federal regulation of health insurance relative to the states. The AHCA empowered states to reduce the essential health benefits that the ACA required insurers to offer; it also allowed states to weaken the ACA's community rating provisions that protected sicker individuals from having to pay higher premiums than healthier people. The CBO estimated that these and other AHCA exchange provisions would result in 9 million people losing coverage as of 2026.[9]

The second act of the repeal-and-replace drama transpired in two scenes that played out in the Senate. The first, which occurred in June and July 2017, featured Senate Majority Leader Mitch McConnell appointing a thirteen-member working group to devise an alternative bill, which emerged as the Better Care Reconciliation Act in late June. With modest exceptions, the bill mirrored the Medicaid template embedded in the House's AHCA. The CBO calculated that over ten years, the bill would reduce Medicaid spending by $772 billion and the number of enrollees by 15 million. The CBO also estimated that the exchange provisions in the Senate bill would lead 7 million people to lose coverage by 2026.[10] Due to opposition from a handful of Republican senators and all their Democratic colleagues, McConnell abandoned this initial legislation and sought backing for several revised versions. But these efforts also failed, and by the end of July repeal-and-replace legislation appeared dead.

The second scene involved efforts by two Republican senators, Lindsey Graham of South Carolina and Bill Cassidy of Louisiana, to resurrect repeal-and-replace. Released in September, the Graham-Cassidy bill also sought to convert the pre-ACA Medicaid program into a capitated block grant. But it departed radically from prior proposals in two major respects. First, the bill called for massive devolution in the form of a new block grant that would, from 2020 through 2026, give states the monies the federal government would have otherwise spent on the exchanges and Medicaid expansion. Federal health insurance regulation and subsidies for people to purchase individual policies in the marketplaces would end in 2020. Each state could then use its block grant to create its own health insurance coverage program from scratch, a massive policy and administrative challenge. Most states would receive less money for this purpose than under the ACA. Second, the Graham-Cassidy proposal reshaped the funding formula for the massive block grant to benefit states that had not expanded Medicaid. New York, for instance, would endure an estimated 35 percent cut in expansion monies from 2000 to 2026, while Texas would increase by 75 percent.[11] A preliminary CBO analysis indicated that the bill would greatly increase the number of uninsured.[12] Like its July predecessors, Graham-Cassidy failed to attract enough Republican support to pass.

The third act of the repeal-and-replace drama took place in December 2017 under the guise of tax reform. With no support from Democrats, Congress approved a major tax bill that President Trump promptly signed. The measure had at least three significant implications for the ACA. First, it repealed the tax penalty for failing to comply with the "individual mandate" to obtain health insurance. Without this penalty, the risk grew that healthier people would decline to buy insurance, and exchange premiums would soar as people with more medical problems disproportionately enrolled. The CBO estimated that 13 million would lose health insurance over a decade as the result of repeal.[13]

Second, the bill limited the federal deduction for individuals paying state and local taxes to a maximum of $10,000. This meant that states with more generous Medicaid programs would likely have to exert greater tax effort to sustain their spending on the program.[14] Many residents in high-tax states had obtained some fiscal relief by deducting their state and local taxes from their income on their federal returns. Under the new law, they would not receive this offset. Their increased tax burden might prompt them to become more resistant to spending on redistributive programs such as Medicaid. Third, the Congressional Joint Committee on Taxation projected that the tax bill would boost the federal debt by over $1 trillion over ten years.[15] This development seemed likely to renew Republican pressure to retrench major health care entitlements, such as the ACA and Medicaid.

In reviewing the congressional politics of repeal-and-replace, political scientists Jacob Hacker and Paul Pierson observe that the Republican repeal drive resulted in "the most unpopular piece of major legislation with a real chance of passage in the past quarter century. . . . Party leaders pursued policies that were manifestly and massively unpopular, yet they came remarkably close to success—the dog that almost barked." Opposed, as well, by nearly all major health care provider groups, the Republican initiative "did more to improve the [ACA's] public standing than the Democrats had in the seven years" since the law's passage.[16]

Sabotage of the Insurance Exchanges

Well before Congress failed to overturn Obamacare, the Trump administration had employed a range of administrative tools to undercut the exchanges. On his first day in office, the president issued an executive order directing administrative agencies within "the maximum extent permitted by law" to "exercise all authority and discretion available to them to waive, defer, grant exemption from, or delay" any statutory provision that would impose a fiscal or regulatory burden on the states, individuals, health care providers, and other stakeholders.[17] Under the banner of this executive order, the administration pursued several key strategies to chip away at the exchanges over the next three years. These included reducing outreach and opportunities for enrollment, cutting subsidies to insurance companies, building multiple off-ramps to lower-quality coverage, and failing to launch a full-throated defense of the ACA's constitutionality in the federal courts.

Reduced Outreach and Opportunities for Enrollment

Concerned to attract healthy younger people to the exchanges to achieve a "balanced risk pool" that would keep premiums down, the Obama administration aggressively promoted the ACA. Among other things, it ran ads, subsidized workers to assist people in signing up for insurance, encouraged the creation of supportive private nonprofit organizations such as Enroll America, and persuaded the Robert Wood Johnson Foundation to fund take-up initiatives.

Upon assuming office, the Trump administration immediately moved to limit advertising and other outreach as well as reduce enrollment windows. In January 2017, the White House pulled $5 million in ads that the Obama administration had authorized. In late July, the White House terminated contracts with two firms that had helped people in certain cities enroll. In early September, the Centers for Medicare and Medicaid Services (CMS) announced that it had nearly halved funding for the ACA's navigator program, which paid frontline workers to assist people in purchasing insurance.[18] Ten months later, and much to the consternation of a coalition of 190 patient organizations (for example, the American Heart Association), CMS announced that it would provide only $10 million for navigator grants in 2019. This sum was $26 million less than in 2018 and $53 million less than the Obama administration had allocated in its last year.[19] In defending these cuts, CMS Administrator Seema Verma argued that it was natural for the exchanges to have large marketing budgets initially, but that spending could subsequently be pared as people became more aware of them. She dismissed research findings advanced by California officials that aggressive outreach would facilitate a better risk pool, thereby lowering exchange premiums by about 3 percent.[20]

The Trump administration undercut the navigators in other ways. The ACA required state insurance exchanges to supplement federal subsidies by using their own funds to establish a grant program for navigators. Existing regulations specified that the exchanges had to fund at least two grantees, and that one had to be a "community and consumer-focused nonprofit group." They also mandated that the navigators be physically present in the exchange service area "so that face-to-face assistance can be provided to applicants and enrollees." In mid-2018, the Trump administration removed both these requirements.[21]

In addition to curbing outreach, the Trump administration often changed its content from positive to negative. For example, the Department of Health and Human Services posted videos on YouTube of people who said they had been burdened by the law.[22] The department also relied on tweets and news releases to portray the program negatively. For example, CMS Administrator Seema Verma kicked off the opening of exchange enrollment on November 1, 2018, with the following tweet: "The big SECRET no one reports: #Obamacare's skyrocketing premiums are destroying affordable options for the unsubsidized including people with preexisting conditions."[23]

The Trump administration also pared enrollment windows. In April 2017, it promulgated a "market stabilization" rule that halved the application period for 2018 from three months to a month and a half—November 1 to December 15, 2017.[24] The rule also restricted the use of "special enrollment periods" for people with health problems who failed to sign up at the beginning of the year. Insurance companies generally supported the Trump administration's market stabilization rule on grounds that it would "decrease the incentives for individuals to enroll only after they discover they require medical services."[25] Rather than enhance the risk pool, however, the rule might worsen it. Shorter enrollment periods, especially when accompanied by enervated outreach, would be unlikely to discourage sicker people with chronic conditions from applying for insurance. But it might well deter healthier applicants with a less immediate need for coverage. The Obama administration supported the longer three-month enrollment period out of a conviction that it would enable the exchanges to attract younger, healthier people who often signed up at the last minute.

Boomerang: Cutting Subsidies to Insurance Companies

The ACA authorized subsidies to health insurance companies in the exchanges to reduce their risk of losing money. Among other things, the law established the "Three Rs"—reinsurance, risk corridors, and risk adjustment—to compensate companies that disproportionately enrolled sicker individuals with greater healthcare costs.[26] *Reinsurance* featured CMS payments to insurance companies for their high-cost enrollees, with these companies and self-insured plans[27] contributing funds to finance these payments. *Risk corridors* involved the federal bureaucracy in collecting funds from insurance plans with lower than expected claims, and redistributing them to plans with higher than anticipated payouts. The ACA envisioned reinsurance and risk corridors as temporary, in effect from 2014 through 2016, to entice insurance companies to participate in the marketplaces and keep premiums down. In contrast, the ACA established *risk adjustment* as a permanent feature of exchange implementation. This provision called on federal officials to perform a highly technical, complex administrative task: computation of an insurance plan's average actuarial risk based on how healthy its enrollees appeared to be. Officials would then redistribute funds from insurance plans with lower risk scores (that is, with healthier enrollees) to those with higher ones.

Political dynamics prior to the Trump administration had already undercut the Three Rs, thereby fueling increases in exchange premiums. Risk corridors in particular had come under siege. The methodology established by the Obama administration had resulted in many more companies qualifying for payments to compensate them for unexpectedly high claims than carriers who had overestimated their costs and contributed to a funding pool. CMS acknowledged that it owed insurance companies over $12 billion in outstanding risk corridor payments for the period of 2014 to 2016. The ACA authorized CMS to draw on its general appropriation to pay this debt. But, starting in December 2014, congressional Republicans approved riders to appropriations bills that required the risk corridor program to be budget neutral, thereby ruling out this option. Insurance companies filed dozens of lawsuits in the federal courts seeking to collect the promised payments. After a court of appeals ruled against the companies in June 2018, they appealed to the Supreme Court, which in 2020 sided with insurers and reversed the lower court.[28]

When the Trump administration arrived in 2017, only risk adjustment among the original Three Rs remained in effect. It had become embroiled in litigation brought by certain insurance companies unhappy with the monies they received as a result of the CMS formula for calculating the health risk scores of their enrollees.[29] Rather than seek to undermine the exchanges by entering this legal thicket, the Trump administration targeted another insurance subsidy, CSR payments. The rationale for these payments stemmed from the fact that exchange insurance in varying degrees required significant cost sharing by patients (for example, deductibles, copayments). To prevent these costs from becoming onerous, the ACA had required insurance companies not to impose them on people with incomes from 100 to 250 percent of poverty. In turn, the federal government would provide CSR payments to compensate insurers for foregoing these patient contributions.

As discussed previously, Congress had persuaded a federal district court that the Obama administration had no authority to make CSR payments without an explicit congressional appropriation. The Obama administration appealed this decision and continued to make CSR payments. The Trump administration initially refused to clarify whether it would continue CSR and persist with the Obama administration's appeal of the district court ruling. This lack of resolve triggered legal action by most Democratic state attorneys general in support of CSR. The attorneys general argued that the Trump administration could not be trusted to defend federal executive branch prerogatives in the courts and that subjecting CSR payments to the annual congressional appropriations process would make the states' "task in regulating and providing health insurance to their residents more complex, unpredictable and expensive."[30] In October 2017, the Trump administration finally announced it would not appeal the lower court ruling, thereby terminating CSR payments unless Congress restored them. In response, the Democratic state attorneys general urged the federal courts to overrule the president and continue CSR. The Trump administration's CSR actions roiled the operation of the insurance exchanges. Some insurance carriers withdrew from the marketplaces while others hiked premiums appreciably.

Soon, however, the forces of federalism caused the Trump administration's CSR strategy to boomerang. Responding to incentives embedded in the ACA, insurance companies strove to compensate for CSR cuts by "silver loading" premium increases. Regulators in forty-one states permitted them to do so.[31] The term "silver loading" has its origins in the color scheme applied to exchange health insurance policies to reflect their actuarial value:

- bronze: 60 percent

- silver: 70 percent (includes the benchmark plan that determines the amount of the tax credit for those with incomes from 100 to 400 percent of poverty)

- gold: 80 percent

- platinum: 90 percent

Actuarial value refers to the cost sharing an average enrollee is likely to experience in such a plan. For instance, up to some cap, a typical enrollee in a silver plan could expect to pay 30 percent of her bills for medical care. In general, people face higher premiums for plans with greater actuarial value.

The ACA designates certain silver plans as the benchmark[32] for enrollees with incomes from 100 to 400 percent of poverty, whose insurance the government subsidizes. This means that within this cohort the tax credit for an individual or family increases to the degree that the premium for the benchmark silver plan rises.[33] The subsidy remains the same even if an individual signs up for a different color plan, which might well have lower premiums than the benchmark silver offering.[34] By loading premium increases on silver, rather than bronze, gold, or platinum plans, insurance companies could generate revenues to compensate for lost CSR payments while simultaneously helping the subsidized group obtain a greater insurance tax credit from the federal government. The practice permitted the federally subsidized purchasers in some states to pay zero premiums for bronze plans and to obtain gold plans (which had less cost sharing for medical services) for lower premiums than silver plans.[35] Hence, despite the steep premiums on silver plans, subsidized individuals still had substantial incentive to enroll in the exchanges. Silver loading also had the effect of shifting a greater share of the overall costs for insurance premiums from subsidized enrollees to the federal treasury. The higher the premium on the benchmark silver plan the greater the premium subsidy to individuals in the 100 to 400 percent income cohort. Ironically, this meant the federal government wound up with a higher tab for these enrollees than if they had continued the CSR payments and had not incentivized insurance companies to do silver loading. Reflecting this development, CBO, in April 2018, categorized a resumption of CSR payments as a deficit reduction measure.[36]

Aware of these developments, the Democratic state attorneys general and ACA advocacy groups had second thoughts about reviving CSR payments. In March 2018, Families USA and the Center on Budget and Policy Priorities affirmed that, given the benefits of silver loading, congressional restoration of CSR might do more harm than good for people with incomes below 400 percent of poverty.[37] In July, the Democratic attorneys general who had sued the Trump administration over CSR reached an agreement with a federal court to dismiss the case. The court did, however, preserve the opportunity for the state attorneys general to refile if the Trump administration subsequently moved to eliminate silver loading.[38]

As 2019 dawned, uncertainty clouded the future of CSR and silver loading. While the Democratic attorneys general had dropped their suit, insurance companies sought CSR relief from the U.S. Court of Federal Claims.[39] In late 2018, this court ruled that the government had to reimburse a Montana co-op nearly $6 million in CSR payments. In November, Blue Cross Blue Shield and its subsidiaries in Florida also sued to compel the government to make these payments.[40] Meanwhile, in March 2018, CMS Administrator Seema Verma expressed concern that silver loading would have adverse consequences for unsubsidized purchasers of exchange products as well as for the federal budget.[41] By late 2019, however, CMS had not prohibited the practice for the 2020 enrollment year.

Off-Ramp to Lower-Quality Insurance: Short-Term Becomes Long-Term

The ACA sought to upgrade the quality of insurance. Of particular importance, it stipulated that small group and individual insurance had to cover ten essential health services (including mental health and maternity care), provide financial protection against bankruptcy in the case of severe illness, and guarantee coverage to those with preexisting conditions without imposing excessive premiums (community rating).[42] Vowing to promote less expensive options for consumers, the Trump administration moved to increase access to coverage that did not meet these quality standards. By so doing, it heightened the risk that healthier applicants would flee the exchanges, leaving them with a more expensive risk pool that would place upward pressures on premiums. These rising premiums would likely fuel declines in exchange enrollments, especially among those with incomes above 400 percent of the poverty line.

Bolstering access to "short-term" health coverage comprised one off-ramp to lower-quality insurance. In October 2017, President Trump issued an executive order titled "Promoting Healthcare Competition and Choice Across the United States."[43] In response, the Departments of Treasury, Labor, and Health and Human Services teamed up to revise Obama-era regulations on short-term, limited-duration insurance. Such insurance was designed to provide people who were temporarily uninsured with an opportunity to purchase some protection until they obtained more permanent coverage. Concerned that short-term products not substitute for exchange insurance, the Obama administration in late 2016 published a rule limiting their duration to three months, with the possibility of renewal for up to one year.

Prodded by Trump's executive order, federal administrators now worked to reverse that decision. In August 2018, they published a revised federal rule that did much to establish short-term insurance as an alternative to the exchanges, affirming that such insurance could last 364 days and be renewed for up to thirty-six months.[44] Companies offering these products did not need to offer the ACA's ten essential health benefits and could reject applicants on the basis of health criteria (for example, those with preexisting conditions, an estimated 27 percent of all non-elderly adults).[45] Federal officials acknowledged that the rule would appreciably increase the number of people buying short-term products and that these individuals would likely be "healthier than average" (p. 38228). They conceded that the rule would worsen the risk pool on the exchanges, leading to a 5 percent average increase in premiums. The rule paid some homage to principles of federalism by granting state insurance regulators discretion to establish more restrictive limits on short-term policies. It also required all short-term products to include a warning that this coverage was not as comprehensive and guaranteed as ACA-compliant insurance on the exchanges.

Many of the 12,000 public comments federal officials received on the proposed rule opposed the changes. Among its opponents, none were more vociferous than advocates for those with mental health problems, maternal care needs, or expensive health needs (for example, HIV), who feared that the short-term plans would not cover these conditions. Seven organizations representing these interests (for example, the American Psychiatric Association, AIDS United, the National Partnership for Women & Families) filed suit against the rule in the District of Columbia federal district court in September 2018.[46] In July, the district court judge found the benefits of the short-term rule to be "undeniable" and sided with the Trump administration. Vowing to block efforts "to expand dramatically the sale of junk insurance," the seven organizations appealed the ruling to a higher court.[47]

Off-Ramp to Lower-Quality Insurance: Association Health Plans

The promotion of association health plans comprised the second key initiative of the Trump administration to increase the availability of cheaper, non-ACA-compliant coverage. Regulated for decades by the Employee Retirement and Income Security Act (ERISA), these plans gave smaller employers (generally those with no more than fifty full-time-equivalent employees) an opportunity to form an association to purchase health insurance coverage. As part of a larger group, these employers stood a better chance of obtaining reasonably priced insurance than if they tried to buy it on their own.[48] The Obama administration had interpreted the ACA and ERISA to mean that many multiple-employer health plans would have to meet the quality standards that applied to the exchanges. Only association health plans that met certain criteria could obtain a special classification that exempted them from the ACA and much state regulation. One such criterion was that the employers forming them had to have a "commonality of interest" (for example, farm or restaurant owners). Another criterion was that small enterprises joining the plan had to have one or more employees in addition to the business owner and spouse. Plans tailored to individuals who worked by themselves as independent contractors or sole proprietors would not escape ACA quality regulation. These and other criteria significantly restricted the spread of association health plans.[49]

In October 2017, President Trump issued an executive order directing the Secretary of Labor to open the gates to noncompliant association plans. After receiving 900 mostly negative comments on a proposed rule, the Department of Labor issued a final regulation in late June 2018.[50] The rule took two major steps to enlarge the numbers of people covered by association health plans that did not meet the ACA's quality standards. First, it expanded the employers who could form them from those with a commonality of interest based on being in the "same trade, industry, line of business, or profession" (for example, farm owners) to occupationally diverse small employers who resided in a defined *geographic* area. Specifically, the rule permitted all employers that have "a principal place of business within a region that does not exceed the boundaries of the same State or the same metropolitan area" to form a plan.[51] Second, the rule expanded the definition of employer to include individuals who were "working owners" with no employees. This group of self-employed people had previously been limited to seeking insurance in the individual market, which had to comply with the ACA's quality standards. The rule now enabled them to form association health plans to obtain cheaper, noncompliant coverage. The only significant requirement was that these individuals work at least twenty hours a week or eighty hours a month.

The Department of Labor estimated that the rule would lead some 4 million individuals to gain coverage from association health plans, with 10 percent coming from the ranks of the uninsured.[52] Officials acknowledged that the new rule would, to some degree, cause healthier individuals to select association health plans, leaving those with greater medical needs disproportionately enrolled in the exchanges—a dynamic that would drive up premiums.

The rule to expand opportunities for association health plans kindled a court challenge. In late July 2018, Democratic attorneys general from eleven states and the District of Columbia sued in a federal district court to block the new rule.[53] The suit charged that the rule compelled states to devote more resources to preventing consumer fraud and abuse. (Association health plans historically had a record of engaging in such practices as failing to pay promised medical benefits.) The attorneys general also claimed the rule would increase costs to the states by destabilizing insurance markets and diminishing the number of people with comprehensive coverage, especially hurting those with preexisting medical conditions. In sum, the attorneys general charged that the rule was a "radical reinterpretation of the term 'employer'" that violated the Administrative Procedure Act by departing sharply from prior, more legitimate understandings of ERISA.[54] In late March 2019, a federal district court sided with the attorneys general and vacated the new ERISA rule. The Trump administration soon filed an appeal of the lower court decision on grounds that the states lacked standing to challenge the new rule because they could not meaningfully demonstrate that it injured them. Meanwhile, the Department of Labor announced that it would not take enforcement action against existing association health plans that did not meet ACA requirements.

State Innovation Waivers: From Helping Hand to Sabotage

The ACA had authorized states as of 2017 to propose Section 1332 waivers to pursue innovative alternatives to achieving the law's goals. The Obama administration had established certain "guardrails" for these waivers to prevent them from watering down the ACA. It insisted that state alternatives provide coverage that was at least as comprehensive and at least as affordable as the ACA. It also stipulated that the waiver cover at least a comparable number of state residents and not increase the federal deficit.

The Trump administration's initial use of these waivers departed sharply from the sabotage that generally characterized its posture toward the marketplaces. From the outset, top officials expressed enthusiasm about prospects for state innovation using Section 1332 waivers. In a letter to governors in early March 2017, then Secretary of Health and Human Services Thomas Price invited states to submit proposals that would slow the rate of premium growth and improve the exchange risk pools.[55] The letter pointed to "reinsurance" as one way to accomplish this. This approach offered subsidies to insurance companies for covering people with more costly medical needs, thereby allowing them to set lower premiums that would presumably help them attract healthier enrollees.

CMS followed up its verbal commitment to reinsurance with action. In mid-2017, the agency approved a 1332 waiver proposal from Alaska that allowed the state to use federal funds to defray the cost of a reinsurance program. In turn, the lower premiums that resulted would reduce the tax credits the federal government had to provide to exchange enrollees with incomes below 400 percent of poverty. By late 2019, eleven more states (Colorado, Delaware, Maine, Maryland, Minnesota, Montana, New Jersey, North Dakota, Oregon, Rhode Island, and Wisconsin) had received CMS blessings to use reinsurance.

The successful proposals largely came from relatively liberal states, with eight of the twelve having voted for Hillary Clinton in 2016. Why did the Trump administration abandon sabotage to approve these waivers to buttress the marketplaces? We lack evidence to answer this question definitively, but it may be that principles of federalism mattered—where the administration's declared commitment to greater state flexibility overrode its desire to undermine the exchanges.

While the initial use of 1332 waivers bolstered the exchanges, the Trump administration subsequently sought to use this tool for sabotage.

In October 2018, CMS issued new guidelines to the states that replaced the Obama guardrails promulgated in 2015. The new guidelines changed the name of the initiatives to "State Relief and Empowerment Waivers." They emphasized that CMS would prioritize access to coverage over the quality ("comprehensiveness and content") of insurance in reviewing state proposals. This step opened the door to state proposals that called on the federal government to subsidize enrollment in noncompliant-ACA products, such as short-term and association health plans. While CMS Administrator Seema Verma denied that the new guidelines would adversely affect people with preexisting conditions, the move heightened the risk that healthier people would exit the exchanges, worsening their risk pools.[56] CMS also made the waiver application process less prone to legislative veto at the state level. The Obama guardrails had insisted that the legislature and the governor sign off on a waiver proposal. The Trump administration relaxed this requirement and made it easier for a governor to submit the waiver application without specific legislative authorization.[57]

Response to the new guidelines divided along predictable partisan lines in Congress. Senator Lamar Alexander, a Republican from Tennessee who chaired the Committee on Health, Education, Labor, and Pensions, praised the action while complaining that Democrats "have elevated Obamacare to the 67th book of the bible and refused . . . to fix even a word of the law's waiver provision."[58] In turn, Senator Ron Wyden, Democrat from Oregon, asserted that the new guidance "rolls out the red carpet for junk insurance."[59]

The degree to which the new CMS guidelines would fuel flight from the ACA-compliant exchanges to lower-quality plans depended on state willingness to pursue such waivers. Six months later, no state had requested waivers in response to the new Section 1332 guidance. Concerned by this lack of interest, CMS Administrator Seema Verma in late April 2019 implored states to take advantage of the new waiver flexibility.[60] Finally, Republican Governor Brian Kemp of Georgia announced in early November that his state would propose a 1332 waiver that would, among other things, allow individuals with incomes below 400 percent of poverty to use their federal tax credits to subsidize the purchase of noncompliant ACA coverage. Whether the Georgia proposal, if approved by CMS, would survive a certain court challenge remained unclear as 2020 dawned.

Zigzagging toward the Nuclear Option in the Federal Courts

U.S. legal doctrine has long assumed that the executive branch would defend laws passed by Congress and signed by a president if challenged in court. Whether the law was deemed constitutional would generally be left to the judicial branch. In recent decades, however, the decision on whether to defend a law in court has become a tool of the administrative presidency. Thus, the Obama administration decided that to advance gay rights it would not defend the Defense of Marriage Act, which affirmed that marriage should be between a man and a woman. In a similar vein, the Trump administration chose not to fully defend the ACA against efforts of state Republican officials to have the entire law declared unconstitutional.

The case arose from a suit filed by eighteen Republican state attorneys general, two Republican governors, and two Texas residents in Fort Worth, Texas. The suit based its argument on the congressional repeal of the penalty associated with the individual mandate the prior December. A Supreme Court decision in 2012 had upheld the constitutionality of the mandate on grounds that it was a tax on those who failed to obtain health insurance. With the tax repealed, the Republican officials and two individual plaintiffs argued that the mandate (without any penalty) was unconstitutional. It required the two Texas residents to buy health insurance they did not want. More dramatically, the plaintiffs argued that the mandate, as the linchpin of the ACA, could not be severed from the law's myriad other provisions (including the Medicaid expansion). Hence, they urged the district court to throw out the entire ACA.

To enhance prospects that a court would undertake such radical action, the Republican plaintiffs engaged in what can be termed "forum shopping squared." Plaintiffs of all ideological stripes routinely seek to file suits in court jurisdictions known to sympathize with their views, but plaintiffs do not typically determine which judge within a district hears their case. However, the Fort Worth Division of the Federal District Court for Northern Texas had only one judge, Reed O'Connor, who had burnished a reputation for being the go-to judge for a spectrum of conservative causes. Thus, Republican plaintiffs picked not only the jurisdiction but the judge who would hear the case.[61]

The Republican suit triggered a response from both the Trump administration and Democratic state attorneys general who filed court briefs in June 2018. Initially, the Justice Department partially defended the ACA. While agreeing that abolishing the tax penalty invalidated the individual mandate,[62] it argued that Republican officials went too far in asserting that this voided the entire ACA. Rather, the specific provisions protecting those with preexisting conditions through guaranteed issue and community rating had to be tossed. Such a step would leave the ACA's Medicaid expansion intact but would gravely threaten the viability of the exchanges.

The Trump administration's halfway posture meant that the full-throated defense of the ACA fell to sixteen Democratic state attorneys general (plus the District of Columbia). The Democratic brief claimed that the Republican suit called for action that was "truly unprecedented" and "profoundly undemocratic" in throwing out a major law approved by elected officials.[63] It presented a panoply of counterarguments asserting that the mandate was constitutional and, anyway, could readily be severed from the rest of the law. The attorneys general pointed out that Republican senators sponsoring tax penalty repeal had affirmed in congressional speeches that it would not adversely affect other ACA provisions. They underscored that any harm to the two Texas residents imposed by the ACA would be far outweighed by the "havoc" an injunction would wreak "on the healthcare market for patients, providers, insurance carriers, and federal and state governments."[64]

But forum shopping squared paid dividends for state Republican plaintiffs. In December 2018, Judge Reed O'Connor lived up to his conservative reputation by striking down the entire ACA. Responding to the ruling, which both conservative and liberal legal experts criticized,[65] the Democratic attorneys general appealed to the Fifth Circuit Court of Appeals in New Orleans. In January 2019, the House of Representatives, now in control of the Democrats, obtained permission from the Fifth Circuit to join the case and file its own brief defending the ACA.

Meanwhile, the Trump administration announced it was abandoning its partial defense of the ACA to join Republican state officials in calling for the law's obliteration. In late March, President Trump accepted the advice of his acting chief of staff, Mick Mulvaney, and the head of the White House Domestic Policy Council, Joe Grogan, to seize the opportunity to have the courts accomplish what a Republican Congress had failed to do: repeal the signature legislative achievement of his predecessor. In doing so, President Trump overrode opposition from Attorney General William Barr and reservations expressed by the White House Counsel and Secretary of Health and Human Services (among others).[66]

Having publicly embraced the nuclear option, however, the Trump administration subsequently backed away from full support of the Republican attorneys general in two respects. First, while providing no specific plan, the Justice Department suggested that the court stop short of eradicating the entire law because some of its provisions had nothing to do with the complaints of the two Texas residents that the ACA required them to buy insurance they did not want. In sum, "the relief awarded to plaintiffs should extend only to the ACA's provisions that actually injure them." By way of example, the Justice Department pointed to ACA provisions that amended "several criminal statutes used to prosecute individuals who defraud our healthcare system." Its brief affirmed that it was "unlikely" that the Texas plaintiffs had standing to challenge the validity of these provisions.[67] The brief clarified that this limitation on dismantling the ACA would not save the Medicaid expansion from termination.

Second, in a last-minute shift of positions during the oral argument before the appellate court, the Trump administration asserted that a ruling invalidating the ACA would apply only to the eighteen states and the two Texans who were plaintiffs. This view departed sharply from the widely held prior understanding that the court decision would apply to all states. If the court accepted this argument, it would mean that the eighteen plaintiff states,[68] all dominated by Republicans, would lose major ACA subsidies. In turn, the remaining states, where Democratic policymakers were stronger, would continue to operate under the ACA. When pressed by appellate judges at the oral briefing to describe how this approach would be implemented, the Department of Justice declined to offer details.

In mid-December 2019, a three-judge panel of the Fifth Circuit concurred, 2 to 1, with the district court ruling that the ACA's individual mandate was unconstitutional even without the tax penalty attached to it. In doing so, however, the appellate court deferred substantially to Justice Department arguments by remanding the case back to Judge Reed O'Conner for further deliberation with explicit instructions to apply a "finer-toothed comb" to the severability issue. It ordered the district court to consider methodically whether each of the ACA's ten titles could be retained in part or fully despite the ruling on the mandate. The appellate court also directed O'Connor to consider the last-minute Justice Department argument that the law be declared unconstitutional only in the Republican states bringing the case.[69] The Democratic state attorneys general and their fellow partisans in the House of Representatives who had intervened promptly appealed the Fifth Circuit decision to the Supreme Court. While the Trump administration argued that the case should be returned to the Fort Worth district court for further consideration, the Supreme Court in early March 2020 agreed to accept it. It appeared likely that the Supreme Court would hear the case in the fall of that election year with a ruling on the ACA's fate to be announced in 2021.

Medicaid: Waivers to Erode Enrollments

The Trump administration belatedly attempted to help persuade the courts to gut the Medicaid expansion.[70] But from the outset, it had initiated other efforts to vitiate Medicaid, drawing on demonstration waivers as a policy tool. Authorized under Section 1115 of the Social Security Act, these waivers have proliferated and profoundly shaped who gets what, when, and how from Medicaid over the last three decades.[71] About 80 percent of the states had these demonstration waivers either operating or pending when President Trump took office. The Trump administration moved rapidly to repudiate key dimensions of the Obama administration waiver legacy. Some initial steps were highly incremental, placating governors in non-Medicaid expansion states. For instance, the Obama administration had used the waiver renewal process in an attempt to motivate resistant states to expand Medicaid. It singled out waivers that allowed states such as Florida, Kansas, Tennessee, and Texas to establish pools that diverted Medicaid monies into subsidies for hospitals rather than insurance for individuals. The Obama administration saw no need to continue these hospital pools when the state could address the problem of uncompensated care by expanding Medicaid. Thus, when Florida sought to renew its hospital pool, CMS announced its intent to phase out the program. Upon taking office, the Trump administration moved rapidly to ease pressure on Florida and other non-expansion states, promising to preserve funds for hospitals.

New Waiver Themes: Work Requirements and Administrative Burdens

Beyond these incremental steps, the Trump administration sought to forge new waiver themes to transform the program. These themes emphasized work mandates, greater premiums, more extensive reporting, and a gaggle of other requirements for the able-bodied, non-elderly adults targeted by the ACA's Medicaid expansion. Collectively, these requirements would greatly increase the administrative burdens on Medicaid applicants and beneficiaries.

Research suggests that administrative burdens on those seeking public benefits assume three basic forms.[72] *Learning costs* capture how difficult it is for individuals to obtain information about a program and how to access its benefits. Keeping up with changes embedded in the new waivers was a demanding, time consuming task for the expansion cohort. Many lost eligibility for unknowingly failing to comply with the new requirements. *Psychological costs* involve program signals about the social worth of its beneficiaries and whether they should be stigmatized for seeking benefits. Many of the new Medicaid waivers played heavily on the theme that the ACA expansion population was undeserving. Work requirements, for example, sent the message that the expansion population tended to be freeloaders and had to be compelled to seek employment. Finally, *compliance costs* refer to the time and effort (for example, documentation requirements) the eligible population must spend to apply for and retain Medicaid eligibility. For example, the Medicaid waiver proposals tended to increase the reporting requirements enrollees faced. Whatever the precise form, the costs imposed by the administrative burdens embedded in the waivers promised to drive down Medicaid enrollments.

To carry out the new waiver policy, Trump nominated Seema Verma to lead CMS. The former head of a health policy consulting firm with a graduate degree from the Johns Hopkins School of Public Health, she had assisted Indiana (under then Governor Mike Pence), Kentucky, and Ohio in developing market-oriented Medicaid expansion waivers emphasizing individual choice and personal responsibility. Once approved by the Senate, Verma quickly joined Secretary of Health and Human Services Tom Price in signaling receptivity to waiver provisions that the Obama administration had rejected. In March 2017, Price sent a letter to all governors that opened the door to "meritorious innovations" that imposed training or employment requirements on Medicaid beneficiaries.[73] It also endorsed premiums and other enrollee cost sharing as well as fees that would penalize enrollees who used hospital emergency rooms for nonurgent care. The letter invited governors to restore some of the barriers that had historically depressed take-up rates.[74] For instance, it welcomed state restrictions on "presumptive eligibility," which health care providers had used to obtain Medicaid funding for uninsured patients who appeared to qualify for Medicaid but had not yet formally applied.

In November, Verma developed these themes more fully. Speaking at a meeting of state Medicaid directors, she promised a "new day" for Medicaid, stressing that the ACA had caused the program to stray from its core mission of helping society's most vulnerable members. In her words: "The ACA moved millions of working-age, nondisabled adults into a program that was created to care for seniors in need, pregnant mothers, children and people with disabilities." This had stretched "the safety net for some of our most fragile populations, many of whom are on waiting lists for critical home-care services while states enroll millions of newly eligible, able-bodied adults" at an enhanced match rate of 90 percent. "If the match rate is a value we place on caring for our neediest citizens, this is backwards."[75]

Having portrayed the expansion population as undeserving and a threat to more meritorious cohorts of Medicaid enrollees, Verma went on to endorse state flexibility to impose work and community engagement requirements on able-bodied adults. In her view, these requirements would help these enrollees "break the chains of poverty" and surmount "the soft bigotry of low expectations consistently espoused by the prior administration."[76] Amplifying this theme, CMS prepared a new website that no longer included "increase and strengthen overall coverage of low-income individuals" as a Medicaid waiver goal.[77] On January 11, 2018, CMS sent a letter to state Medicaid directors justifying work requirements on grounds that they would "promote better mental, physical and emotional health" for beneficiaries "in furtherance of Medicaid program objectives."[78]

Several states responded favorably to CMS's new posture on Medicaid waivers. As of early December 2019, ten states (Arizona, Arkansas, Indiana, Kentucky, Michigan, New Hampshire, Ohio, South Carolina, Utah, and Wisconsin) had obtained CMS approval for work requirement waivers, with another eight awaiting the agency's decision on their proposals.[79] These work initiatives mirrored partisan divisions. All but two of the states with approved or pending waivers had a Republican governor at the time of waiver submission; all but two had voted for Trump in the 2016 presidential election.

The partisan outcomes of state elections often affect the waiver count. Maine had obtained approval of a work waiver under a Republican governor but withdrew it after the election of a Democratic successor in 2018. In late 2019, the newly elected Democratic governor of Kentucky announced he would do the same. Virginia's Democratic governor indicated he would withdraw that state's pending work waiver after the 2019 election gave his party control of both legislative houses. Waiver proposals varied in their work provisions, but they typically mandated that a specified cohort of non-elderly, able-bodied adults be employed for at least twenty hours per week. "Work" generally encompassed such activities as employment, education or training, and job search. The waivers also tended to allow enrollees to meet the requirement through various forms of community engagement, such as volunteering with a nonprofit group.

In weighing whether to approve work requirements, CMS officials could count on supportive public opinion. Survey data indicated that 70 percent of Americans backed such requirements.[80] But CMS also anticipated that advocates would challenge the legality of the waivers in court. While policymakers had long supported waivers, legislation, and other measures to impose work requirements on certain welfare and food stamp recipients, they had not applied them to Medicaid enrollees. This legacy prompted the agency to move guardedly in reviewing the waiver proposals and to reject certain state requests.

One brake on waiver approval derived from the fact that about half of the states proposing work requirements had not expanded Medicaid at the time they submitted their waiver requests. This raised the possibility that Medicaid enrollees in nonexpansion states would face a catch 22 in the form of a "subsidy cliff." This denotes a situation where compliance with the work requirement would cause a Medicaid enrollee to lose insurance coverage. Consider, for example, Mississippi, which had not expanded Medicaid and where only able-bodied adults with incomes up to 27 percent of the poverty level qualified for the program. If these adults found work paying the minimum wage, they would become ineligible for Medicaid; many of them would also still be in poverty and ineligible for exchange coverage (which targets people above the poverty line). Faced with this conundrum, CMS, in May 2018, urged several waiver applicants to reconsider their proposals to mitigate the threat of the subsidy cliff.[81]

State work requirements would by themselves sap Medicaid enrollments. But the degree of enrollment decline also depended on other administrative burdens embedded in the waivers. Reporting requirements comprised one such burden. These requirements become more burdensome if they must be done more frequently, call for more information to be submitted, and afford enrollees limited communication channels for reporting. Several of the approved work requirement waivers featured burdensome reporting requirements, with Arkansas providing an especially vivid illustration. This state required able-bodied enrollees age nineteen through forty-nine to report the status of their work efforts on a monthly basis, and it limited the venues for communicating this information. Despite the fact that many enrollees had no or limited computer skills, they had to report electronically through a special web portal the state created. If enrollees did not have access to the Internet at home or through mobile devices, county offices would have portals available during work hours. To use the portal, an enrollee needed an email address, a password unique to the portal, and a reference number that Medicaid officials had sent in a multipage letter. Once linked to the portal, enrollees had to click through several different screens to report their work and community engagement activities.

The requirement for electronic filing promised to tamp down the administrative costs of the work initiative. These costs are no small matter for states pursuing work requirement waivers. Although CMS does not take administrative costs into account in determining whether a waiver proposal is budget neutral, these costs tend to be substantial. Arkansas had further incentive to rely exclusively on an electronic portal because the federal government covers 90 percent of state administrative costs for pertinent information system development while subsidizing only half of most other administrative costs.[82] It is hardly surprising, therefore, that one Arkansas official commented: "If you implement it in the old-fashioned way of 'Come in to our county offices,' we would have to hire so many people—and that just doesn't make sense."[83]

Not surprising, this reporting structure precipitated sharp declines in Medicaid enrollments. The Arkansas waiver stipulated that beneficiaries who failed to comply with work requirements for three months would be locked out of coverage for the remainder of the calendar year. In September, three months after waiver implementation began, state officials announced that over 4,300 people would lose coverage for failing to report. By the end of 2018, nearly 17,000 had lost coverage.[84]

Lock-out periods in many of the approved waivers also placed burdens on enrollees. These periods refer to the length of time a beneficiary loses coverage for failure to comply with Medicaid requirements. For instance, the Kentucky waiver established a six-month disenrollment for beneficiaries who did not report changes in income or employment status promptly. Former enrollees could shorten the lock-out period by completing a financial or health literacy course.

Some of the approved waivers also imposed new financial burdens on enrollees through cost sharing provisions. Medicaid law permits some cost sharing by enrollees but generally prohibits states from charging premiums to beneficiaries with incomes below 150 percent of poverty. Some of the approved waivers departed from that norm. For instance,

Kentucky's waiver required enrollees to pay a monthly premium[85] according to the following schedule based on household income:

- 0 to 25 percent of the poverty line: $1 per month

- 26 to 50 percent of the poverty line: $4 per month

- 51 to 100 percent of the poverty line: $8 per month

- 101 to 138 percent of the poverty line: $15 per month (with premiums to rise after two years)

According to Kentucky officials, the purpose of the premiums was to discourage "Medicaid dependency by preparing individuals for the costs associated with commercial or Marketplace coverage."[86] Those in poverty would not lose their Medicaid eligibility if they failed to pay but would become subject to various copayments. Those with incomes above poverty who neglected to pay premiums would be disenrolled and generally not permitted to reapply for six months. Among the states receiving CMS approval for their work requirement waivers, seven had proposed new premium provisions.[87]

CMS was not responsive to all initiatives embedded in the state waiver proposals. It did not, for instance, sign off on Wisconsin's proposal to impose mandatory drug screening for poor, childless, able-bodied Medicaid applicants from age nineteen through sixty-four. Nor did it accept that state's proposal to establish a four-year time limit on eligibility for this Medicaid cohort. CMS also turned down several state proposals to reduce Medicaid eligibility for the expansion population from 138 percent of the poverty line to 100 percent. Despite showing some restraint with these and other requests, however, the Trump administration's waiver approvals clearly threatened to erode Medicaid enrollments. Not surprising, litigation to block these initiatives soon emerged.

The Battle in the Federal Courts to Limit Work Waivers

Opponents over two years filed suits to block the waiver initiatives in Kentucky, Arkansas, and then New Hampshire, Indiana, and Michigan. In late January 2018, three advocacy groups—the National Health Law Program, the Kentucky Equal Justice Center, and the Southern Poverty Law Center—sued Kentucky on behalf of fifteen state residents. The suit alleged that in approving the Kentucky waiver, the Trump administration aimed to "comprehensively transform" and "re-write the Medicaid Act," while bypassing Congress.[88] The plaintiffs attacked multiple waiver provisions, including work requirements, lock-out periods, and premiums as "arbitrary and capricious."[89] The suit claimed that CMS had violated the Administrative Procedure Act by announcing its new orientation toward Medicaid waivers via a letter to state officials rather than the formal rulemaking process. Citing Trump's open hostility to the ACA, the plaintiffs charged that the new waiver policy violated the president's constitutional duty to "take care that the laws be faithfully executed."

Faced with the suit, Kentucky's Republican Governor Matt Bevin struck back. He championed the Trump administration's abortive efforts to shift the case from the federal district court in the District of Columbia to one in Kentucky, where he believed the judge would be more sympathetic to the waiver. He sued the Kentucky plaintiffs involved in the case only to have a federal judge rule that he lacked standing to so. Doubling down on his defense of the waiver, Bevin filed court papers indicating that the state would end its Medicaid expansion if the judge threw out the waiver, thereby terminating benefits for an estimated 400,000 enrollees.[90]

Despite Governor Bevin's' efforts, the court ruled against Kentucky and the Trump administration in late June 2018. In doing so, Judge James Boasberg (an Obama appointee) did not explicitly address whether Medicaid law permitted work requirements or other provisions, let alone whether the waiver was unconstitutional. Instead, he more narrowly vacated the waiver on grounds that the Secretary of Health and Human Services had "entirely failed to consider Kentucky's estimate that 95,000 persons would leave its Medicaid rolls during the 5-year project." This failure was all the more "stunning" because some stakeholders commenting on the waiver had estimated likely coverage losses to be even greater.[91] Boasberg believed that these enrollment declines were inconsistent with the coverage goals embedded in the Medicaid statute.

Facing at least a temporary defeat, Governor Bevin quickly retaliated. Blaming the court ruling, state officials announced plans to cut dental and vision benefits for a half million enrollees in early July 2018.[92] More generally, however, the Trump administration expressed confidence that they could overcome Judge Boasberg's concerns. Rather than appeal the ruling to a higher court, they pledged to offer a more detailed rationale for the waiver after opening a new public comment period. But the additional deliberation yielded only modest changes in the Trump administration's justification for the Kentucky waiver. After reviewing their arguments again, Judge Boasberg voided the waiver in March 2019.

Prior to that, in August 2018, the National Health Law Program and the Southern Poverty Law Center opened a second litigation front by challenging the Arkansas work waiver. Joined by Legal Aid of Arkansas and three state residents, they again sued in the District of Columbia district court.[93] Over the objection of the Trump administration, the court assigned the case to Judge Boasberg. The plaintiffs' arguments echoed those they had voiced in their Kentucky suit, and especially stressed that the Arkansas waiver would fuel significant enrollment declines. As noted previously, steep monthly declines had ensued in Arkansas in September and continued into 2019. These losses generated concern among various players in the Medicaid policy arena. For instance, chair of the Medicaid and CHIP[94] Payment and Access Commission (MACPAC),[95] Penny Thompson, noted in mid-September that the advisory body had "a serious level of concern" about the Arkansas waiver. MACPAC member Christopher Gorton went further, saying: "I hope these [enrollment] data scare the pants off the people in Arkansas, because if you're running a program, this is not very good."[96] In late October, MACPAC formally communicated its doubts about the waiver and work requirements to the Department of Health and Human Services.

But CMS and Arkansas officials refused to budge. Republican Governor Asa Hutchinson said that while he wished fewer enrollees were losing coverage, the waiver was "compassionate" and that the enrollment decline would save the state $30 million.[97] For her part, CMS Administrator Verma stressed that it was too soon to judge the waiver and "that it is not compassionate to . . . create greater dependency on public assistance as we expand programs like Medicaid."[98] With disenrollment increasing month after month, Arkansas officials in December 2018 indicated that the targeted beneficiaries would also be able to report their work activities by phone as well as the special portal and promised to provide greater outreach to enhance compliance.[99] But these actions did not save the waiver in the courts. Judge Boasberg suspended operation of the Arkansas demonstration the same day he ruled against Kentucky. In response, the Trump administration appealed the Arkansas and Kentucky rulings to the District of Columbia circuit court, which in February 2020 upheld the district court ruling invalidating the Arkansas waiver. (The court did not rule on the Kentucky work requirement waiver because a newly elected Democratic governor had withdrawn it.)

Meanwhile, the National Health Law Program joined with New Hampshire Legal Assistance and the National Center for Law and Economic Justice to file suit against New Hampshire's work waiver on behalf of four of the state's Medicaid beneficiaries. Again, the plaintiffs brought the case to the District of Columbia federal court; again, the court assigned it to Judge Boasberg. Despite the suit, New Hampshire officials promised to launch implementation of the waiver on June 1, 2019. In early July, however, state officials announced they were postponing enforcement of this mandate for 120 days. In doing so, they acknowledged difficulties in notifying thousands of the targeted Medicaid enrollees who were at risk of losing coverage. State officials pledged to ramp up outreach efforts to this cohort. But these actions failed to mollify Judge Boasberg. Asserting that "we have all seen this movie before," he struck down the New Hampshire initiative in July 2019.[100] Encouraged by these early victories, the National Health Law Program and other advocates sued the Indiana Medicaid program over its work requirement waiver in September 2019. Soon thereafter, Michigan officials also faced a legal challenge to their waiver. By the end of Trump's third year in office, the implementation of work waivers had ground to a halt.

Tamping Down "Alien" Enrollments: The Public Charge Initiative

While the Trump administration's initiative to curb Medicaid enrollments primarily relied on waivers, it opened another front to achieve this goal in October 2018 when the Department of Homeland Security issued a proposed rule to change "public charge" policies. "Legal aliens" are foreign nationals permitted by law to reside and often work in the United States. The Trump administration's public charge rule focused on aliens seeking to extend their stay or change their status (for example, from temporary to permanent resident). Federal administrative action had since 1999 permitted immigration officials to take into account whether an alien had received government cash benefits, such as welfare, as a negative factor in deciding these cases. The Trump administration now sought to include receipt of noncash benefits, such as enrollment in Medicaid, as a negative in evaluating alien requests.[101] In so doing, federal officials would incentivize individuals otherwise eligible for Medicaid not to apply for benefits for fear of losing their legal right to be in the country.

With minor revisions, and after receiving over 265,000 comments (the "vast majority" negative), the Department of Homeland Security promulgated a final rule in early August 2019.[102] The impact on Medicaid enrollments seemed likely to be substantial. Drawing on a federal data set, researchers at the Kaiser Family Foundation estimated that disenrollment rates among Medicaid and CHIP beneficiaries living in households with one noncitizen would range from 15 to 35 percent. This would translate into Medicaid enrollment reductions ranging from approximately 2 million to nearly 5 million people.[103]

Publication of the final rule on public charges kindled a host of lawsuits. At least three different cohorts of Democratic state attorneys general (over twenty in all) each filed a suit opposing the regulation. Private entities, such as the California Primary Care Association, also challenged the regulation in the federal courts.[104] As 2019 ended, the federal courts were considering numerous lawsuits aimed at blocking implementation of the public charge rule. However, the Supreme Court ruled in February 2020 that the federal government could implement the new rule while the lower courts deliberated.

Meanwhile, President Trump continued to target immigrants on other health care fronts. In October 2019, he issued a presidential proclamation that required immigrants lawfully seeking to enter the country to prove that they would not "financially burden" the country's health care system. The proclamation defined burdensome immigrants to include those who would qualify to purchase federally subsidized insurance on the exchanges.[105]

Other Trump Administration Initiatives

Beyond the public charge and work requirement initiatives, other administrative measures to erode Medicaid surfaced during the third year of the Trump presidency. In May, the Office of Management and Budget proposed a revision in methodology that would lower official estimates of the inflation rate. This change would affect calculations of the poverty level in a way that reduced the number of people who could qualify for means-tested programs like Medicaid.[106]

In January 2020, CMS also announced its willingness to consider waiver proposals from states that would convert Medicaid to a block grant for non-elderly, able-bodied adults (the ACA's Medicaid expansion cohort). Proposals of this kind would undercut Medicaid as an open-ended fiscal entitlement to a state by capping or placing a limit on federal funding to it in exchange for affording the jurisdiction more flexibility to design its Medicaid program. Critics of the proposal worried that some states would impose significant cost sharing on enrollees and reduce the scope of health services offered to them.[107]

CMS also began work on a proposed rule to allow states to curb access to health care for Medicaid enrollees by denying them transportation for nonemergency services. Recognizing that many beneficiaries did not have a way to get to their medical appointments, federal officials in 1969 had promulgated an administrative rule requiring state Medicaid programs to offer this benefit. The Trump proposal would make its provision optional for states. In addition, CMS announced in November 2019 that it would overhaul regulations to drive down state errors in granting Medicaid benefits to those who do not meet eligibility criteria. The procedures designed to reduce these eligibility errors typically increase the administrative burdens of application and redetermination. These burdens, in turn, increase the ranks of those who could qualify for Medicaid but remain unenrolled.[108]

The Administrative Presidency Victorious?

The Trump administration's executive actions vis-à-vis Obamacare vividly illustrate the dynamics of an uncommonly hostile takeover. This takeover not only featured the typical antipathy of Republican presidents toward liberal programs; it was also driven by an intense desire to gut a signature program of the prior president—a fervently stated objective of the Republican Party ever since the ACA's passage. The repeal effort had symbolic overtones that went well beyond the specifics of health policy. It channeled the partisan animosities of much of the Republican base toward Barack Obama himself. These factors encouraged the Trump administration to pursue strategies to sabotage the exchanges and Medicaid. President Trump openly predicted that the ACA would fail and hoped to orchestrate its demise.

In his quest, the president employed multiple tools. Students of the administrative presidency have from the outset stressed the role of loyal, capable political appointees in accomplishing presidential ends. After a rocky start, which featured the early resignation of Tom Price as Secretary of Health and Human Services, Trump placed several appointees in key leadership roles who were both competent and loyal conservative ideologues. For instance, CMS Administrator Verma had received a Master in Public Health from Johns Hopkins University and founded a health policy consulting firm in 2001. In the years leading to her appointment, she worked on countless Medicaid and other health policy initiatives, frequently at the behest of Republican governors. It would be hard to find another conservative appointee as well versed in the day-to-day nexus between health policy and federalism as Verma.

Having used the power of political appointments, the Trump administration turned to other familiar administrative tools to accomplish its ends, with executive orders, formal rulemaking, and funding cuts being particularly prominent. Trump officials also employed waivers, a pervasive tool of executive federalism since the Clinton years. These included Section 1115 demonstration waivers imposing work requirements and administrative burdens on Medicaid enrollees. They also encompassed Section 1332 innovation waivers, in part to provide another off-ramp to cheaper, lower-quality insurance. In extraordinary ways, the Trump administration also used the Justice Department to sabotage the ACA. Its failure to mount a robust defense of the law in the face of a suit brought by Republican state officials and a district court decision obliterating the ACA stand out in this regard. The administration also used less formal administrative tools, such as guidelines or letters to state Medicaid directors, to encourage states to pursue new directions. Finally, an array of more informal top-level communications and signals (for example, tweets, social media messages, and speeches) hostile to the ACA strove to influence state officials, program beneficiaries, federal administrators, and other stakeholders. On balance, the Trump administration pushed the full-throated, multifaceted administrative presidency forged by President Reagan and most of his successors to unprecedented levels in the health arena.

To what degree did the Trump administration succeed in undermining the ACA? After three years, considerable uncertainty shrouds the answer largely because legal challenges to its major initiatives remain unresolved in the federal courts. Of dramatic importance, the appeals of the Fort Worth decision await resolution. If the Fort Worth ruling obliterating the ACA stands, the Trump administration would have abetted eradication of health insurance benefits for nearly 20 million Americans.[109] To be sure, such a development would only in part be about the triumph of the administrative presidency. It would also be about the unprecedented ascendance of state attorneys general and the courts as ever more powerful actors and veto points in the American separation-of-powers system. While the Supreme Court has historically vetoed a number of domestic distributive and redistributive programs approved by Congress, we know of no instance where it stripped benefits from so many people *after they were receiving them* as in the possible case of the ACA.

If the nuclear option aborts, the question persists as to whether the Trump administration's other executive branch initiatives will cripple the ACA. Again, much depends on how the federal courts rule in various cases. So, too, possible state policy responses heighten uncertainty about the efficacy of the Trump administrative presidency. The CSR boomerang, for instance, vividly illuminates how administrative sabotage can go awry. Faced with CSR funding cuts, insurance companies promoted and the great majority of states approved silver loading, thereby shoring up the exchanges. Going forward, state policy responses with respect to insurance regulation and waivers also matter greatly. New Jersey policymakers have, for instance, approved an individual mandate with a tax penalty for failing to obtain health insurance. California prohibited the sale of short-term health plans as of January 2019.[110] The degree to which other states take similar steps will strongly shape whether individuals have off-ramps to lower-quality insurance if the courts approve these initiatives.

State interest in the Trump administration's waiver initiatives also remains to be seen. As of late 2019, only Georgia had expressed interest in submitting a 1332 proposal that would make lower-quality insurance available. Whether waiver requests to impose work requirements and other administrative burdens on Medicaid enrollees have peaked is also unclear. To some degree, the partisan and ideological leanings of states may well predict their waiver and policy responses to the Trump administration. This could lead to a division of the country into red and blue state policy models, with the former helping the president realize his executive initiatives. Still, some state decisions may not be so predictable based on partisan and ideological factors. That 80 percent of states permit silver loading testifies to this possibility.

Despite these uncertainties, the available evidence casts some light on the degree to which the ACA has been eroded under Trump. (This evidence begs the issue of causality—the degree to which the Trump administration caused certain trends.) One measure of exchange vitality is insurance company participation in them. Greater participation gives people more opportunity to choose insurance products and fosters market competition. Decline on this metric had set in under Obama as many carriers grappled with financial losses on the exchanges. In 2014, the first year of marketplace operations, an average of five companies per state participated. This number increased to six in 2015 before declining to 5.6 in 2016 and 4.3 in 2017. Under Trump, the average number of insurance carriers dropped still further, to 3.5 in 2018. Thanks in part to state and insurance company adaptations, such as silver loading, this figure crept upward to 4 in 2019 and to 4.5 in 2020, slightly more than when Trump took office. Many insurance companies do not participate in all areas of a state, with fewer serving rural areas. Here, too, the data suggest improvement since 2018. While 26 percent of enrollees living in 52 percent of the counties had just one exchange insurer in 2018, these figures declined to 10 percent of enrollees in 25 percent of the counties in 2020.[111]

The affordability of insurance premiums comprises another indicator of exchange vitality. The available evidence points to the following core developments during the initial Trump period. First, in part due to such Trump initiatives as cuts in CSR payments and the resultant silver loading, average insurance premiums rose sharply in 2018. For instance, average premiums for certain silver plans increased by 37 percent in 2018, compared to 27 percent in the prior year.[112] Second, having secured hefty premium hikes for two consecutive years, insurance companies faced less pressure to raise them in 2019; average premiums stabilized and, in many areas, declined. This decline would likely have been appreciably greater had Congress refrained from repealing the tax penalty associated with the individual mandate as of 2019.[113] Preliminary evidence suggested that premiums would change little in 2020 and drop in some areas.[114] Third, premium increases primarily discouraged enrollment by those with incomes above 400 percent of poverty. People with incomes below that line received federal subsidies that substantially absorbed the costs of rising premiums. In some exchanges, silver loading made it possible for this income cohort to obtain a bronze plan for no premium. In sum, Trump administration initiatives further fueled the premium hikes that had begun under Obama. But these increases abruptly halted, at least for the time being, as Trump entered his third year in office.

Enrollments also speak to the fortitude of the exchanges. Under Trump, these enrollments have eroded but have proven more resistant to sabotage than many observers expected. After three years of enrollment gains under the Obama administration, sign-ups on the exchanges ebbed by about 4 percent in 2017 and 2018, respectively. The decline in 2019 was less than 3 percent.[115] Early returns suggest that exchange enrollments in 2020 will approximate those of the prior year.[116] This relatively modest erosion in exchange enrollments (especially considering the 2019 termination of the tax penalty for failure to obtain coverage) partly reflects the ingenuity of the states and insurance companies in facilitating silver loading. It also stems from the response of civil society to Trump initiatives. For instance, in the face of Trump budget cuts for outreach, private nonprofit groups and volunteers (for example, Get

America Covered), along with insurance companies and brokers in some states, doubled down on their outreach. The eleven states (along with the District of Columbia) that fully operate their own marketplaces also picked up some of the slack left by the thirty-nine federally administered exchanges. State-run exchanges witnessed slight enrollment upticks of nearly 2 percent in 2017, 1 percent in 2018, and nearly another 1 percent in 2019.[117] The better performance of state-run exchanges probably reflects greater ideological support for the ACA in these states. In 2016, Hillary Clinton won all of these jurisdictions except Idaho, and 64 percent of them had Democratic governors. The ideological commitment of these states to the exchanges manifested itself in such practices as longer enrollment periods and greater commitment to outreach. Meanwhile, five states with Democratic governors (Nevada, New Jersey, New Mexico, Oregon, and Pennsylvania) moved to take over operation of the exchanges from the federal government in 2019.

These moderate declines in exchange enrollments should not mask the threat that the Trump administration's sabotage efforts pose over the longer term. While CMS announced that it would not forbid silver loading for the 2020 enrollment year, its willingness to tolerate the practice beyond that point is unclear. Moreover, the off-ramps to cheaper, lower-quality insurance that the administration has built could, if the courts approve, siphon off growing numbers of healthy people from the marketplaces. It would not be easy for any future Democratic presidential administration to take down these off-ramps rapidly. The lengths to which the Obama administration went to grandfather and grandmother in substandard insurance point to the reluctance of policymakers to take coverage away from people.

In the case of Medicaid, CMS openness to waiver themes (for example, work requirements and administrative burdens) that prior presidential administrations had rejected threatens program enrollments. By early 2019, about a third of the states had waiver proposals of this kind either pending or already approved. The Trump administration also used speeches and social media to stigmatize the Medicaid-expansion cohort as able-bodied people seeking a kind of welfare handout while avoiding their moral obligation to work and contribute to the community. In essence, these waivers rest on the principle that health insurance should be a reward for work and accomplishment rather than a universal right applicable to all. It deserves note that an estimated 80 percent of able-bodied, non-elderly adult Medicaid enrollees are in working families, with close to 60 percent employed themselves.[118] The unemployed in this cohort disproportionately suffer from behavioral health and other chronic conditions (for example, hypertension).[119] Given this and other factors, the work requirement waivers could precipitate significant enrollment declines if approved by the courts. One study estimates that from 600,000 to 800,000 enrollees would lose coverage in nine states with CMS-approved waivers.[120] The Trump administration's "public charge" initiative may also prove damaging to program enrollments as pressures intensify on legal noncitizens to refrain from enrolling their children and themselves in Medicaid and CHIP.

Comprehensive data on Medicaid and CHIP enrollments from 2014 to 2019 also suggest some reversal of fortune under President Trump. From January 1, 2014 (when the Medicaid expansion commenced), to January 1, 2017, when Obama left office, monthly enrollments grew by 22 percent to more than 75 million beneficiaries, an average annual growth of over 7 percentage points. During the first two years of the Trump administration, monthly enrollments declined by 2.5 percent and continued their downward trajectory as 2019 unfolded.[121] The causal dynamics underlying this reduction remain unclear, but it seems likely that Trump administrative initiatives contributed to the decline.

In considering the negative implications of the Trump administration for Medicaid enrollments, a caveat deserves note. However much the Trump administration has tried to stigmatize the Medicaid expansion cohort, public support for providing health benefits to this group remained strong. The number of Medicaid-expansion states grew from thirty-one (plus the District of Columbia) when Trump took office to thirty-three (Maine and Virginia added) his third year on the job. Moreover, voters in three conservative states, Idaho, Nebraska, and Utah, passed ballot measures endorsing the Medicaid expansion in 2018.[122] Subsequently, elected policymakers in the three states dragged their feet and sought waivers (including work requirements) as part of moving forward with expansion. Nonetheless, considerable momentum for expansion existed in all three states as 2019 closed.

Beyond Medicaid and the exchanges, President Trump's administrative war on the ACA began to ripple through the health care system. The Census Bureau's annual reports on health insurance coverage found that the ranks of the uninsured grew slightly in each of the first two years of the Trump administration, with the overall percentage of those without coverage amounting to a little under 9 percent of the U.S. population in 2018.[123] However, more fine-grained analyses present a less sanguine picture. Drawing on other census data, a study reported that "in 2017, the number of uninsured . . . increased by nearly 700,000 people, the first increase since implementation of the ACA."[124] Over a similar period, the number of uninsured children grew by about 400,000.[125] For its part, Gallup found a nearly 3 percentage point increase in the proportion of adults without health insurance from the last quarter of 2016 to the final quarter of 2018.[126] While the precise causal dynamics driving these trends are foggy, Trump administration initiatives to vitiate the ACA in all probability contributed to this erosion.

In sum, the case of the ACA suggests the complexities of assessing the administrative presidency as a hostile takeover after an incumbent's first three years in office. Much depends on pending court decisions. For instance, the Trump administration's initiative to promote work waivers would represent an abject failure if higher courts refuse to overturn district court rulings invalidating these initiatives. Meanwhile, President Trump's prediction that key elements of Obamacare would explode, a prophecy his administration worked diligently to fulfill, was not realized. In many ways, the exchanges and Medicaid proved quite resilient. To be sure, enrollments in both programs have slightly eroded. But even if the administration prevails in a series of court decisions concerning work waivers, short-term insurance, and association health plans, the damage to Medicaid and the exchanges during Trump's first term, while significant, would be limited. Alternatively, of course, higher court ratification of the Fort Worth decision to destroy the ACA, which the Trump administration's legal strategy has mostly abetted, would radically alter this assessment. It would be a victory of historically unprecedented proportions for the Trump administrative presidency.

FOUR

Search and Destroy in Climate Change Policy

Donald Trump would not be the first president to employ administrative presidency tools to reverse or soften the impact of environmental policies that had been embraced by his predecessors. Ronald Reagan used his powers of appointment and regulatory interpretation to dial back Carter-era air and water quality and waste management provisions, making environmental deregulation a major thrust of his first term. George W. Bush sought to inject more flexibility into the application of key Clean Air Act (CAA) provisions that his father had signed into law in prior decades. But Trump would take this approach to new levels, both rhetorically and in the scope and depth of his actions. He acted systematically, through his own unusually aggressive use of administrative presidency powers, to attempt to eviscerate every major step on climate change policy his immediate predecessor, Barack Obama, had taken during his two terms.

A good deal of this effort would ultimately take the form of regulatory repeal and, where necessary, some form of a considerably more modest replacement under the larger framework of comprehensive deregulation. All this stemmed from Trump's numerous declarations on the 2016 campaign trail that Obama administration efforts to sign the Paris

Agreement on climate change and reinterpret the CAA to mitigate green-house gas emissions represented an assault on American workers and the nation's economic future. He made no secret of his revulsion toward these policies, often dramatizing them against the declining fortunes of the coal industry and its iconic miners, despite substantial evidence that coal faced far more serious threats from increasingly cost-competitive natural gas and renewable energy sources than from federal regulation. Trump further discredited the evidence and analysis on climate change that motivated these policies, disparaging climate science as a hoax being propagated by China to imperil the United States by manipulating it to take steps to reduce emissions. Why should the federal government do something about a problem that really did not exist? And even if there were something to climate change, why should the United States act uni-laterally to reduce emissions and threaten economic growth unless all other nations did at least as much and perhaps more?

Trump said little in specific terms during the campaign on just how he would reverse course, however, other than promising big shake-ups shortly after taking office. Ultimately, he avoided nuclear-style efforts that might have dealt a singular and devastating blow to Obama climate initiatives. Unlike Presidents Clinton, Bush, and Obama, Trump made no efforts to advance his preferred climate policies through engagement with Congress, even during his first two years, when Republicans con-trolled both legislative chambers. Statutory repeal of key Obama policies would have been relatively straightforward in terms of crafting legis-lation bundled as amendments prohibiting the application of the 1990 CAA amendments to carbon dioxide and methane. This represented an opportunity for a landmark legislative accomplishment, but the presi-dent never proposed such a strategy, and neither the House nor Senate ever considered such a bill.

Moreover, the Trump administration also shied away from a fun-damental assault on the findings of a landmark 2007 Supreme Court case that provided scientific and legal underpinnings to all of Obama's administrative efforts. Neither legislative nor administrative channels would be used formally to confront the question of whether climate change was real and, if not, directly undermine the endangerment chal-lenge to public health and safety that the Obama administration had used to legitimize regulatory steps under the CAA. The president would continually dismiss climate change as a fake issue and yet resist advice to launch a comprehensive assault on the scientific and legal underpinnings of all Obama policy.

Instead, Trump would deploy a diverse set of administrative presidency tools, but in segmented and selected ways. This began with high-level appointments of loyalists and continued with a range of withdrawal notifications and regulatory reversals that cut across multiple economic sectors and related policies. The goal would be to either erase prior policy wherever legally and politically feasible or settle for regulatory freezes or suspensions where all-out evisceration was not possible. Eschewing the nuclear option of a one-shot victory, Trump, instead, adopted a search and destroy approach. This entailed looking for weaknesses in every separate provision of the Obama plan and then selecting administrative presidency tools to neutralize them.

The phrase "search and destroy" originated as a military term, perhaps best known for its role in guiding American military strategy during extended portions of the Vietnam War. It entailed rapid deployment of concentrated military personnel into a defined region of hostile territory, with the charge of searching for enemy forces, destroying them in short order, and then moving on toward another target.[1] It avoided taking more comprehensive or decisive steps and did not focus on rebuilding after the anticipated victory.

The adoption of this approach meant the Trump administration had settled on an alternative to confronting climate endangerment formally, meaning that it did not officially challenge the finding that climate change was real or worthy of policy responses. Instead, it worked to cripple existing policies piece by piece rather than through one comprehensive and devastating attack.

The Trump approach to climate change represented an administrative presidency search and destroy mission unique across the half-century since the federal government first engaged environmental protection through far-reaching legislation that cut across environmental media of air, water, and land. If Trump's initiatives were sustained and fully implemented, American greenhouse gas emissions would be higher than they would have been under Obama-era regulations. This would be billed as a net benefit to the nation given anticipated expansion of economic performance and negligible environmental consequences.

But even a determined president employing multiple administrative presidency tools confronts limitations. Each step in this search and destroy process would face significant resistance, though not from Congress under either unified Republican control from 2017 to 2019 or split party control through 2021. Instead, the real governmental opposition emanated from coalitions of states that issued legal challenges and vowed to expand their own climate mitigation policies. Federal courts would provide, at least initially, receptive venues for many of these legal challenges, regardless of whether judges had been appointed by Democratic or Republican presidents. Even the most visible step taken by Donald Trump on climate change—American withdrawal from the Paris Agreement—could not legally take effect until the day after the 2020 election. Even then, that decision could quickly be reversed by a future president. Consequently, the Trump administration deployed the vast set of options available to a president determined to systematically eliminate or weaken each and every policy step that had been taken by his immediate predecessor, all without ever turning to Congress.

This approach would also be applied to other environmental policy areas, including water pollution and wetlands protection, reflecting approximately eighty regulatory reversal processes launched during Trump's first term.[2] As with climate change, there were no new policy initiatives designed to improve environmental quality but, rather, an attempt to eliminate or soften existing regulatory provisions linked to prior presidencies, primarily that of Barack Obama. Somewhat defensively, the president would claim in mid-2019 that America had a "clean climate" and that its air and water were "crystal clear."[3] Given this, he argued, additional regulations were unnecessary and contrary to overarching economic goals, thereby justifying his unleashing of multiple weapons in the administrative presidency arsenal.

There was, however, no singular approach to federalism across these respective administrative presidency initiatives for climate change. Instead, the Trump administration engaged in a form of selective federalism that could either expand or constrain state latitude in pursuit of the overriding goal of completing a search and destroy assault on every climate policy action undertaken by Obama.

In transportation, the sector with the largest share of total national emissions, the Trump approach would involve a historic effort to reverse a longstanding policy designed to facilitate state policy innovation. The overall goal here was to constrain state climate policy through federal preemption of state authority and, ultimately, engage in a high-decibel federalism battle with the state that was most directly impacted by and opposed to this move. For electricity and methane from the energy and waste management sectors, the Trump approach emphasized state empowerment. In these instances, Obama-era federal regulations were defenestrated through a series of regulatory steps, either easing pressures on states to make significant emissions reductions or entirely eliminating newly created forms of federal oversight.

Points of Hesitation: Trump Limits

The most straightforward approach to reversing most Obama climate initiatives would have involved a single piece of legislation amending the CAA, which had last been revised in 1990. Such legislation could have declared that carbon dioxide, methane, and other greenhouse gas emissions were not to be considered air pollutants under any section of this legislation. Or it might have placed specific sectors—such as electricity, transportation, oil and gas production, manufacturing, and solid waste management—off limits from any attempt to apply the CAA to them in terms of greenhouse gas releases. Many Republican members of the House and Senate had been outspoken in their opposition to any CAA use for these purposes, and a unified legislative strategy could have yielded historic legislation that closed one major path toward climate mitigation efforts with a single stroke. This might have paralleled Republican efforts, albeit ill-fated, to repeal the Affordable Care Act with legislation rather than the multifaceted administrative sabotage discussed in chapter 3.

But such an idea never emerged from the president, his administration, or Republican leaders in Congress. No such bill was ever introduced in either chamber, much less reviewed in committee, as the legislative branch approached its fourth consecutive decade of silence on the relationship between the CAA and climate change. Even early congressional threats to use the Congressional Review Act to strike down some key Obama-era climate provisions never materialized. Use of this 1996 act seemed particularly plausible for decisions finalized toward the end of Obama's second term, given its time limitations on rendering recent regulatory action to be "of no force or effect."[4] In turn, the act can have particular power beyond the presidency in which it is adopted, as it precludes subsequent adoption of future regulations that are "substantially the same," thereby leaving only future legislation as a viable path to restore a particular regulatory approach.[5]

Congress did approve fourteen Congressional Review Act resolutions during 2017, including several in the environmental arena.[6] However, these addressed such issues as coal mining waste and federal public land management rather than those expressly focused on greenhouse gases.

One major effort to use this tool to reverse climate regulations outside the orbit of the CAA led to an embarrassing political setback in 2017. A repeal resolution on new methane release regulations on oil and gas production on federal lands implemented by the Bureau of Land Management passed the House but failed narrowly in the Senate, given unanimous Democratic opposition and defections from Republicans Susan Collins, Lindsey Graham, and John McCain. These Republican legislators expressed concern that the resolution would not only stop the proposed regulations but would chill future efforts to curb methane, which is a potent greenhouse gas but also a conventional air quality contaminant. In turn, Congressional Review Act cases risked use of considerable floor debate time and filibusters in a Senate that had other pressing priorities, including tax cut legislation and presidential nomination approval.[7] Consequently, this one seemingly plausible tool to not only reverse regulations but block subsequent introduction of comparable ones in the future never surfaced as a serious option.

Even the signature legislative achievement of Trump's first three years in office, the 2017 Tax Cuts and Jobs Act and related extender bills, did not eliminate a number of existing tax system incentives for either renewable energy or fossil fuel generation, or purchase of alternative technologies such as electric vehicles. A number of early proposals included accelerated phaseout of production tax credits for wind and solar energy and attacks on provisions supporting specialized areas, such as geothermal energy, small wind turbines, combined heat and power facilities, and stationary fuel cells. But most of these, ultimately, were retained alongside new provisions encouraging expanded use of carbon capture and storage technology, indicating considerable political ability by supportive constituencies to "lock-in" support for tax preferences once granted initially. This reflected aggressive political pressure from proponents of these technologies, many of which had established considerable footing in Republican-led districts. As House Ways and Means Committee member Republican Kenny Marchant noted, "They just don't give up."[8]

The Trump administration also eschewed a strategy favored by some members of its transition team, an immediate and sweeping executive order that would repudiate the EPA's 2009 endangerment finding. Leaders of some think tanks that dismiss the credibility of climate science and oppose essentially all policy that would reduce greenhouse gas emissions also endorsed this approach.[9] Such a step would have struck at the heart of the key scientific interpretations on climate change that led to the

2007 Supreme Court case on endangerment and 2009 EPA acceptance of this finding, discussed in chapter 2. This opened the path toward far-reaching climate regulatory innovation under Obama.

But direct assault on endangerment would have represented a scientific, political, and legal high-wire act, particularly given the ever-expanding body of evidence from the natural and physical sciences concerning the realities and risks of human-induced climate change. This approach would also have required the administration to repudiate ongoing research on climate change from numerous federal government units with considerable scientific expertise and longitudinal databases, including the EPA and the Departments of Commerce and Interior. Some early drafts of Trump executive orders linked to climate change included text to reverse the endangerment finding, but these quickly vanished once the administration took office. As in the cases of comprehensive repeal legislation or aggressive use of the Congressional Review Act, the Trump administration avoided this option, although it is possible that this strategy might be revisited in a second term, particularly given Supreme Court personnel shifts that might be friendlier to this approach than the one Trump inherited.

The administration also recoiled from a frontal assault on established measurements of the "social cost of carbon," a formal consideration of the estimated societal costs attributable to carbon emissions. This followed comprehensive Obama administration analysis of this issue, leading to consideration of both domestic and global costs and an estimate of approximately $50 per ton of released carbon that was subsequently used when considering new emission-reduction policies. The Trump administration took a more modest approach, eliminating an interagency task force on the social cost of carbon and withdrawing technical guidance for agencies. It also allowed individual agencies considerable latitude in making their own assessments, leading to substantial reductions in federal social cost of carbon estimates without a full and formal review that would have required rigorous involvement of the natural, physical, and social sciences.[10] This approach facilitated rapid pursuit of more segmented regulatory targets but remained likely to re-emerge in future legal and political deliberations and prove a potential stumbling block to implementation.

Instead of all-out political and legal war, the Trump administration launched search and destroy assaults on a set of high-profile Obama policies after making some initial decisions on staffing its leadership team. The overarching goal appeared to be damaging President Obama's policies as much as was politically and legally feasible, retreating or re-strategizing only when necessary. Oklahoma Attorney General Scott Pruitt was nominated to replace Gina McCarthy as EPA administrator, underscoring the dramatic transition that was to follow. Both McCarthy and Pruitt came to federal service through state leadership positions, as was true of many prior EPA leaders. But McCarthy helped launch cap-and-trade and other climate policies in Massachusetts and Connecti-cut while Pruitt secured national visibility as a leading opponent of the Obama climate strategy when serving as Oklahoma Attorney General. Pruitt led multistate litigation challenges to more than a dozen Obama climate initiatives and had been particularly outspoken in leading the charge against the Clean Power Plan (CPP) for the electricity sector.[11]

Pruitt was highly unsuccessful in court with these challenges, facing defeats in a majority of these cases, including some swift dismissals and rhetorical rebukes from federal judges. But he emerged during the second Obama administration as a leading national voice of opposition, building strong alliances with the Republican Attorneys General Asso-ciation and firms engaged in oil and gas production. During his confir-mation hearings and in early media appearances, he indicated that the Trump administration would embrace federalism principles designed to provide states maximum latitude in developing and implementing their own environmental and energy policies. "Every statute makes clear this is supposed to be a cooperative relationship," he explained in a February 2017 *Wall Street Journal* interview, noting "that Congress understood that a one-size-fits-all model doesn't work for environmental regulation, and that the state departments of environmental quality have an enor-mous role to play."[12] Pruitt further emphasized that the Obama admin-istration had looked down upon citizens of energy-producing states such as Oklahoma and Texas and that he intended to usher in a new era of "cooperative federalism" that was respectful of state prerogatives. His opprobrium was most intensively directed at the CPP: "The past ad-ministration just made it up," he lamented. "They reimagined authority under the statute. There's a commitment with the new administration to have a pro-growth, pro-environment approach to these issues, but also to respect rule of law."[13]

Pruitt assembled his leadership team largely with political appointees drawn from Oklahoma political circles and the fossil fuel industry, par-ticularly for positions with a direct link to climate policy. Appointments requiring Senate confirmation were made at a very slow pace compared to prior administrations, and Pruitt made little effort to cultivate relationships with career EPA staff with extensive experience in climate science, law, or policy.[14] Pruitt rapidly emerged as the leading Trump administration voice on all dimensions of climate and environmental policy, eclipsing other leaders such as Secretary of State Rex Tillerson even when international questions were involved. Pruitt, however, also emerged as a lightning rod for controversy, including concerns over personal finance and ethics. Questions also arose over his (and his team's) legal and technical competence, given a number of quick reversals in federal court cases that drew comparisons with his litigation setbacks as a state attorney general. Pruitt's 2018 fall from power led to his replacement by Andrew Wheeler, a lawyer with extensive experience as an energy industry lobbyist after earlier work at the EPA and as a Senate staffer. Wheeler dialed back the melodrama that routinely surrounded Pruitt, replacing it with a far stronger reputation for professional competence and the ability to recruit skilled associates with considerable prior CAA experience. This included advisers with experience in previous Republican administrations, including George W. Bush–era efforts to use administrative presidency tools for air quality policy.

Notification of Withdrawal: Exiting Paris

Trump's transition team proposed that the president sign a comprehensive executive order within hours of his January 2017 inauguration. They recommended the order cover many dimensions of climate policy, leading with the announcement that the United States was withdrawing from the Paris Agreement. However, not only did an early and broad executive order fail to emerge but a formal announcement on Paris was delayed until June, reflecting considerable disagreement among senior administration members. Secretary of State Tillerson and Secretary of Defense Jim Mattis strongly supported retaining Paris membership, as did many business leaders. In contrast, Pruitt and presidential adviser Steve Bannon actively sought withdrawal. Trump ultimately sided with Pruitt and Bannon and announced U.S. withdrawal in June 2017 at a Rose Garden event where Pruitt served as master of ceremonies, Tillerson was absent, and the president announced that "Today, we put America first." Trump repeated campaign statements declaring that Paris was a feckless agreement that disadvantaged American economic interests, including the alleged transfer of coal-related jobs to other nations. He declared: "I was elected to represent the citizens of Pittsburgh, not Paris."[15]

As a presidential-executive agreement, American participation in Paris could be rescinded though a formal notification of withdrawal without any form of congressional approval. Such agreements have been struck by many presidents, ranging from Richard Nixon's 1973 Vietnam peace agreement to Bill Clinton's 1993 North American Free Trade Agreement (NAFTA), although the latter was subsequently approved by Congress.[16] As Norma Riccucci has noted: "Critics, especially the U.S. Congress, have railed against such agreements and there continues to be a good deal of uncertainty about them, particularly from a political standpoint. Presidents often pursue these agreements to circumvent the U.S. Congress. In this sense, executive agreements are an international analog to executive orders or, more broadly, the unitary executive or administrative presidency model."[17] While they are relatively easy to issue, they can face limitations, including the possibilities that Congress might balk at funding them or find other ways to undermine them. These limitations may make them largely symbolic or even voluntary in nature, with considerable risks of implementation setbacks over time.

In the Paris case, the most significant limitation involves the nonbinding nature of national emission-reduction pledges.[18] Nations are under no pressure to submit any particular numeric emission target and face no penalties or sanctions other than moral suasion if they fail to achieve these goals. In turn, one limitation the Paris structure imposed upon Trump stemmed from the fact that withdrawal cannot be completed immediately given the pact's design. As a result, the State Department (despite the objections of Secretary Tillerson) notified the United Nations Secretary General on June 1, 2017, that the United States intended to provide formal notification of withdrawal "as soon as it is eligible to do so." This would be on November 4, 2019. One year after that date, American withdrawal can formally take place.[19] This would occur one day after the 2020 elections seal the fate on Trump's bid for a second term. The only option for an earlier exit would involve formal negotiations with other participating nations. Their response was overwhelmingly negative to the American plan, and there has been no indication they would offer the United States a generous early-departure package. Trump contended in his Paris withdrawal speech that "we will start to negotiate, and we will see if we can make a deal that's fair."[20] However, there has been no indication of any such negotiations since that announcement, and Trump has largely avoided subsequent international meetings devoted to climate change.

At the same time, many American states registered their opposition to Trump's Paris withdrawal and formed an organization pledged to honor the agreement within their own boundaries.[21] Under the banner of the U.S. Climate Alliance, Democratic governors from California, New York, and Washington cochaired an effort to launch a state-based alternative to an American Paris exit, proclaiming that "Alliance states are stepping up."[22] Fourteen states and Puerto Rico were founding members in 2017, representing 36 percent of national gross domestic product. These jurisdictions were generally located along both coasts and, with only two exceptions, were led by Democratic governors.[23] They generally ranked among states that had some of the lowest greenhouse gas emissions per capita and already had achieved the most significant emission reductions during prior decades. Moreover, many states faced considerable difficulties translating these bold pledges into new policy by early 2020. In many cases, action plans and executive orders proved far more common than new legislation, raising questions about policy durability and state ability to deliver on their promises after supportive governors leave office.

Nonetheless, they received considerable media and international attention as an alternative force for collective action in the federal system.[24] Their pledges are not formally registered under the Paris process, yet these states are generally treated internationally as counterparts to participating nation states, almost as if they constitute an alternative American governing order from the Trump administration. "Together, we are a political and economic force and we will drive the change that needs to happen nationwide," said California Governor Jerry Brown when the alliance was announced.[25] This coalition expanded markedly during 2018–2019, largely in cases where Democrats replaced Republicans in state governorships after 2018 elections. Montana became the twenty-fifth state to join the coalition when Governor Steve Bullock announced plans to join in mid-2019. Membership covers states that produce more than half of gross domestic product and has expanded to include a number of Midwestern states. All members continue to pledge to meet their share of Paris emissions reductions, 26 percent below 2005 levels by 2025, as well as "accelerate new and existing policies to reduce carbon pollution and promote clean energy development at the state and federal levels."

The Climate Alliance case represents a pattern whereby every Trump administration step taken to reverse an Obama-era climate policy initiative faced rapid assembly of a multi-state oppositional coalition. This largely paralleled the Obama administration experience, except for very different sets of states aligning in opposition. In general, most members of the Climate Alliance did not have significant fossil fuel deposits or attempt to develop them if they did. However, three major production states, Colorado, New Mexico, and Pennsylvania, joined during 2019. They included regulatory efforts to reduce methane emissions from oil and gas production and expand the use of renewable energy as part of their commitment.

Waiver Withdrawal and Regulatory Freeze: Vehicle Emissions

Transportation sector greenhouse gases received considerable attention during President Obama's first term. As noted in chapter 2, his signature climate policy achievement of those years involved the merger of distinct vehicle emission and fuel economy programs into a unified effort to reduce carbon emissions from future car and truck fleets. Other areas of climate policy dominated his second term, yet transportation sector emissions continued to climb, passing the electricity sector in 2016 as the largest single source. The Obama administration realized it had no viable political path toward legislative options for this sector, such as a tax on oil and gas used in transportation, after the 2010 collapse of cap-and-trade legislation. Consequently, it doubled down on its administrative strategy for vehicle emissions through its very final days in office. This included an EPA review in 2016 and January 2017 that was designed to analyze progress to date and accelerate by more than a year its original schedule for achieving emissions reductions in concert with greater fuel economy through model year 2025. It reflected an aggressive administrative effort to complete a review with unusual speed and protect this extension as a key plank in the climate legacy of the outgoing president.

The EPA possessed legal authority under the CAA, facilitated by the endangerment finding, to adopt greenhouse gas emission standards measured in grams of carbon dioxide per mile through the middle of the 2020s. But the National Highway Transportation Safety Administration (NHTSA) of the Department of Transportation, which oversaw the fuel economy portion of this presidentially brokered partnership, was statutorily prohibited from making such long-term commitments and was formally required to conduct interim reviews. Consequently, there could be no final resolution of future NHTSA directions on fuel economy provisions under the Energy Policy and Conservation Act prior to Obama's departure from office.

These midterm reviews coincided with a steep and sustained drop in fuel prices that began in 2014 and discouraged purchase of new vehicles with greater fuel economy. There had been some evidence of short-term gains in reducing greenhouse gas emissions and improving fuel economy in new vehicles produced after the policy was launched. This reflected significant advances in the use of turbocharging, transmission gears, and idle shutoff systems as well as in air-conditioning efficiency, tire design, and window glazing.[26] But these advances began to slow alongside gas price declines, and American-based manufacturers such as General Motors, Ford, and Fiat Chrysler faced some significant efficiency lags across their respective fleets. EPA actions very late in the Obama administration faced considerable opposition from manufacturers, who challenged both the accelerated review process and the proposed timetables for further reductions. Republican members of Congress also expressed concerns and threatened to use the Congressional Review Act to reverse any extension. Some Republican legislators threatened to go farther, including Texas Congressman Joe Barton, who recommended in December 2016, one month after national elections, that carbon emission and fuel economy standards for vehicles be scrapped "in their entirety."[27]

One might have expected this would present the incoming forty-fifth president with an opportunity to seek a far-reaching reversal of not only the proposed regulatory acceleration but, potentially, the entire program of merging vehicle emissions with fuel economy. This could have begun with an invitation to Congress to terminate the accelerated process through a Congressional Review Act resolution. This might have paved the way for bolder action, either through a regulatory reinterpretation of the endangerment finding or a statute to disable any application of existing air quality or fuel efficiency legislation to carbon emissions. But no such steps were taken, and it remained unclear just how the incoming Trump team would manage this issue as it assumed office.

Tellingly, candidate Donald Trump said very little about the vehicle emissions issue during the 2016 campaign, even though he campaigned intensively in major manufacturing states such as Michigan and Ohio. In theory, he might have argued that emission regulations were burdening American manufacturers and adding to new vehicle costs, but he said relatively little about this, even in addresses where he discussed energy and manufacturing concerns. This likely reflected a political calculation to focus more on the electricity sector and the CPP, linking this attack with his case for restoring coal as a central plank of his domestic policy platform while also maximizing natural gas output. This approach was unveiled in his first major energy speech of the campaign in September 2016 to natural gas industry leaders in Pittsburgh.

January 2017 confirmation hearings for Trump appointees to prominent EPA and Transportation positions relevant to the future of vehicle emissions policy did not provide a clear roadmap on likely steps. But one hearings issue that surfaced frequently involved the status of the 2013 CAA waiver the EPA gave to California as a linchpin of the new policy. Would that waiver endure under a Trump administration? EPA chief nominee Pruitt approached this issue gingerly during his combative hearings. He routinely reiterated his commitment to a state-based form of "cooperative federalism" while indicating misgivings as to whether the California waiver fit under that umbrella. This produced concerns from many legislators, including Massachusetts Senator Ed Markey, who noted: "When you sue from the oil and gas perspective, and you represent Oklahoma, you say they have a right to do what they want to do in the state of Oklahoma. But when it comes to Massachusetts and California, and it comes to that question of those states wanting to increase their production for the environment, you say there, you're going to review."[28] Pruitt declined multiple requests to be more specific on his intentions for the waiver, though he did agree if confirmed to honor a request from Oklahoma Senator Jim Inhofe that he would work with the incoming Transportation Secretary to review the EPA's recent decisions.

The results of the EPA-NHTSA review were disclosed just two months later by President Trump during a Detroit appearance, part of his broader emphasis on protecting American industry from unfair foreign competition. "Today I am announcing that we are going to cancel that executive action," said Trump. "We are going to restore the originally scheduled midterm review, and we are going to ensure that any regulations we have protect and defend your jobs, your factories."[29] An accompanying joint announcement by the EPA and Transportation was more measured, noting only that they would begin work on a review. However, this announcement declared that NHTSA's views had not received adequate consideration during the EPA's analysis and that the upcoming review would balance both perspectives. This action led to significant speculation as to how far this review might go and whether it could lead to the first reversal of a California waiver in a half-century once it had previously been granted by the EPA.

The joint review represented a type of "regulatory custody battle" that is common when two federal agencies are forced to work collaboratively and reconcile differences between competing statutes that define their respective approaches.[30] The EPA and NHTSA had little prior history of working closely together, but they were compelled to collaborate because of presidential action in the absence of new legislation to clarify the huge differences between a pair of very different statutes. The EPA was guided by a half-century of experience fielding waiver requests from a single state that had unique air quality challenges linked to vehicle emissions and had taken major regulatory steps long before the federal government; NHTSA was guided by an established statute that was focused on fuel economy and designed to reduce American dependence on imported oil, formally preempting all state policies and with no history of waiver experience.

This partnership worked during the Obama presidency but began to unravel under Donald Trump. This became increasingly evident as the Trump-led NHTSA articulated concerns that increased fuel economy provisions might significantly increase vehicle costs, deterring new vehicle purchases and slowing economic growth. In turn, NHTSA also expressed worries that intensified focus on fuel efficiency might create pressures to purchase smaller vehicles that it felt might be more dangerous for occupants than larger ones. EPA career staff strongly disagreed with these interpretations, reflected in leaks to news media and regulatory comments on draft proposals. These included multiple textual insertions that "EPA does not agree with this conclusion" and a request that "EPAs name and logo should be removed."[31] EPA staff objections did not drive the final analysis, however, as reflected in an April 2018 EPA report that dismissed a highly technical 1,217-page Obama-era analysis in favor of tighter regulations with a thirty-eight-page document that emphasized the negative impacts of such a step. The report concluded that the strategy adopted by the EPA in January 2017 "presents challenges for auto manufacturers due to feasibility and practicality, raises potential concerns related to auto safety, and results in additional costs on consumers, especially low-income consumers."[32]

This approach was further reflected in the EPA's August 2018 introduction of a proposed Safer Affordable Fuel-Efficient (SAFE) Vehicles rule. This would freeze vehicle emission and fuel economy standards at 2020 levels through 2026 rather than increase them. The rule was linked to the withdrawal of California's 2013 waiver supporting its vehicle emission standards as well as implementation of its zero-emissions vehicle (ZEV) program, placing the status of this well-established federalism model under unprecedented uncertainty. It contended that the Energy Policy and Conservation Act for fuel economy preempted states from designing policy in this area and reiterated concerns about safety and cost ramifications under the now-replaced Obama rule. EPA Administrator Wheeler contended that the new provision "would allow the industry to meet aggressive yet attainable standards, reduce the price of new vehicles and help more Americans purchase cleaner, safer and more efficient vehicles."[33]

President Trump made periodic references to this proposed policy step in 2018 and 2019, most pointedly in blasting California's approach to vehicle emissions regulation as "ridiculous" and "out of control," leading to the waste of billions of dollars.[34] But he did not claim credit for this initiative with the frequency or visibility of his commentary on withdrawing from Paris or replacing the CPP. Nor did he go any farther in dismantling the existing dual regime of vehicle emissions control and fuel economy. Nonetheless, resistance to this initiative was swift and intense. This reflected both economic concerns from the very industry he was proposing to free from excessive regulatory burdens and legal questions posed by numerous states and environmental groups concerning federal authority to revoke a waiver. This would place the administration in a difficult situation approaching the 2020 elections, reflecting prolonged delays in issuing a final rule that further compounded the controversy and uncertainty of this step.

Industry Divides

Vehicle manufacturers had complained to the entering Trump administration about the late Obama regulatory efforts, seeking some form of relief from a demanding and accelerating transition through the mid-2020s. But it is unclear just what they sought beyond increased compliance flexibility, particularly because various manufacturers faced different issues in terms of their capacity to comply with tightened standards.

They also held varied views on the desirability of any transition toward electric vehicles in the United States and globally. Firms such as Volkswagen appeared well positioned for such a shift; others, for example, like Fiat Chrysler, were more fully focused on gas-powered vehicles and were deeply opposed. There is no evidence that manufacturers collectively sought a waiver revocation along with an extended regulatory freeze on fuel economy standards. They all clearly feared the possibility of protracted resistance by California and allied states and any possibility of a split national market requiring industry to adhere to markedly different emission and fuel economy standards in different parts of the nation. In contrast, oil and gas production and refining interests welcomed the proposed regulatory changes, encouraging sustained use of their primary product by discouraging additional movement to vehicles with greater fuel efficiency or reliance on electricity as a power source.

But these divides presented the Trump administration with a political challenge, particularly given the distribution of vehicle manufacturing and assembly jobs in states where the president was victorious or competitive in 2016 and planned to campaign actively in 2020. In turn, the vehicle industry actively encouraged the president and California Governor Gavin Newsom, in June 2019, to find ways to bridge their differences. Industry divides were further reflected as the Trump administration attempted to sort out differences prior to the issuance of a final replacement rule, including statements in public hearings by elected officials from major vehicle production states. Michigan Democratic Representative Debbie Dingell served a Detroit area district with a major stake in the vehicle industry and noted in 2019 hearings in her district: "This industry cannot afford to have two separate standards. If we want to stay at the forefront of innovation and technology, money needs to be going into research and development, not a court battle that is going to go on forever that is going to give this industry uncertainty."[35] She further noted that she was "really not interested in a pissing contest" between the Trump administration and California officials, indicating that it could do considerable economic harm to her district and state.[36]

State Divides

Any prospects of intergovernmental harmony on this issue, however, appeared highly unlikely. The EPA and NHTSA stood steadfast behind their proposals while encountering delays given considerable legal and political hurdles before producing any final rule. California elected leaders, including the governor and attorney general, remained adamant that the CAA and a half-century of precedent made the emission waiver a cornerstone of American environmental federalism. The industry-wide Alliance of Automobile Manufacturers endorsed intergovernmental negotiations and some compromise, and heads of nearly all major vehicle manufacturing firms wrote both President Trump and Governor Newsom with a similar message, but there was little sign of serious negotiation between the parties.

Initial meetings between leaders from federal and state agencies began with baked goods and pleasantries but routinely devolved into acrimony, failing to produce any hint of an alternative path forward. Lead EPA officials ultimately refused to testify before Congress alongside state counterparts, and both sides turned hearings into finger-pointing at the intransigence of the other side. In his written testimony, Wheeler wrote that his direct counterpart, California Air Resource Board (CARB) head Mary Nichols, "was unable or unwilling to be a good faith negotiator. Her testimony that EPA professional staff were cut out of this proposal is false. Her testimony that California was cut out of the development of this proposal is her own doing."[37] Nichols, in turn, found Wheeler's assertions "shocking" and contended that any invitation from the EPA to submit a counterproposal was laced with the "determination to treat you as illegitimate." As Nichols had noted at an earlier stage of this process, "the backup plan is divorce. I don't mean we're going to secede from the Union. We will reassert our CAA authority and move forward with our program, possibly with some improvements. We will do that, and if EPA tries to block us, we'll be in court."[38]

Courtrooms and other venues for prolonged intergovernmental combat appeared increasingly likely. California promptly found its position supported by a substantial body of elected and appointed officials from other states, all eager to join forces in court or through allied policy adoption to build a multistate coalition opposing Trump administration efforts. At an exceptionally early stage of the federal position shift, sixteen state attorneys general joined forces with California Attorney General Xavier Becerra in filing an opening legal salvo against the Trump administration in federal court. *State of California et al. v. U.S. Environmental Protection Agency* stood on somewhat uncertain legal ground, since it responded only to an April 2018 *Federal Register* notice on the proposed shift rather than a final rule. But the legal arguments represented a blistering assault on every step of the federal review process, including allegations of sloppy and biased scientific analysis, failure to consult and engage California in constructive negotiations, and indifference to possible economic and environmental risks that would stem from dividing the nation into zones with separate emission standards.

California also had at least two other forms of intergovernmental alliances to retaliate against any waiver removal effort, as well as a pair of unusual partnerships that stole thunder from the federal effort. First, under Section 177 of the CAA, all other states may formally adopt the California vehicle emissions standard as their own once a waiver is authorized. This reflects the bandwagon effect introduced in chapter 2, which has frequently resulted in past decades in a California-approved waiver subsequently attracting a number of other partner states, often ultimately compelling the EPA to adopt California policy as federal policy to secure national consistency. Twelve states approved alignment with the California waiver policy during the Obama administration. Colorado subsequently joined those ranks in early 2019, and two other states pledged to join later in the year.[39] Collectively, this represented more than 40 percent of the national vehicle market and suggested a fundamental split in regulatory standards for vehicle manufacturers if that coalition held together.

Second, it appeared increasingly possible that this coalition might expand, as twenty-four governors signed a pledge in July 2019 supporting California in its efforts to maintain its vehicle emissions policy in the face of Trump administration opposition. This involved all of the Section 177 states and added twelve additional states, four of which Trump won in 2016 and two of which were likely 2020 swing states: Pennsylvania and Wisconsin. This declaration stated: "We, the undersigned 24 governors—a bipartisan coalition representing 52% of the U.S. population and 57% of the economy—stand together in calling for one strong, national clean car standard and support preserving state authority to protect our residents from vehicle pollution."[40] The combination of sizable state coalitions of attorneys general and governors further indicated the possibility of a prolonged political and legal struggle over implementation of the proposed regulatory freeze and waiver reversal.

The potential opposition coalition to the Trump initiative further diversified and deepened in 2019 when the Canadian government formally embraced the California standards and waiver during a visit to Sacramento by Foreign Minister Catherine McKenna to Governor Newsom and CARB Chair Nichols. Canada has long followed the American lead in setting vehicle emission standards, reflecting its smaller market and considerable supply-chain interdependence with the United States. By pledging to adhere to the California standards, given their own climate policy commitments, Canada further opened the possibility that other nations, including those of the European Union, might choose to join forces with California rather than Washington, D.C., in designing vehicle emissions standards amid growing global concern about climate change, potentially isolating the Trump position.

One final alliance announced in July 2019 was particularly surprising and lacked precedent in the history of vehicle emissions policy. Newsom and Nichols announced an agreement with four major vehicle manufacturers (Ford, Volkswagen, BMW, and Honda) on a compromise of sorts, whereby they agreed to honor a slightly less aggressive version of California's emission-reduction targets on a national basis. The manufacturers secured a partial reduction in the California standards, including a fuel economy rate increase of 3.7 percent rather than 5 percent per year through 2026. They also secured bonus credits for electric vehicle purchases and elimination of requirements to include emissions from electricity generated for use by these vehicles in calculating environmental impact. This agreement made no reference to the more modest standards proposed by the Trump administration or whether other leading manufacturers might join the coalition over time. But it threatened a fundamental industry split alongside the established divide among states in coming to terms with the Trump effort to freeze standards on a national basis.

Newsom and Nichols heralded this as a breakthrough and a model of effective compromise between government and industry. They called upon other manufacturers to join the agreement and for the Trump administration to endorse it as a national model through negotiated compromise. The Trump administration, however, took a very different view, with the White House, EPA, and the Department of Transportation asserting that California had gone even farther than before in encroaching on federal authority and, thereby, demonstrating that it was not a trustworthy partner for serious negotiation. A White House spokesperson derided the agreement as a PR stunt, and media reports confirmed direct involvement by an outraged president in exploring a range of aggressive retaliatory options. Ultimately, the Trump administration doubled down on its aggressive posture when the Justice Department informed California and the participating vehicle manufacturers that they were being reviewed for possible antitrust violations that could restrict production of less costly and less fuel-efficient vehicles that citizens wanted to purchase. However, Trump officials ended this review in early 2020 and thereby ended this threat.

This led to a September 2019 announcement that the California waiver would be formally withdrawn through one final rule, and that a second final rule would be issued later that would likely freeze fuel economy standards without any adjustments from 2020 through 2026. It contended that California had exceeded its authority in attempting to regulate vehicle greenhouse gas emissions and mandating purchase of certain numbers of zero-emissions vehicles. Transportation Secretary Elaine Chao said: "No state has the authority to opt out of the nation's rules, and no state has a right to impose its policies on everybody else in our whole country. To do otherwise harms consumers and damages the American economy." EPA Administrator Wheeler concurred and said: "We embrace federalism and the role of states. But federalism does not mean that one state can dictate standards for the entire country."[41] The final rule included a formal request that any litigation should receive initial review in the U.S. Court of Appeals for the District of Columbia Circuit, skipping lower level court review and possibly resulting in a final decision before the end of Trump's term in 2021.

Almost immediately, a coalition led by Becerra and consisting of twenty-two other state attorneys general from the Democratic Party and the District of Columbia filed suit in the U.S. Court of Appeals for the District of Columbia Circuit. In *State of California et al. v. Elaine Chao et al.*, these states contended that the Trump administration had contradicted the 2007 Supreme Court decision on climate endangerment with its final rule, as well as two lower court rulings from that period that limited the applicability of fuel economy preemption provisions to vehicle emission programs.[42] They contended that the Department of Transportation had exceeded its authority, failed to complete and release required technical and economic analysis, and stripped California and allied states of their authority to implement EPA-approved "longstanding and fundamental parts" of their "efforts to protect public health and welfare in their states, to meet state goals for the reduction of harmful air pollution including greenhouse gases, and to attain or maintain federal air quality standards."[43] They countered the Trump appellate court request with an endorsement of initial review in the U.S. District Court for the District of Columbia, preferring a more deliberative and longer review process that would more likely extend beyond the 2020 election.

California officials launched and sustained a volley of criticisms of the final rule and pledged to continue to "advise" vehicle manufacturers to honor their standards during any period of litigation. Nichols reflected on her many decades of service to the state and noted in a press conference: "This is the fight of a lifetime. We have to win this, and I believe we will."[44] Newsom endorsed those views at the same event. He asked: "Where is the Republican Party right now? Why aren't they pushing back? They believe in federalism, they believe in state rights—at least they assert that. And they're nowhere to be found on this." All thirteen bandwagon states pledged continued commitment to their California partnership, and governors of both Minnesota and New Mexico announced plans to join this contingent after the federal final rule withdrawing the California waiver.

This state response triggered a barrage of presidential tweets deriding the California position and a blistering letter from EPA's Wheeler to CARB's Nichols alleging that "California has failed to carry out its most basic tasks under the Clean Air Act," leading to "the worst air quality in the United States." Wheeler indicated that California's entire state implementation plan under the CAA would undergo review and that the state could face highway funding and air quality permitting sanctions as possible penalties.[45]

Financial penalties had been an EPA option to secure compliance for decades but had never been used to reduce any state's transportation funding. Additional threats via EPA letters and presidential tweets focused on water quality issues and possible federal funding cuts to the state.[46] Alongside an aggressive response from California authorities and leaders of bandwagon states, the Environmental Council of the States (ECOS), representing lead environmental agency officials of all fifty states, wrote to Wheeler: "ECOS is seriously concerned about a number of unilateral actions by U.S. EPA that run counter to the spirit of cooperative federalism and to the appropriate relationship between the federal government and the states who are delegated the authority to implement federal environmental statutes."[47]

ECOS Executive Director Donald Welsh sought a meeting with the EPA to review this situation. The EPA, however, responded promptly, dismissing criticism of its role and the meeting request. Its letter noted support for the EPA approach from several ECOS members, including lead environmental officials from Arkansas, Florida, Mississippi, West Virginia, and Wyoming. Following this exchange, the Sierra Club filed suit against the EPA for alleged failure to impose similar pressures on a dozen other states that also faced ongoing compliance challenges with air quality standards but did not receive a letter comparable to the one sent to Sacramento.

Intergovernmental hostilities continued to intensify in early 2020, as did divides among vehicle manufacturing firms. Two coalitions representing the majority of vehicle manufacturers, the Association of Global Automakers and the Coalition of Sustainable Automotive Regulation, intervened on behalf of the Trump administration position in the pending court case and received laudatory tweets from the president.[48] In November, thirteen states with Republican leadership filed a motion to intervene in the court case, claiming that approval of California's waiver would increase car prices, reduce vehicle sector jobs, and threaten manufacturing. They also noted federalism concerns with the waiver's granting of too much power to a single state, contending: "In our Republic, no State is more equal than others. Allowing California alone to evade otherwise preemptive law upsets that balance, and the intervening States have an interest in recalibrating it."[49]

California matched these efforts with renewed expressions of outrage over the waiver reversal, repeatedly characterizing the Trump administration's actions as an assault on both the climate and federalism. State officials began to refer to the four vehicle manufacturers supporting the California position as the "fabulous four" and announced that future state vehicle purchases would involve only their products. In turn, the California Air Resources Board announced that, for the first time, it would not participate in the annual Los Angeles Auto Show while hinting that it might attend "off-campus" events involving their four corporate allies. State leaders reiterated that they would continue to fight this federal policy shift in every imaginable venue. Speaking about President Trump, Attorney General Becerra said: "He is a bump in the road of what we're trying to do. So I'm just figuring out, do I go over the bump or around the bump?"[50]

The Trump administration hinted in early 2020 at a possible willingness to adjust the federal fuel economy rule, potentially allowing modest annual increases averaging 1.5 percent. This represented an attempt to address industry preference to avoid appearing implacably opposed to limited efficiency improvements while refusing any bargaining with California. Industry remained deeply divided on this issue, with the Ford-led alliance of four manufacturers continuing to side with California, while the General Motors and Toyota-led alliance of eight firms supported the Trump administration position. Three other firms, Daimler AG, Volvo, and Jaguar Land Rover, did not take a formal position. Amid this uncertainty and considerable controversy over the scientific and economic analysis underpinning the Trump administration review process, any final rule was delayed until 2020, and prolonged litigation seemed likely to extend beyond the November election.

It was not clear, however, that any version of this policy would have major impacts on greenhouse gas emissions without further policy linked to congressional action. Sustained low gasoline prices due to expanding oil production and the absence of any federal carbon tax fostered record sales for large pick-up trucks and SUVs. Fleet shifts away from passenger cars to far bigger vehicles undermined the environmental gains from the installation of efficiency technology. In turn, California's hopes for a major increase in demand for vehicles powered by electricity were dashed by national purchase rates that hovered around 2 percent despite sustained federal subsidy programs and complementary efforts in some states.

Regulatory Repeal and Replacement: The Clean Power Plan

Donald Trump had no ambivalence about undertaking a high-profile and far-reaching assault on the segment of Barack Obama's administrative-driven climate policy applied to electricity sector emissions. The CPP was developed without congressional input through executive action during the second Obama term. It represented a massive expansion of CAA authority to address carbon emissions from the burning of coal, natural gas, and oil in power plants, justified in considerable part on projected benefits that were global rather than domestic. Ironically, that sector would have received the most immediate and intensive focus had federal cap-and-trade legislation passed Congress in 2010. It was also the sector in which significant emission reductions had already occurred, linked to marked declines in coal use in favor of expanded natural gas and renewables. Many states, including a number of predominantly Republican ones with expanding natural gas and renewable power production capacity, anticipated continued carbon emission declines in coming years. Ten states had adopted and implemented their own versions of cap-and-trade for power plants using fossil fuels, further propelling a shift toward renewables. The CPP was designed to build on these changes, accelerating them in coming decades by setting fixed emission-reduction targets for each state but allowing them to propose their own preferred strategy from a broad menu of options.[51] It was designed to play a central role in the Obama plan to meet Paris emission-reduction targets.

The 2015 issuance of the final CPP rule was celebrated at an EPA headquarters event, where it was signed by Administrator Gina McCarthy. But it almost instantly was challenged by litigation filed in federal courts, led in part by the person who would succeed McCarthy, Scott Pruitt. Ultimately, twenty-seven states joined forces behind that suit, and Senate Majority Leader Mitch McConnell implored states in an op-ed to refuse to comply or undertake any efforts to draft state implementation plans.[52] The 2016 Supreme Court stay halted most federal and state plan development, although some states continued with their efforts. All this created a highly uncertain context for the future of the CPP, although the Obama administration assumed that a Hillary Clinton presidency would lead the fight in federal court and work to preserve and possibly expand the program.

Trump, however, viewed the CPP as a poster child of regulatory excess that harmed American workers and provided no obvious benefit to the nation. In particular, his strong campaign focus on coal production and electricity use gave him considerable opportunity to hold a number of campaign events in coal-based states that featured coal miners and pledges to restore their jobs if elected. Even with the Supreme Court stay, however, there was no simple path toward eviscerating the CPP. It had been finalized too long before Trump took office for the Congressional Review Act to be an option. In turn, the decision not to undo the endangerment finding meant that any plan repeal had to offer a replacement that arguably had some potential for reducing carbon emissions from the electricity sector. Consequently, the Trump administration sought and secured court approval for abeyance of further CPP review, given its plans to pursue transition toward an alternative.[53]

This set the stage for preparation of a sweeping executive order that would include many provisions designed to promote "American energy independence." Trump traveled to Kentucky to unveil the order in March 2017 and made the CPP a primary focal point in his remarks: "Perhaps no single regulation threatens our miners, energy workers, and companies more than this crushing attack on American industry."[54] Some Trump supporters expressed concern that the executive order would lead to CPP replacement rather than outright elimination. Myron Ebell of the Competitive Enterprise Institute, a lead member of the Trump environmental transition team and a strident opponent of the CPP, explained: "I think it is acceptable given the fact that they haven't taken on the endangerment finding, so they have to regulate CO_2 emissions from new and existing power plants in one way or the other. This is clearly a minimal regulation. I can live with it but I think the question is whether the courts will be able to live with it."[55]

Like Ebell, coal-focused industries and utilities also were generally on board with the regulatory replacement process, in part because this would complicate efforts in any future administration to rehabilitate the CPP.[56] Moreover, there was considerable confidence in conservative legal circles that Trump's efforts to appoint to the federal courts judges who would be ideologically hostile to such a policy could further serve to legally protect any modest replacement regulation.

Seven months after the executive order issuance, the Trump administration scheduled another event in Kentucky, this one announcing its plans to file an Advance Notice of Proposed Rulemaking confirming its plan to repeal the CPP. Pruitt declared that "the war on coal is over," and Trump had begun to describe the replacement as a done deal even before the proposed rule was issued. As noted in chapter 1, he declared at a September 2017 rally in Alabama: "Did you see what I did to that?

Boom. Gone."[57] But this regulatory replacement process would prove far more complex as the Trump administration worked toward development of its alternative, which would ultimately take the form of the Affordable Clean Energy (ACE) rule. Unlike the vehicle sector and the reversal of the California waiver, the CPP-to-ACE transformation would be portrayed as empowering states by giving them greater latitude to shape their own electricity system free of heavy federal interference.

The completion of the final ACE rule would take nearly two additional years, introduced by Pruitt's successor, Andrew Wheeler, with far less hoopla than the initial promises. A proposed rule was not completed until August 2018, with the final version following in June 2019. The ACE represented a "minimalist interpretation of EPA's authority" in replacing the CPP, working with provisions of Section 111 of the CAA to require the "best system of emissions reduction" (BSER) for operational power plants.[58] The ACE did not endorse any specific technology or set fixed emission-reduction targets for individual plants or states. Instead, it encouraged states to select their own emission-reduction targets and begin consideration of possible ways to improve facility efficiency for coal-generating units. Cost-effective strategies such as emissions trading, which had been a CPP centerpiece, were formally prohibited for consideration as a path toward ACE compliance, as were fuel-switching from coal to natural gas, expanded renewable energy use, or installation of carbon sequestration and storage technology.

The ACE also proposed a prolonged process of state plan development and federal review, possibly delaying any actual implementation until the mid-2020s. It offered states up to three years to submit initial state implementation plan proposals, followed by one year for EPA review. If the EPA found these proposals unacceptable, it was given up to two years to craft and impose a federal plan option. In turn, the EPA decided through the ACE process to abandon Obama administration efforts to include an assessment of "co-benefits," namely other air quality gains that would be achieved through any of the steps taken to reduce carbon emissions. Reduction of particulate matter releases was a major consideration in CPP development, but the ACE ruled these out because they would move a number of states beyond compliance with standards that were already being met.

The ACE final rule issuance triggered a thunderstorm of negative reaction, much as had been the case for the CPP. There were some state losers in this transition, even though there was no electricity emissions waiver process that designated particular authority to California or any other state. The ten states already operating cap-and-trade programs had anticipated highly favorable terms of entry into the CPP, expecting credit for early action and emissions reduction, nonfactors under the ACE. In turn, California had never halted its CPP planning process and actually submitted a formal state implementation plan to EPA in 2017, while other states, such as Minnesota and Pennsylvania, had sustained their planning efforts despite the Supreme Court stay and uncertainty about the fate of the regulation. Indeed, nearly half of the states reported few concerns over anticipated compliance, particularly in cases where they were already experiencing rapid transition from coal toward other energy sources and had developed their own policies to continue that shift. Even states where attorneys general had gone to court to attack the CPP often had productive discussion among executive officials on implementation options, sometimes including quiet negotiations with neighboring states about possible emission trading options.[59]

Many of these states would form coalitions to oppose the ACE. This included twenty-two Democratic attorneys general, all from states that had already adopted renewable portfolio standards that required steady increases in the volume of electricity produced from renewable sources. Lawyers from seven major cities led by Democratic mayors also joined the suit. The American Lung Association and the American Public Health Association filed suit first, within hours of ACE's unveiling, but states and cities promptly jumped into the fray. As Misha Tseytlin, a lawyer who represented utility interests during CPP hearings, noted: "It's hard for litigation to be quite as intense as the CPP. But obviously [the ACE] is going to be a battle royal, with a large number of players on both sides."[60] The suit was filed in the U.S. Court of Appeals for the District of Columbia Circuit in August 2019.

One area of likely legal and political attack is the possibility that the ACE might serve to increase power sector carbon emissions rather than reduce them in any way, at least in some states. EPA's Regulatory Impact Analysis accompanying the final rule acknowledged this possibility, particularly if states pursued refurbishing of established coal-burning plants rather than closing them. This could result in operating such plants with greater intensity and for longer time periods than would have occurred without the rule. This could lead not only to expanded carbon emissions but also increases in other air contaminants linked to coal usage, potentially triggering cross-border complaints from states downwind from these "rebounding" power plants.

States opposed to the ACE immediately decried the lack of any common national performance standard and the possible reversal of past sectoral gains in reducing carbon and conventional emissions. A 2019 economic analysis of the ACE concluded that 28 percent of plants could have higher emissions by 2030 when compared to a scenario in which no policy had been adopted. This would result in very modest overall national emission reductions, reflecting averaging that anticipated increases of up to 8.7 percent in eighteen states plus Washington, D.C.[61]

These rebound effect projections, however, played out amid continued transition away from coal use in American electricity. Both natural gas and renewable energy prices continued to decline, making coal increasingly uncompetitive, particularly when mined in key states like Pennsylvania where extraction costs are high and Trump had focused his pro-coal messaging. Forty-four generation units at twenty-two coal plants closed during 2018, a pace exceeding prior years and one that appeared likely to continue regardless of the fate of the ACE. In 2019, no new coal plants were being built anywhere in the United States, and a majority of operational plants are more than four decades old.[62] Indeed, more coal plants closed during Trump's first two years in office than in Obama's entire first term. At the same time, a growing number of states adopted new policies in 2018 and 2019 to further accelerate their transition away from coal and toward more carbon-friendly sources, including states in the Midwest and Mountain West regions that had not been leaders in this policy area during the prior decade.

As in the vehicle emissions case, it seemed inevitable that the ACE and the larger issue of federal regulation of electricity sector carbon emissions would not be resolved prior to the 2020 elections. A Trump administration victory through future rounds of litigation could serve not only to thwart the greater ambitions of the CPP but also make it quite difficult for any successor administration to revisit the CAA as a path toward new carbon policy for electricity generation given the structure of the ACE. But a reversal could force the hand of a more rigorous regulatory initiative, assuming Congress continued to sit on the sidelines.

While billing the CPP-to-ACE transition as a hallmark of its climate federalism approach to state empowerment, the Trump administration took an unexpected step in late 2019 designed to constrain state authority in the electricity and related sectors. As with vehicles, California would be in the crosshairs of this effort to dial back state climate policy innovation. At the same time federal-state relations on vehicles were disintegrating, the Department of Justice confronted California with threatened litigation over its cap-and-trade collaboration with the

Canadian province of Québec. This partnership had followed years of negotiation and Québec's decision to join the cap-and-trade system in 2014, along with neighboring Ontario, building on longstanding patterns of state and provincial collaboration on climate-related policy.[63] This system initially focused on electricity emissions but has begun to expand to other sectors over time, using a series of allowance auctions to set a carbon emissions price and allocate auction revenue for associated climate-related purposes.[64]

This cross-border collaboration was part of a broader set of partnerships between California and other sub-federal governments but was unique in the Americas for its development of parallel carbon pricing systems. The Department of Justice contended that Québec was operating an "independent foreign policy" and, thereby, was encroaching on federal constitutional terrain. It noted that former Governor Arnold Schwarzenegger had characterized California as a "nation-state" and as the "modern equivalent of the ancient city-states of Athens and Sparta," thereby demonstrating the state's allegedly exaggerated understanding of its role under the American Constitution. Newsom responded by contending that the Trump administration was "yet again continuing its political vendetta against California."[65] In December 2019, Justice officials sought an expedited decision on this matter from a district court judge, contending that it represented an encroachment on federal powers. In February 2020, California's Xavier Becerra and Democratic attorneys general from thirteen other states formally countered that the emissions trading agreement with Québec was simply an exercise of state authority to regulate pollution.

Regulatory Withdrawal, Replacement, Repeal, and Suspension: Methane Emissions and the Three Amigos

Donald Trump made no secret of his displeasure with NAFTA, either during the 2016 campaign or after assuming the presidency. He routinely characterized it as "the worst deal ever made" and contended that it had ultimately served to drain America's manufacturing job base. Either terminating NAFTA or negotiating a replacement that would represent a superior deal was a major priority during his first term, which led to a new pact, the United States-Mexico-Canada Agreement, in September 2018 that was approved by Congress in January 2020. Trump was, however, much less loquacious about another North American agreement struck by his predecessor during the final year of his presidency, a so called Three Amigos pact reached with Canadian Prime Minister Justin Trudeau and then Mexican President Enrique Peña Nieto. This was a presidential-executive agreement, with some parallels to the Paris Agreement, whereby these three neighboring nations agreed to reduce their methane emissions from oil and gas production by 40 to 45 percent from 2012 levels by 2025. All three nations included this commitment in their Paris greenhouse gas emissions–reduction pledges and further agreed to extensive technical collaboration in improving the measurement of methane emissions and evaluating mitigation strategies.

Methane represents a distinctive challenge for mitigation but also an enormous opportunity. It emanates from oil and gas production and distribution, as well as the agricultural and solid waste sectors. The United States estimates that 10 percent of its total greenhouse gas emissions comes from methane, although actual numbers may be considerably higher based on recent research. Globally, methane is estimated to have caused one quarter of the global warming that has already occurred. It has far greater warming capacity than carbon dioxide during its first century in the atmosphere, so reduction in its releases can offer both short-term and long-term climate benefits. However, it is difficult to measure methane with considerable confidence, particularly in the oil and gas sector with long supply chains and possibility of leaks and in the agricultural sector given sources from livestock, manure, and some crop production techniques. In turn, neither federal nor state governments have invested extensively in state-of-the-art monitoring technology.

The 2016 North American agreement focused on energy-based methane, particularly at the point at which these energy sources are extracted from below the surface of the ground. All three nations are major fossil fuel producers, and the advent of hydraulic fracturing and horizontal drilling led to particularly large increases in American production. Methane is a primary element of natural gas and can be vented to the atmosphere if not captured during production. Large oil basins, such as the Permian in Texas and New Mexico and the Bakken in North Dakota and Montana, often produce unexpected and expanding volumes of methane during drilling. In cases where producers cannot make a profit on this gas if prices are low or if they are located in remote areas where gas capture infrastructure is not available, they frequently flare methane by placing a flame at its release point. This converts methane into carbon dioxide, a less potent greenhouse gas during its first century in the atmosphere, along with volatile organic compounds and other toxic air emissions released by this combustion.

Methane linked to energy production on private- or state-held lands has long fallen under the primary regulatory jurisdiction of states, in many cases going back generations, when state oil and gas commissions set regulatory standards. These have historically been highly deferential to industry, fearful that requiring tougher regulatory standards could lead energy production investments to migrate in search of more favorable terms.[66] Methane became a growing concern in many energy producing states during the last decade as shale boom output expanded. This reflected concerns about methane's contribution to climate change and a wider set of air quality issues, leading in some cases to CAA noncompliance due to methane concentrations. In turn, methane releases also constituted the permanent loss of a nonrenewable natural resource. This raised concerns from property owners hosting drilling operations who were denied royalty payments for flared or vented methane and for state governments that were denied revenues from production or severance taxes.

States proved generally slow to revisit this arena through new regulatory or taxation strategies, with a few notable exceptions, including Colorado and Pennsylvania. Consequently, the Obama administration entered into this area with new regulatory provisions in May 2016 before the agreement on the Three Amigos pact. As with the CPP, these relied on CAA provisions, where the EPA could address methane as a conventional air contaminant but also as a climate threat under the endangerment finding. What emerged was a set of performance standards focused on methane release minimization. This entailed detailed provisions for more frequent monitoring of fugitive emissions and requirements to repair any leaks that were detected during such review. It also established performance standards for pumps and other equipment and required greater industry disclosure and transparency. These and similar regulatory provisions for drilling on federally held land overseen by the Department of Interior gave Obama a credible platform to negotiate the North American agreement in July 2016.

One significant attraction of this approach from an economics standpoint is that numerous studies have concluded that methane from oil and gas production represents "low-hanging fruit," presenting many cost-effective options for achieving significant reductions. Indeed, reducing methane leaks to as close to zero as possible was critical in any strategy to propose transition from coal to natural gas as a climate-friendly strategy. Natural gas has essentially half the greenhouse gas impacts of coal as long as related methane releases are negligible, but these advantages fade as the rate of releases climbs.[67]

Canada and Mexico have subsequently designed and begun to implement methane-reduction regulations, honoring the Three Amigos agreement. The path forward, however, has been rocky in the United States, reflected in the fact that Congress never vetted the agreement or provided legislative support for implementation. Within weeks of the announcement of the North American plan, thirteen states, all Republican attorneys general, filed suit in federal court against new EPA standards that would be essential to meet the continental targets, claiming they were "arbitrary, capricious, an abuse of discretion and not in accordance of law." This group of states was led by West Virginia and included a few states with little or no oil or gas production, such as Wisconsin and Michigan. North Dakota and Texas filed separate but complementary legal challenges. This position squared with that of many oil and gas production firms who endorsed the proposed rule, as did the Independent Petroleum Association of America. A few larger producers, such as ExxonMobil, were more lukewarm, favoring some aspects of the Obama regulations.

Before these legal cases or the continental partnership had advanced very far, President Trump took steps to reverse these Obama initiatives, thereby placating the litigating states. The Obama-era EPA methane regulations were targeted in the same executive order that launched a regulatory repeal-and-replacement process for the electricity sector. As in the case of the CPP, replacement rather than full elimination proved to be a more prudent path, and regulatory revision proposals were introduced in September 2018. These proposed considerable softening of monitoring and leak repair protocols as well as exemptions from some equipment use requirements. Moreover, the proposed replacement regulations allowed states to opt out of federal requirements if they could demonstrate that their own rules were "equivalent." Indeed, EPA took the unique step of announcing that six states (California, Colorado, Ohio, Pennsylvania, Texas, and Utah) would immediately be recognized as achieving equivalency and, thereby, free of federal regulations. EPA officials acknowledged that these steps would lead to increases in methane releases of greenhouse gases, volatile organic compounds, and hazardous air pollutants compared to scenarios under the Obama regulations. But they countered that reduced compliance costs would approach $500 million through 2025 and outweigh any foregone benefits, prompting their plans for milder regulatory replacements.

Ironically, an entirely new coalition of thirteen states formed to declare their opposition to this proposed regulatory alteration, in anticipation of likely litigation once final regulations were issued.[68] This represented a flip from the earlier opposition cluster of production states and generally involved states led by Democrats. Many had no oil and gas production, such as Connecticut, Maine, and Massachusetts. They opposed the reforms, contending that they would suffer climate and air quality consequences from emissions released in other regions of the country. Two of the production states cleared for regulatory equivalency, California and Pennsylvania, joined this group, as did one other major production state, New Mexico. These three were among the very small set of states that had pursued major methane regulatory reforms of their own and likely faced the most modest transition costs under any federal plan implementation.

The EPA's path to completing a final rule, however, was complicated by unexpected concerns about some of the regulatory replacement provisions. These objections were raised by some of the very production states that had opposed the Obama plan. They fell short of outright opposition to the replacement plan but involved states that had not made any major changes in their own regulations or legislation guiding methane oversight in recent decades and backed some elements of the Obama approach. In the case of North Dakota, its Department of Health argued in December 2018 public comments that more frequent monitoring would, in fact, be beneficial and should be maintained in any federal replacement regulation. They encouraged the EPA to consider a "sliding scale," whereby companies with higher methane-reduction performance records would be granted greater latitude than lower-performance production firms, recognizing enormous differences between firms operating in their states.[69] In the case of Oklahoma, Department of Environmental Quality officials proposed "retaining the semi-annual monitoring frequency for non-low production well sites which are located in areas designated nonattainment for ozone." Officials from some other production states also registered concerns with the proposal, often finding merit in some Obama policies and recommending that the EPA offer a less sweeping replacement in final form. Ironically, these states retained authority to take such steps on their own but had declined to do so, while seemingly favoring a federal role that constrained them despite their role in litigation.

If anything, the Trump administration began moving in a different direction in 2019, considering even more draconian shifts that might eliminate any direct federal methane regulation of oil and gas production. EPA Administrator Wheeler noted in a May 2019 speech that the agency was considering dividing environmental oversight of the oil and gas industry into separate sections of the production and supply chain, thereby arguing that methane emissions from any one segment would be insufficient to warrant federal regulation. "With the sources split, it's not clear whether the level of greenhouse gas emissions will be high enough to trigger the significant attribution criteria, which are required to set emission standards under the Clean Air Act," Wheeler said in a speech to the U.S. Energy Association.[70] This announcement coincided with mounting concerns over major increases in flaring volumes in the Bakken and Permian Basins and an ever-expanding body of studies indicating that methane flaring and venting from oil and gas sector production was considerably higher than had been acknowledged under existing reporting protocols.[71] However, aside from Colorado and New Mexico, few states took additional steps to tighten their methane regulatory oversight during 2018–2020, leaving many questions about decentralized environmental stewardship of oil and gas production as output continued to climb.

In August 2019, the EPA introduced a proposed rule to carry through on its far-reaching methane deregulatory threat of previous months, although it was unclear how much progress it would make toward final rule development prior to 2020 elections. Industry groups immediately divided in response as a required public comment period began. A number of larger oil and gas producing firms with deep financial reserves had already begun to invest in state-of-the-art methane capture technology. They expressed serious misgivings about the proposed deregulation, since their path to compliance was easier and they faced growing public doubts about natural gas advantages over coal given methane release concerns. In contrast, smaller production firms with tighter pockets and greater problems with methane mitigation expressed strong support. Many of the states who had led opposition to the earlier regulatory changes were most outspoken in their response to this latest round, likely leading to a litigation challenge if a final rule was produced in 2020.

Methane on Federal Lands

The Trump administration also attempted major regulatory changes from the Obama era on methane flaring and venting on federal land, primarily involving a set of Western states with a large historic federal presence in land use.[72] The Obama administration's Waste Prevention Rule would fall under different statutes and Bureau of Land Management auspices but was designed to complement EPA efforts focused on privately held and state-owned lands to reduce methane-related emissions. This included required submission of waste minimization plans before drilling began, mandatory leak detection and repair programs, and requirements to capture increasing amounts of methane for use rather than waste through flaring and venting. It also opened the possibility of adopting major proposed increases in royalty levels on produced oil and gas that are paid to the federal government and endow a trust fund that supports state land and wildlife conservation efforts.

The initial Trump strategy involved use of the Congressional Review Act, leading to the narrow Senate failure to pass a resolution discussed earlier in this chapter. The administration responded by proposing in December 2017 a one-year suspension of the Obama rule, but this was rejected two months later in federal court, leading to rule reinstatement. A repeal-and-replace strategy ensued, leading to the issuance of a new rule in September 2018 that weakened while not eliminating nearly all key provisions and reducing the possibility of future royalty increases.

As with other Trump regulatory efforts, final rule issuance triggered immediate formation of a state opposition coalition. In this case, the Democratic attorneys general of California and New Mexico stepped forward, launching a litigative response on the same day the repeal rule was issued.[73] This reflected major concerns about methane concentrations and related air quality concerns in both states, particularly in Kern County, California, and the San Juan Basin of New Mexico. A federal district court vacated the Trump royalty reversal in April 2019, citing serious Administrative Procedure Act violations. Judge Saundra Brown Armstrong, a George W. Bush appointee, wrote that the Department of Interior repeal "was effectuated in a wholly improper manner."[74] However, the balance of the rule remained in operation as the Trump administration also attempted to expand and accelerate approvals of drilling permit requests on federal lands.

Similar developments occurred in offshore drilling for oil and gas, as the Trump administration worked to weaken new regulatory provisions added by the Obama administration after the 2010 Deepwater Horizon disaster.[75] These included loosening monitoring provisions, third-party inspection certification, and blowout preventer standards. Additional Trump proposals to expand drilling in the Gulf of Mexico and along both the Atlantic and Pacific coasts triggered substantial opposition from states governed by both parties, reflecting an unusual example of bipartisan state opposition to federal regulatory reforms.

Methane from Landfills

The Obama administration viewed methane emission reductions from solid waste landfills as highly cost-effective and technically feasible. Landfills are the third largest source of methane in the United States, following oil and gas production and agriculture. They are relatively few in number and remain stationary over many decades, monitored closely and inspected regularly by state and local governments for a number of public safety and environmental protection considerations. Methane is also vented or flared through a limited number of pipes that are highly visible from a considerable distance, and there is already substantial industry precedent for capturing landfill methane gas and bringing it to market as an energy source. Nearly a dozen states define such biogas as a renewable energy source because landfills continually produce it as their contained solid waste decomposes. The EPA began regulation of landfill methane in the 1990s under the CAA and so developed considerable experience in this area.[76]

The EPA developed a two-fold strategy, combining new regulations on landfill methane capture and use alongside expansion of a Landfill Methane Outreach Program that offered technical and financing advice for landfill gas distribution and marketing. The agency issued a final rule in 2016, with guidelines for both existing and new landfills that sought a 30 percent increase in the amount of landfill gas captured rather than released. Its new regulations required installation of gas collection systems, expanded the number of landfills that would be required to collect gas, and expanded facility monitoring efforts. States were required to prepare implementation plans for EPA approval by May 30, 2017, which shifted approval to Obama's successor.

This regulation did not trigger the creation of a multistate coalition or litigation or a firestorm of controversy. It was seemingly destined to be one of the easier provisions of the Obama climate strategy to launch and sustain. The Trump administration did not attempt to repeal or reverse the landfill methane rule but did borrow a tool from the Reagan administration regulatory playbook and undertook suspension of its operation.[77] This would delay the EPA's deadline for state plan submission for two years and extend the timetable for compliance with other stages in the regulatory process. In cases where no state plan was approved and a federal plan had to be developed, implementation would not occur until at least March 2023.

The EPA contended that it needed more time to complete its work in developing plans, as did states. But this immediately met stiff opposition from states that had already submitted plans and were awaiting EPA responses (Arizona, California, Delaware, and New Mexico) or were nearing plan completion when the suspension was announced. West Virginia was not normally an opponent of Trump administration strategies to reverse federal climate regulations but was upset by the suspension and proceeded to complete its plan, submitting it to the EPA in September 2018. Its Department of Environmental Protection argued that states "should not be penalized and required to duplicate their efforts when no substantial amendments were proposed" to the suspended rule by the EPA.[78]

As in other areas, Democratic state attorneys general joined forces to challenge this interpretation in federal courts in late 2018. This nine-state coalition was smaller than those for transportation, electricity, and methane from oil and gas. It consisted of California, Illinois, Maryland, New Jersey, New Mexico, Oregon, Pennsylvania, Rhode Island, and Vermont. California Attorney General Xavier Becerra served in the lead role and argued that all states would have already secured an approved state plan or a federal plan and begun implementation had the EPA not suspended its rule. He lamented: "The adverse impacts of the proposed Delay Rule on human health and welfare—the very things Congress has tasked EPA with safeguarding—will be significant."[79]

The lawsuit received a near-immediate boost in the U.S. District Court for the Northern District of California, when Judge Haywood Gilliam Jr., an Obama appointee, dismissed EPA requests to dismiss or stay the litigation in December 2019. Gilliam subsequently rejected EPA arguments that states lacked "special standing" to challenge its methane landfill rule interpretation. In May 2019, he issued a ruling requiring the EPA to complete review of submitted state plans within four months and release a federal rule within six months. "EPAs self-inflicted inconvenience, by itself, does not satisfy the 'especially heavy' burden necessary to warrant more than six months to promulgate a federal plan," wrote Gilliam.[80] The EPA subsequently approved plans submitted by Delaware, New Mexico, and West Virginia, while continuing to file requests for additional delay in 2020.

Climate Policy Lessons from the First Three Trump Years

The initial three years of Trump administration engagement on climate policy demonstrates the large and diverse arsenal of administrative presidency tools that a determined executive can apply in a search and destroy effort to obliterate as much of his immediate predecessor's legacy as was politically and legally feasible in just a few years. Trump and his team tailored various strategies that could be applied across each of the areas where Barack Obama's administration had launched major new climate protection initiatives. These included withdrawal from presidential-executive agreements involving other nations, aggressive appointment power use to place loyalists in leading posts, regulatory repeal and replacement, state waiver withdrawals and regulatory freezes, and regulatory suspensions. There was no consistent approach to federalism evident across these initiatives. Some were designed to constrain the authority of states pursuing unilateral policy development (vehicles), whereas others were intended to expand state latitude to chart their own course free of federal constraints (electricity and methane).

The results in just three years include significant inroads in ending involvement in international agreements on carbon dioxide emission reductions. Major domestic policy assaults were launched in the transportation, electricity, oil and gas production, and waste management sectors. Unlike the issue of health care, none of these efforts involved Congress, despite the fact that the president's party controlled both the Senate and the House during his first two years in office and much of the Obama approach could have been derailed through legislated CAA amendments prohibiting their application to carbon emissions. Once an attempt to adopt a Congressional Review Act resolution to nullify methane regulations on federal lands collapsed in the Senate, thanks in part to Trump nemesis John McCain, Congress reverted to its prolonged pattern of irrelevance on climate policy regardless of partisan control. Indeed, neither Trump nor congressional allies ever articulated any serious plan to reverse the Obama actions through legislation that would amend the CAA provisions they found troublesome, much less introduce legislation to that effect.

Instead, all the action would involve the executive branch. Trump reframed American climate policy during the 2016 campaign and carried through on his promises during these initial years in office. He took denial of climate change to dramatic highs, suggesting the possibility of a global conspiracy led by China to manipulate climate science to scare weak-kneed Americans into sacrificing jobs through a foolish environmental crusade. Trump declared, both on the campaign trail and from behind the presidential lectern, unilateral efforts to reduce national greenhouse gas emissions to be pointless and threatening to coal miners and other American workers. The CPP would serve as Exhibit A for his outrage and face an aggressive obliteration attempt.

But no Obama-era policy linked to climate change would escape some significant repeal, reversal, reinvention, freeze, or delay. When carbon emissions continued their recent pattern of decline during his first year in office, credit was claimed, even though the idea that this would accomplish anything useful had been disparaged. When emissions rose subsequently, nothing was said. No new proposals that would in any way promote carbon emission reduction would be unveiled as he neared the end of his first term in office, making Donald Trump the first resolutely pro-carbon emission president in American history. More broadly, Trump also broke new presidential ground by not developing administrative or legislative proposals to strengthen any area of environmental protection during his first three years in office.

Nonetheless, Trump's search and destroy strategy faced serious limitations, as did the initial American experiment with search and destroy operations during the Vietnam War. The president and members of his leadership team decided not to confront the 2007 Supreme Court endangerment finding that had opened a path for Barack Obama to reinvent the CAA administratively as a multifaceted climate policy tool. They did not formally repeal or replace the Obama social cost of carbon metric. And they did not attempt to eviscerate every regulatory provision that had been developed, in some cases settling for prolonged delay (such as landfill methane) or a freeze in standards (such as vehicle emissions) rather than outright reversal or elimination. They faced some near-immediate setbacks in federal courts, including stinging rebukes from judges appointed by prior Republican and Democratic presidents, with the possibility that these would continue even as Trump increased the number of his own appointees serving on the federal bench.[81] The prospects of additional court setbacks loom in coming years as major regulatory shifts completed in 2019 and 2020 face significant court tests. Many of Trump's major steps could also likely be reversed rapidly by a subsequent president without congressional involvement. This could begin with restoring American participation in the Paris Agreement, whereby no final decision could be made until the day after the 2020 election. That decision could be promptly altered by the forty-sixth president in either 2021 or 2025.

Trump also faced one relentless foe that showed signs of growing larger and more hostile over time: a coalition of opposition party attorneys general and state governors committed to rebut him at every step. Coalitional membership shifted from issue to issue but generally expanded after the midterm 2018 elections brought sizable increases in the number of Democrats holding elected state executive office. These state leaders worked relentlessly to discredit and challenge Trump, whether through unilateral efforts to adopt new policies or by launching aggressive attacks in the federal courts almost immediately after new rules or interpretations were issued. This represented the latest iteration of a growing trend in American federalism, whereby states dominated by the political party that did not control the federal executive branch would launch intergovernmental assaults to try to disparage, block, or reverse administrative policy steps taken by a sitting president. This coalition had an entirely different set of state members than the one that formed to oppose every administrative presidency effort on climate change policy undertaken by the forty-fourth president. But it defined the primary political and legal opposition that emerged to confront the forty-fifth president once he unveiled his own administrative presidency approach to the same policy topic.

FIVE

REVERSAL IN FEDERAL EDUCATION POLICY

Fewer Regulations, More Choice, and Civil Rights Shift

On the cover of *The Economist* on February 4, 2017, the bright red headline read: "An insurgent in the White House."[1] With no public sector experience and guided by practice and culture in a family business, President Trump was keen on using unilateral actions to advance his priorities of federal withdrawal in most domestic areas, especially social policy. The administration made serious efforts to dismantle key Obama administration initiatives in elementary and secondary as well as higher education.[2]

Between late January 2017 and early June 2019, the Trump administration issued six executive orders, two memoranda, five key policy letters, eighteen proclamations, and twenty-three sets of agency guidance in K–12 and higher education. As indicated in table 5-1, Trump's first executive order in education closely resembled a 2010 Obama order that increased the capacity of historically black colleges and universities (HBCU). Trump emphasized the importance of the private sector in strengthening HBCUs. Early in his presidency, Trump also issued an executive order that prohibited federal agencies from infringing on state and local control in education issues.

The Trump administrative presidency paid great attention to guidance documents as a key policy instrument in K–12 and higher education. In 2007, the Office of Management and Budget (OMB) had gone to some lengths to define this administrative tool in the *Federal Register*.[3] The OMB bulletin recognized the growing reliance on guidance documents by executive branch departments and agencies to inform the public and to provide policy direction to staff at the federal, state, and local levels. It defined "guidance document" as "an agency statement of general applicability and future effect . . . that sets forth a policy on a statutory, regulatory, or technical issue or an interpretation of a statutory or regulatory issue."[4] Guidance documents were not intended to impose requirements beyond those under applicable law. There were also particular types of guidance documents, including a "significant guidance document," which led to an annual effect of $100 million or more on the economy,

TABLE 5-1. *Executive Orders in Education Issued by President Trump*

Executive Order	Purpose
13779 (February 28, 2017)	White House initiative to promote excellence and innovation at historically black colleges and universities
13791 (April 26, 2017)	Enforcing statutory prohibitions on federal control of education
13801 (June 15, 2017)	Expanding apprenticeships in America
13845 (July 19, 2018)	Establishing the president's National Council for the American Worker
13853 (amended 13845) (December 12, 2018)	Establishing the White House Opportunity and Revitalization Council
13864 (March 21, 2019)	Improving free inquiry, transparency, and accountability at colleges and universities

Source: Federal Register, 2017–2019.

and an "economically significant guidance document," which had similarly broad annual effects on the economy without including federal expenditures and receipts. Actions to rescind guidance documents issued by the Obama administration became central to Trump's efforts to chart a new course in education. The Department of Education also used other informal tools, such as Dear Colleague letters, to shape policy. But in addition to executive orders, the Trump administration also employed formal tools, such as administrative rulemaking.

In elementary and secondary education, the Trump administration broadly envisioned a federal government that would fundamentally depart from the activist role that has evolved across several presidencies since the Great Society era of the Lyndon Johnson administration. The first three years of the Trump administration witnessed specific steps toward that broad vision of restraining the federal role, where education policy would be governed by stronger state rights and less federal involvement in civil and student rights. Signs indicating Trump was attempting to repurpose federal education policy include:

- scaling back federal direction and shifting substantial decision making to state and local government

- expanding federal support for a broad portfolio of school choice that went beyond the preceding administrations, including vouchers for parents to enroll their children in public and private schools (including religiously affiliated ones), federal tax credit scholarship programs, and charter schools

- easing possible entry of for-profit providers in K–12 education

- placing limits on federal capacity to promote equal education access, such as limiting the scope of Title IX enforcement

- reducing investment in data and research infrastructure

In higher education, the Trump administration focused on revising Obama-era policies, such as those pertaining to sexual misconduct and racial/ethnic diversity. But above all, it sought to roll back Obama-era efforts to curb abuses by the for-profit sector. As discussed in chapter 2, the Republican position on for-profits had morphed from skepticism under President Reagan to enthusiastic embrace under George W. Bush. Congressional Republicans had become staunch supporters of the for-profits and were richly rewarded for their support with campaign contributions from this sector. This was not because federal student loan repayments were no longer a problem. As of late 2018, for instance, only 24 percent of federal student loans were regularly being reduced by at least one dollar of principal and interest payment. Forty-three percent of outstanding student loans ($505 billion) were classified as being in "distress," meaning that student repayment plans were inadequate to the task of making the government whole, the loan payments were at least thirty days delinquent, or students had defaulted.[5] Compared to those enrolled in private nonprofit or public colleges, a much higher proportion of students in the for-profits had federal loans (roughly 90 percent) and subsequently defaulted on them (close to 25 percent of borrowers).[6] To the degree that the dire fiscal situation concerned the Trump administration, their efforts appeared mostly to focus on limiting the procedural rights of the borrowers.

This chapter illuminates many of the strategies the Trump administrative presidency employed in an effort to achieve its K–12 and higher education goals. The first section describes distinctive features of the education policy arena that tended to undermine the impact of Trump executive actions compared to the ACA and climate policy spheres. The following two sections focus respectively on clusters of initiatives intended to leave a mark on elementary and secondary education: namely, the promotion of school choice, along with reduced federal oversight and regulation. We then turn to an assessment of Trump's attempts to reshape policy toward higher education with actions directed at for-profit educational institutions and student borrowers front and center. We also gauge efforts of the Trump administration to reverse course on campus issues related to sexual misconduct and racial/ethnic diversity.

Distinctive Features of the Education Policy Arena

In considering the Trump administrative presidency, certain distinctive features of the education arena deserve note. Unlike the ACA and climate policy domains, some of the most important policy and governance issues in K–12 were resolved by bipartisan congressional legislation toward the end of the Obama presidency. The 2015 Every Student Succeeds Act, following eight years of delays, offered a strong bipartisan framework on the role of the federal government in supporting state and local school improvement. ESSA placed clear restrictions on federal intervention and the imposition of common standards on all states. The 2015 law granted states the primary responsibility for defining academic standards, adopting various measures of academic performance, identifying schools for improvement, and mapping the scope of turnaround interventions for failing schools. ESSA essentially replaced a federally driven regulatory framework with a state-defined agenda of education reform.

The Trump administration supported the ESSA framework. On September 24, 2018, the Department of Education released guidance to support states in meeting regulatory requirements to implement valid and reliable state assessment of students and clarified the department's obligation to conduct a peer review focused on the technical quality of state assessment systems.[7] The guidance further clarified: "Within the parameters noted above [statutory requirements in the Elementary and Secondary School Act as amended by Every Student Succeeds Act], each State has the flexibility and the responsibility to design its assessment system."[8]

The Trump team did not launch unilateral actions to disrupt ESSA implementation. Nor in its budget proposal did the Trump administration espouse major cuts for categorical programs that had long received bipartisan support. In her March 13, 2017, letter to the Chief State Schools Officers on a revised consolidated state plan for ESSA, Secretary Betsy DeVos highlighted the administration's commitment to "maintaining essential protections for subgroups of students, including economically disadvantaged students, students with disabilities and English learners."[9] President Trump even proposed slight funding increases over President Obama's FY2017 budget proposal in several areas, including certain grants to local education agencies, as well as for rehabilitation services and disability research.

In higher education, congressional leaders were ready to replicate their successful legislative outcome in K–12. Reauthorization of the 2008 Higher Education Act was long overdue. During Trump's first term, Republican Senator Lamar Alexander of Tennessee and Democratic Senator Patty Murray of Washington held a series of hearings, facilitated bipartisan deliberation, and made steady progress toward a comprehensive package that covered financial aid, a revised GI Bill, educational accountability, and student rights. While their efforts failed to yield new legislation by spring of 2020, the bipartisan initiative reduced the political incentive for the Trump White House to launch major executive actions in this sphere.

A second distinctive feature of the education domain is that the delivery of core services in both K–12 and higher education are primarily a state and local government responsibility. The states and well over

10,000 local school districts substantially shape K–12 education policy, its implementation, and its outcomes throughout the United States. States also play a large role in the case of higher education, though public universities sustain substantial autonomy within state governance structures. Given this setting, the federal government's role in shaping education policy is significant but far from determinative. A president faces more institutional barriers to influencing policy than in the case of the ACA or climate policy. Lower levels of government may, of course, be eager allies of an administrative presidency. For instance, Republicans dominated a majority of state governments after the 2016 election, thereby broadening the political support for Trump's education policy during his first two years in office.

Finally, state and local governments primarily finance education, with federal grants focused on supplementary services. In its budget proposals, the Trump White House maintained federal funding for major K–12 categorical programs, such as those focused on education for students with disabilities. The ESSA reporting requirement on performance among student subgroups remained a key legislative focus, an area Trump did not attempt to dismantle.

States also have responsibility for funding public higher education. In this sphere, however, most states have retreated from this commitment and increasingly relied on colleges and universities to make up for reduced funding by charging higher tuition. State spending per student dropped by 26 percent from 1990 to 2010, while the share of state budgets devoted to higher education declined from 8 to 4 percent. Between 1971 and 2011, the mean cost of attending public four-year colleges (including tuition, room, board, and fees) as a proportion of family income grew from 6 to 9 percent. Increases on this metric were much greater for families in the bottom, second, and middle-income quintiles of the population, more than doubling for each of these cohorts.[10] The state retreat on public higher education funding elevated the significance of federal policy concerning student grants and loans. In this regard, Trump budget proposals sought to cut Pell Grants and divert those funds to the space program and other policy initiatives. The proposal generated little support in Congress, however.

In sum, the higher degree of bipartisanship in Congress and elsewhere on matters of education policy and the limited direct role of the federal government in the governance and financing of K–12 and higher education reduced the salience of this arena for the Trump administrative presidency. Its executive initiatives did not seek the radical change the Trump White House pursued in the case of the ACA and climate policy. Still, as the rest of this chapter shows, the Trump administration did pursue several significant executive initiatives to refashion who gets what, when, and how in the education sphere. In the case of K–12, Trump strove to bolster the already substantial discretion states and localities had over a wide range of matters. In the higher education sphere, it sought to reverse Obama policies related to sexual misconduct and ethnic/racial issues while empowering for-profit institutions and curbing the rights of federal loan recipients.

K–12: The Trump Administration Champions School Choice

The appointment of Betsy DeVos as the U.S. Secretary of Education signaled a strong commitment to school choice from the Trump administration. Unlike her predecessors, Secretary DeVos had to receive a tie-breaking vote from Vice President Mike Pence for her Senate confirmation. During the Senate hearings, DeVos showed her passion on school choice but was unable to address other critical issues confronting public schools.[11]

Secretary DeVos's reliance on school choice as a primary federal strategy was grounded in her own activism in this domain. She was the chair of the American Federation for Children and provided financial support to a number of school choice initiatives, including vouchers for private schools. In her capacity as Secretary of Education, DeVos believed the federal government should play a catalytic role in promoting school choice. In her prepared remarks at the February 23, 2017, Conservative Political Action Conference, Secretary DeVos stated: "The education establishment has been blocking the doorway to reforms, fixes and improvements for a generation." She then announced: "We have a unique window of opportunity to make school choice a reality for millions of families."

In her meeting with leaders of HBCU on February 27, 2017, DeVos initially characterized HBCUs as "pioneers of school choice." Further, in his first presidential appearance before a joint session of Congress on February 28, 2017, President Trump asked Congress to pass an education bill "that funds school choice for disadvantaged youth, including millions of African-American and Latino children." He went on: "These families should be free to choose the public, private, charter, magnet, religious or home school that is right for them."

To be sure, this was not the first time a president endorsed school choice. Ronald Reagan was a strong proponent of it, but was unable to gain much congressional support. President George H. W. Bush was receptive to the notion of charter schooling when American Federation of Teachers President Albert Shanker first proposed it in the 1980s. Further, President Bill Clinton popularized charter schools with federal start-up funding, a position endorsed by both presidents George W. Bush and Barack Obama.

Unlike his predecessors, Trump hoped to scale up his school choice initiatives with a large infusion of federal funds. He first made this promise on the campaign trail, pledging $20 billion in federal funding. In his first presidential appearance before a joint session of Congress in late February 2017, Trump echoed his campaign promise, proposing a bill that provided federal funding for public and private school choice.

During the first two years of the Trump presidency, the governing landscape favored school choice expansion. First, the flexibilities built into ESSA opened up opportunities for the administration to work more directly with the states. Second, with nearly two-thirds of the states under one-party Republican control in both legislative bodies, Trump's school choice initiative received favorable responses in several state houses. Third, charter schools continued to be popular among parents in minority communities (though some organizations, including the NAACP, became more critical). According to a 2018 national poll, 44 percent of the public supported charter schools.[12]

In 2017, 2018, and 2019, President Trump signed presidential proclamations honoring National School Choice Week.[13] The 2018 proclamation stated:

> Charter schools empower families to pursue the right educational fit for their children, helping to ensure that there are paths to the American Dream that match the needs of students striving to achieve it. . . . My administration is committed to reducing the outsized Federal footprint in education and to empower families, as well as State and local policymakers and educators, with the flexibility to adapt to student needs.[14]

President Trump also highlighted in the proclamation that his budget request included an increase in funding for the Federal Charter Schools Program from $440 million to $500 million. Further, the 2019 proclamation affirmed that "out-of-zone public schools, public charter schools, magnet schools, sectarian and secular private schools, home schools, and online education programs have expanded opportunities for students regardless of background or economic status." The proclamation claimed the number of students receiving the DC Opportunity Scholarship increased by nearly 50 percent and the Tax Cuts and Jobs Acts improved 529 tax shelter plans to cover elementary and secondary school tuition.

In his 2019 State of the Union message, President Trump proclaimed, "The time has come to pass school choice for America's children." For Fiscal Year 2020, the administration wanted to double the federal allocation to the Opportunity Scholarship program. Further, Secretary DeVos, with support from Republican Senator Ted Cruz and other pro–school choice legislators, strongly endorsed the Education Freedom Scholarships and Opportunity Act. The bill proposed a $5 billion annual federal tax credit for donors who contributed to state-designated scholarship funds to subsidize students who wanted to attend private schools. Senator Cruz claimed that the competition among K–12 schools that the bill would stimulate "will enhance the quality of education to kids all across the country." Seventeen states currently had some form of tax credit scholarship program, and the Cruz bill sought to expand that number.[15]

States also employed other tools to facilitate enrollment in private schools. As of 2019, twenty-nine states were implementing sixty-two voucher programs. These included twenty-six traditional voucher programs that used public funds for private school enrollment and five educational savings account programs.[16] In the face of the Trump administration's efforts to expand school choice, the National Association of Secondary School Principals and other professional associations expressed concern that the Trump plan would siphon off resources from public schools.[17]

The Trump administration moved to ease the administrative burdens of states to support school choice and services for private school students. On March 13, 2017, Education Secretary Betsy DeVos wrote a letter to the Chief State School officers, stating:

> I indicated that the U.S. Department of Education planned to develop a revised consolidated State plan template that would require only descriptions, information, assurances and other materials that were "absolutely necessary" for consideration of such a plan. . . . Today, I am pleased to provide you with the revised template for the consolidated State plan that promotes innovation, flexibility, transparency and accountability, and reduces burden to help ensure every child has a chance to learn and succeed.[18]

The revised guidance streamlined state plan templates to provide flexibility for state and local education leaders. Further, DeVos stated, "Parents may use this information [in the States plans] to help choose the right educational environment for their child and to help their schools and their educational programs grow and improve."[19]

At times, the Department of Education evinced impatience with the states for not taking more advantage of the new flexibility it was providing to advance school choice. In an address to the Council of Chief State School Officers in March 2018, DeVos noted: "This law [Every Student Succeeds Act] gives you that chance [the flexibility and opportunity to address state's unique challenges]. The trouble, I don't see much evidence that you've seized it. . . . Just because a plan complies with the law doesn't mean it does what's best for students. Whatever the reasons, I see too many plans that only meet the bare minimum required by the law."[20]

The Trump administration emphasis on funding services for students in private schools, including religiously affiliated ones, persisted. In April 2019, the Department of Education released a draft guidance document, which replaced guidance provided in the second Bush and the Obama administrations, concerning the use of federal monies to support these services. The new guidance stressed the need for local school districts,[21] in consultation with appropriate private school officials, to provide children attending private K–12 schools with services and other benefits comparable to those that public school students received. Faith-based educational organizations welcomed this new guidance. The director of public policy for the National Catholic Education Association commented, "The Association may not be excluded as providers simply because Catholic is in our title." The Vice President for Federal Affairs for Agudath Israel of America highlighted the importance of the new guidance: "The Secretary's decision is groundbreaking in that it brings the Department in line with the Supreme Court's rejection of anti-religious discrimination."[22]

In March 2019, the Trump administration further reinforced its commitment to assisting religious schools. In a letter to House Speaker Nancy Pelosi, DeVos declared that the Education Department found portions of ESSA to be unconstitutional, referencing the Supreme Court decision in *Trinity Lutheran Church of Columbia, Inc. v. Comer, 137 S. Ct. 2012 (2017)*. The letter asserted that the Education Department aimed to "refrain from enforcing, applying, or administering these provisions."[23] In a 7 to 2 decision, the Supreme Court had ruled that the Missouri Department of Natural Resources violated the Trinity Lutheran

Church's First Amendment rights when the agency denied the church's grant application for planting recycled trees in the playground for its preschool program. DeVos's letter to Pelosi affirmed that because of the ruling, the Department of Education "decline[s] to enforce the specific requirement" that service providers "be independent . . . of any religious organization." The department's decision signaled how the Trump administration had expansively interpreted the court decision in favor of its policy position to increase federal support for religious schools.

The Trump administration also supported litigation designed to expand access to private schools. To be sure, it had not by the end of 2019 formally intervened in a case that the Supreme Court was scheduled to hear on a Montana tax credit program that allowed students to enroll in private schools, including religious ones. A lower federal court had struck down the program on grounds that it violated constitutional doctrines on the separation of church and state.[24] The Justice Department did, however, support three families seeking to require the state of Maine to pay tuition for their children to attend religious high schools.[25] The Justice Department's Statement of Interest in this case referenced the Supreme Court ruling on the Trinity Lutheran Church case over forty times. The statement concluded that the state's "exclusion of students who attend religious private schools from the generally available tuition program violates the Free Exercise Clause."[26] In June 2019, the federal district court ruled in favor of the school district, indicating that no state funds can be used to pay tuition in religious high schools. The plaintiffs immediately appealed the ruling to the First Circuit in Boston.[27]

Finally, Education Secretary DeVos joined Republican lawmakers in championing legislation that would allow states to provide individual and corporate donors dollar-for-dollar tax credits for contributing to scholarship programs that help families pay private school tuition and other educational expenses.[28] DeVos released an op-ed in *USA Today* coauthored by Senator Ted Cruz and Representative Bradley Byrne in support of this legislation.[29]

The Trump administration's efforts to expand school choice received considerable support in states that were predominantly under Republican control. Between February 2017 and July 2019, six states with Republican governors introduced bills aimed at providing families tax credit toward paying for private school tuition, while two states with Democratic governors did the same. For example, Republican Governor Nathan Deal of Georgia signed HB 217 in 2018 that increased the number of tax credits available to subsidize enrollment at private schools.

Republican-controlled legislatures were twice as active as their Democratic counterparts in introducing bills related to creating or expanding an education scholarship program that would benefit private schools.

K–12: Streamline Regulations and Roll Back Oversight

In addition to shaping K–12 education policy by fervently supporting school choice, the Trump administrative presidency emphasized a greatly reduced federal role in monitoring and regulating the practices of states and their school districts. Historically, equity has been a key justification for federal involvement in K–12 education. Since the civil rights movement and the Great Society, federal education programs have sought to promote equal educational opportunities for all students. Title I of the Elementary and Secondary Education Act of 1965 was part of President Johnson's War on Poverty. Since the presidency of Ronald Reagan, the federal government has broadened its focus to include performance-based accountability. Reagan entered the White House with the intention of abolishing the Department of Education, introducing school prayer, and promoting tuition tax credits. None of these became reality. Instead, Reagan became an advocate of the recommendations of his commission that issued the widely cited report, *A Nation at Risk*. At a time when the federal role in education was largely measured in terms of funding support, Reagan elevated the importance of school performance. Consequently, the federal government had embraced both equity- and performance-based accountability since the 1980s.

The Trump administration strove to redefine the federal-state relationship with respect to both equity and accountability. In doing so, it enjoyed certain political advantages. Above all, the 2015 ESSA legislation has rebalanced intergovernmental relations by granting states much more control over school accountability and improvement strategies when compared to the No Child Left Behind Act. The Trump administration now pushed even further to expand state flexibility in implementing ESSA.

Weakening Federal Oversight of ESSA

During the first several months of Trump's presidency, the White House, with support from the Republican leadership in Congress, scaled back many of the Obama rules on oversight and accountability in ESSA. For example, to provide Secretary DeVos with the opportunity to leave her mark on ESSA, Congress employed the Congressional Review Act to repeal the Accountability State Plan regulations the Obama administration had published late in his presidency.[30] The congressional repeal was comprehensive in scope, targeting such requirements as the mandates that schools must include at least 95 percent of the students in the annual assessment and must forge accountability protocols for teacher preparation programs. Hence, Secretary DeVos was able to build on the ESSA platform to further reduce federal influence over state implementation of the law.

Ultimately, one of the most significant initiatives to empower states and school districts involved revision to the federal rule on "supplement not supplant." Since 1969, the federal government has relied on this dictum as a regulatory framework to ensure state and local compliance in using Title I of the Elementary and Secondary Education Act for targeted high needs schools and students. Supplement not supplant served well the redistributive intent of Title I across different administrations.[31] In the absence of supplement not supplant, some state and local agencies might replace federal goals with their own priorities. Under these circumstances, services intended for the targeted populations would receive reduced funding.

Not surprising, the Trump administration viewed the supplement not supplant requirement as "restrictive and burdensome—to the point that some school districts made ineffective spending choices to avoid noncompliance."[32] In June 2019, the Department of Education issued its final guidance that gave school districts "significant flexibility" in meeting the federal requirement. Districts were allowed to allocate local and state funds without regard to the Title I status of the schools. This guidance did not anticipate additional local funding to compensate schools that lost money in the process.[33] In these and other ways, the Trump administration's revision of supplement not supplant signaled a retreat from federal oversight as to how well local school districts targeted Title I funds to those most in need.

Reversal on Civil Rights

The Trump administration pursued extensive reversal of Obama's executive actions in civil rights. Withdrawal from pertinent information collection was one element of this retreat. Secretary DeVos conducted an assessment on whether the Department of Education's Office for Civil Rights should continue an effort that began in 1968 to collect biennial data on schooling opportunities and quality in public schools throughout the country. Since 1968, the Civil Rights Data Collection (CRDC) has been widely used by policy researchers and by states and districts for service improvement for all students.[34]

In her letter to the Council of Chief State School Officers on March 13, 2017, Secretary DeVos indicated that the federal government would require "only descriptions, information, assurances and other materials that were absolutely necessary." Consequently, the Office for Civil Rights (OCR) stopped requiring schools and districts to submit data on several elements as of the 2017–2018 school year. The dropped elements included student participation in high school equivalency examinations by subgroups as defined by race, gender, disability, English Learner status, and absence from school fifteen or more days. It eliminated similar subgroup breakouts for student participation in AP examinations and computer science courses. The OCR also made some data submissions optional, such as the number of computer science classes taught by teachers with certification in that subject and whether the school had Wi-Fi access in every classroom.

Reduced civil rights enforcement also characterized the Trump administrative presidency. An internal memo issued by Candace Jackson, the acting head of the OCR before being promoted to deputy general counsel in the department, indicated that the department would scale back investigations into civil rights violations in the nation's public schools and universities. This represented a substantial change from the Obama administration policy, which called for investigators to broaden their inquiries to identify systemic issues.[35] Two months after this decision, *Politico* found that the Education Department had already closed over 1,500 civil rights complaints at the nation's schools.[36] The OCR closed a total of 17,797 cases in 2017 and another 14,074 cases in 2018.[37] In contrast, the Obama administration closed 8,637 cases during its last year in office. These differences between the Trump and the Obama years were closely related to the policy shift from focusing on systemic conditions to individual complaints. The OCR also revised the guidebook on investigation by removing the procedures to be used in establishing systemic bias. The Assistant Secretary for Civil Rights summarized the Trump approach as having the civil rights office become "a neutral, impartial law enforcement agency."[38] The pace of case closures and dismissals was much faster than that of previous administrations, particularly Obama's, which had required signoffs from D.C. headquarters for all case closures.

The reversal on civil rights enforcement also found expression on issues pertaining to racial/ethnic discrimination in school disciplinary actions. The Obama administration had issued guidelines putting schools on notice that they could be violating federal law if racial disparities in student discipline and punishment existed in their schools.[39] The Department of Justice and the Department of Education jointly issued a letter notifying schools of their withdrawal of the policy guidance that the Obama administration had issued on nondiscriminatory school discipline in 2014.[40] The Trump administration justified its action on grounds that "states and local school districts play the primary role in establishing educational policy." The decision triggered sharp opposition from Democratic lawmakers and civil rights organizations. The House education committee chair, Robert Scott (D-Virginia), asserted that "rescinding the guidance will stall, if not reverse our progress toward addressing these disparities."[41]

Not all Trump administrative actions signaled steady reversal from a concern with civil and student rights. The case of sexual misconduct stands out in this regard. The Department of Education withdrew from the Obama-era policy regarding sexual misconduct in schools, calling, instead, for ensuring the rights of both the complainant and the accused to be heard in misconduct cases. Seeking to avoid the public perception that the administration was withdrawing from sexual misconduct investigations with the launching of the new policy, the department flexed its oversight muscle in selected cases. For example, in September 2019, based on investigations conducted during the Obama administration in 2015 and 2016, the Assistant Secretary of Education for Civil Rights announced an agreement with the Chicago Public Schools requiring the district to implement specific steps to comply with Title IX in addressing sexual harassment and abuse.[42] The executive director of the Chicago schools pointed out that the district had already implemented significant changes on sexual misconduct, including the creation of a new Office of Title IX. The September 2019 agreement with the OCR required Chicago schools to broaden the authority of the Title IV Coordinator, provide Title IX training to school personnel, and strengthen the monitoring system on sexual misconduct.[43] Student advocacy organizations expressed hope that the Department of Education would not stop with one case but pursue sexual misconduct cases across the country.

Reversal: The Case of Transgender Students

Letters from the Justice and Education Departments notified the Supreme Court and the nation's public schools that the Trump administration was changing its position on transgender bathroom protections. The Obama administration had interpreted Title IX, which prohibits sex discrimination in education, to include the right for transgender students to use bathrooms and locker rooms of their chosen identity. The Trump administration terminated that policy and challenged the Obama administration's stance that transgender rights were an extension of Title IX, saying the former administration's guidance did not "explain how the position is consistent with the express language of Title IX."[44] In a Dear Colleague letter dated February 22, 2017,[45] Secretary DeVos cited recent litigation and declared that "there must be due regard for the primary role of the States and local school districts in establishing educational policy." The Education Department confirmed it was no longer investigating complaints from transgender students barred from school bathrooms that matched their gender identity.

These and other administration actions with respect to transgender students sparked resistance in several venues. In April 2019, for instance, the House Education Committee Civil Rights Subcommittee Chair Suzanne Bonamici (D-Oregon) skeptically questioned Secretary DeVos regarding her transgender student guidance. So, too, protests involving several hundred people occurred outside the White House.[46] In addition, the courts increasingly became involved in issues of transgender rights for students. Of particular importance, the Supreme Court prepared to hear the case of Gavin Grimm, a transgender high school student from Virginia whose school had denied him access to male bathrooms. Two lower courts had already sided with Grimm. After the Trump administration's reversal of Obama-era guidelines, Grimm's case was sent back to the district court. Public attention turned to the case as a possible crucial reinterpretation of Title IX law.[47] In August 2019, the federal district court ruled in favor of Grimm.[48] The court rejected the school board's argument that allowing transgender students to use the bathroom based on their gender identities violated the privacy of other students. The decision also required the local school district to change the gender status in Grimm's school record. As of early fall 2019, the local school district had not appealed the court decision.

State legislative reactions to the Trump administration's transgender stance largely, though not completely, reflected partisan polarization. In

October 2018, the Iowa Department of Education released a statement reiterating the protections for transgender students under Iowa law.[49] The same month, the New Jersey Department of Education issued new guidance on the rights of transgender students.[50] In May 2019, the Colorado legislature passed a bill simplifying the process for transgender individuals to seek a change in gender designation on their birth certificate; it required the state registrar to issue new birth certificates to such individuals rather than amend preexisting ones.[51] The bill stipulated that a third gender category, "X," that is neither male nor female, be included on newly issued birth certificates. Rhode Island Governor Gina Raimondo also endorsed a third gender category on the state driver's license. In July 2019, a federal judge in North Carolina approved a settlement to resolve litigation on transgender students' right to access the bathroom of their identity. The settlement was proposed by civil rights groups and Democratic Governor Roy Cooper.

At the same time in 2018, state legislatures in such Republican-controlled states as Kentucky, Missouri, Oklahoma, South Dakota, and Tennessee considered bills to ban transgender students from accessing restrooms according to their gender identity.[52] The Missouri legislature considered a bill to require "all public restrooms, other than single occupancy restrooms, to be gender-divided."[53] Some of these legislative proposals were approved at the committee level but did not advance to become legislation.

Meanwhile, challenges to school district practices with respect to transgender students continued in the courts. The Supreme Court had not ruled on transgender bathroom protections since the Trump administration's withdrawal of Obama-era guidelines.[54] But federal district and appellate courts did hand down rulings and attracted the attention of state attorneys general.

One such case involved Drew Adams, a senior at Nease High School in Ponte Vedra Beach, Florida, who came out as transgender in his freshman year and underwent surgery.[55] When the district told him he would have to use the gender-neutral or the girls' bathroom, Adams and his mother sought a court injunction, contending that the district's policy violated Title IX regulations and constitutionally protected rights under the Fourteenth Amendment. In July 2018, a federal district judge ruled that Adams could use the boys' bathroom, but the school board appealed the ruling to the Eleventh Circuit Court of Appeals in Atlanta. A coalition of twenty-one Democratic attorneys general, led by Leticia James of New York, filed an amicus brief in the appeals court arguing that the district policy did not offer any benefits and that its "sole function is to stigmatize a particular group."[56] In a statement, James said, "Educational institutions have a responsibility to protect and educate their students—neither of which involve denying students access to the bathroom that aligns with their gender identity. My office will ensure that all students are treated with dignity and respect."[57]

In logic opposite to the Adams case, parents affiliated with the anti-LGBTQ organization *Parents for Privacy* filed suit against the Dallas School District in Oregon in 2017 for accommodating the bathroom preferences of transgender students. They argued that such accommodations violated the "bodily privacy" of nontransgender students. The ACLU, in turn, argued that federal law prohibiting gender discrimination in education (Title IX) supported the position taken by the Dallas School District. The federal district court sided with the school district, but plaintiffs appealed the decision to the Ninth Circuit Court of Appeals.[58]

Meanwhile, the Trump administration continued undercutting the rights of transgender students by turning its attention to athletics. The Department of Education launched an investigation concerning the rights of transgender athletes to compete with peers in their self-defined gender group. At the time, seventeen states allowed transgender athletes to compete in high school sports based on their declared gender identity. Seven states placed restrictions that made it difficult for transgender athletes to compete in high school sports. A conservative nonprofit organization, the Alliance Defending Freedom, filed a lawsuit on behalf of student athletes and their parents in Connecticut, claiming the full participation of transgender athletes had resulted in unfair sports competition.[59] The Office for Civil Rights in the Department of Education formally launched an investigation into Connecticut's policy on transgender athletes in August 2019.

Reversal: Students with Disabilities

In 1990, Congress reauthorized legislation in place since 1975 that sought to ensure that public schools provide students with disabilities the same opportunity for a sound education as other students. In implementing the 1990 legislation, which Congress had renamed the Individuals with Disabilities Education Act (IDEA), presidential administrations had issued guidance documents to shape state and local practices. The Trump administration set about shrinking this guidance.

In October 2017, the Education Department scrapped seventy-two guidance documents that fleshed out students' rights under IDEA.[60] The documents were meant to help schools and parents understand how the law applied in different situations. The guidance included information on local use of federal funds to support students with disabilities. This move came as part of the top-to-bottom regulatory review undertaken by the Education Department to carry out President Trump's February 2017 executive order to "alleviate unnecessary regulatory burdens."[61] In a hearing prior to the decision to scrap the documents, many disability rights groups and other education advocates pressed officials to keep the guidance in place. After the special education guidance documents were eliminated, Representative Robert Scott (D-VA) called the move "the latest in a series of disturbing actions taken by the Trump Administration to undermine civil rights for vulnerable Americans."[62]

The Trump administration's policies regarding people with disabilities, within and beyond the education system, contributed to a swelling of disability rights activism. Activists staged a "die-in" at Republican Senate Leader Mitch McConnell's office in June 2017, the disability rights organization ADAPT opened over ten new chapters in 2017, and preexisting ADAPT chapters saw increases in membership and donations.[63]

Meanwhile, the federal courts intervened on behalf of students with disabilities. In 2017, the Supreme Court handed down a decision in *Endrew F. v. Douglas County School District*, which plaintiffs had initiated before Trump took office.[64] In a unanimous decision, the court held that under the Individuals with Disabilities Education Act, "a school district must offer the special needs student an Individualized Education Plan (IEP) that is reasonably calculated to enable a child to make progress appropriate in light of the child's circumstances."[65] This raised the bar for school districts in their services for students with disabilities at about the same time the Trump administration moved to reduce federal guidance on this issue.

In March 2017, the Trump administration also encountered court resistance when it opted to delay a rule that would have required states to determine whether racial disparities existed in school districts' identification, discipline, and treatment of students with disabilities.[66] The department's action was challenged by the Council of Parent Attorneys and Advocates. In *COPAA v. DeVos*, a federal district court ruled that the Department of Education had engaged in an "illegal delay" of the 2016 Equity in IDEA regulations. In May 2019, the Department of Justice filed a Notice of Appeal in *COPAA v. DeVos*. The press release announced: "The filing of this Notice of Appeal does not stay the district court order or alter the fact that the December 19, 2016 Equity in IDEA regulation on significant disproportionality is currently in effect."[67] In September 2019, the Trump administration withdrew the appeal.

Some states responded to the weakening of federal support for students with disabilities by bolstering their own protections for this group. California, for instance, sought to strengthen anti-discrimination provisions for students with disabilities enrolled in charter schools. Though charter schools by law must admit any student who applied (or decide admissions based on lottery when they are overenrolled), reports of disparities in enrollment were prevalent, particularly for students with disabilities receiving poor grades. Following the U.S. Education Department's 2017 decisions to revoke IDEA guidance documents and to discontinue its investigations of systemic civil rights issues in public schools, California Democratic Governor Gavin Newsom proposed to crack down on discrimination in charter school enrollment through tightened regulation.[68] The move came at the recommendation of the *Uncharted Waters* study conducted by the California School Boards Association in 2018.[69] Recognizing a gap in the "piecemeal federal protections" against discrimination in public schools, New Hampshire lawmakers also took initial action. The Governor's Advisory Council on Diversity and Inclusion in the state had repeatedly heard complaints about persistent discrimination in schools without adequate resolution or redress processes. Legislators introduced a bill to prohibit discrimination against students with disabilities as well as age, sex, gender identity, sexual orientation, race, color, marital status, familial status, religion, or national origin.[70] In July 2019, the New Hampshire Senate and House passed Senate Bill 263 on anti-discrimination protection for students in public schools. Other states had previously approved measures to protect the rights of students with disabilities.

Higher Education: For-Profits, Student Loans, and Civil Rights

Unlike K–12, the story of the Trump administrative presidency in higher education is much less about devolving greater authority to lower levels of government. To be sure, the Department of Education sought to reverse Obama initiatives aimed at promoting racial diversity and gender equity related to sexual misconduct on the nation's campuses. But the posture of the Trump administration in these two spheres was not about deregulating colleges and universities. Instead, the administration had a different agenda: to make it more difficult for institutions of higher education to factor race into admissions decisions and to caution them about going too far in shifting the burden of proof away from the alleged victims of sexual misconduct to those accused of engaging in it.

Beyond these two issues, the Trump administration also faced the massive problem of defaults on federal student loans and how to deal with two major stakeholders: the for-profit postsecondary institutions that disproportionately fueled this problem and the thousands of student borrowers burdened with substantial debt and unfulfilled occupational aspirations. Between the two, the Trump administration assigned top priority to accommodating the for-profit institutions, a muscular interest group fully engaged in what economists call rent seeking.[71] The for-profits depended heavily on the federal student loan program to survive and, in part through generous campaign contributions, had cemented a firm alliance with Republican policymakers. Following a path forged by President George W. Bush, the Trump administration strove to accommodate this interest group through executive actions.

Gainful Employment: A Trump Victory

As noted in chapter 2, the Obama administration had in 2014 issued a Gainful Employment (GE) rule in an effort to curb the excesses of for-profit postsecondary institutions. This rule established measures for determining whether certain postsecondary institutions prepared students for employment that was sufficiently remunerative to enable them to pay off their federal loans. At its core, the rule relied on a ratio of student debt to earnings. Failure to sustain an acceptable ratio could cause the educational institution to lose eligibility for the federal student loan program. The Obama rule was supported by recent studies that found that students who enrolled in for-profit online programs were mostly disappointed with their employment prospects and frustrated by their debt loads.[72] African Americans were overrepresented in these programs. A study found that the GE rule tended to slow the enrollment of low-income students in for-profit institutions, in part due to federal oversight on employment and debt issues.[73]

Like the administration of George W. Bush, the Trump White House sought to placate the for-profit lobby, which strongly opposed the GE rule. On March 6, 2017, the Acting Assistant Secretary for Postsecondary Education announced that the department would delay implementation of the rule "to further review the GE regulations and their implementation."[74] On June 14, 2017, the department further stated that it "intends to develop fair, effective and improved regulations to protect individual borrowers from fraud, ensure accountability across institutions of higher education and protect taxpayers." In doing so, it insisted that the GE requirement was "overly burdensome and confusing for institutions of higher education."

The delay in implementing the GE rule was only the first step in the Trump administration's effort to dismantle it. Convinced that the rule was unfair to for-profit institutions, the Department of Education initiated a process of negotiated rulemaking. This process allows the federal agency to meet with interest groups in an effort to devise a rule satisfactory to all parties. The stated purpose of the process was to "evaluate the accuracy and usefulness" of the GE rule methodology and come up with a new regulation that could be applied to all programs. The negotiated rulemaking process failed, in this case, to yield a consensus on this issue.

In the wake of this failure, the Department of Education launched a formal rulemaking process that resulted in the GE regulation being rescinded in July 2019. In justifying its action, the department criticized the debt-to-earnings measure as "an inaccurate and unreliable proxy for program quality." It stressed that the indicator primarily reflected "demographics," the fact that the for-profits "serve larger percentages of African-American students or single mothers." The department stressed that the Obama rule "unfairly target[ed] career and technical education programs" rather than colleges and universities. Education officials also claimed they lacked the capacity to compute the debt-to-earnings ratios for institutions because the Social Security Administration had declined to sign a memorandum of understanding agreeing to furnish the needed earnings data. (The rule did not clarify the reason for this refusal by Social Security officials.) Having eliminated the GE requirement, the Department of Education proposed as an alternative to augment consumer information in choosing an educational institution. It promised to develop and implement an enhanced "College Scorecard" designed to help students avoid making "poor educational investments." The transparent scorecard would include such items as the median federal debt of students in the program and their expected monthly payments.[75]

Many Democrats in Congress condemned the rollback of the GE rule, with House Speaker Nancy Pelosi calling it a "shameful giveaway to special interests."[76] Meanwhile, Maryland, Maine, Oregon, Washington, New York, and California introduced legislation to strengthen regulation of for-profit colleges in response to the Trump administration's actions.[77]

Federal Retreat in Protecting Student Borrowers

The Consumer Financial Protection Bureau (CFPB) during the Obama years led the process in gathering complaints from thousands of student loan borrowers regarding poor business practices of financial service companies, including payment errors and mismanagement.[78] Obama-era guidance to strengthen consumer protections for student loan borrowers was withdrawn by Secretary of Education DeVos in a letter dated April 11, 2017, to the Chief Operating Officer of Financial Student Aid.[79] DeVos's letter stated the process had been subjected to a "myriad of moving deadlines, changing requirements and a lack of consistent objectives."

The Trump administration took additional steps to weaken consumer protection for student borrowers. Secretary DeVos terminated a data-sharing agreement between the CFPB and the Department of Education, thereby ending the monitoring capacity to track student complaints of poor business practices. Further, the Office of Management and Budget dismantled a CFPB division that focused on student loan problems in 2018. Secretary DeVos also declared that states did not have the authority to intervene in problems related to federal loans. The administration's retreat immediately faced legal challenges. While a federal district court rejected a challenge to the Trump actions regarding student loans, the U.S. Court of Appeals for the Seventh Circuit ruled in favor of students in Illinois to sue the federal loan servicer, Great Lakes Education Loan Services. The Court of Appeals found that poor loan services were subject to state financial protection laws.[80]

Indeed, a growing number of states focused on oversight of loan services. In Connecticut, California, Massachusetts, and Washington, D.C., licensing agencies began building their own enforcement procedures through existing laws. Colorado, Illinois, Maine, Missouri, New Jersey, New York, and Washington were considering similar practices in the absence of federal protections.[81] Efforts to ensure oversight of student loan services also gained support from Republican leaders in several states. For example, Republican Governor Larry Hogan of Maryland signed into law new oversight over loan service companies.[82]

Weakening the Borrower Defense Rule

Protecting student borrowers remained an ongoing policy challenge.[83] Under the Borrower Defense to Repayment (BDR) rule promulgated by the Obama administration in 2016, student borrowers could request loan cancellation if the education programs they attended engaged in misinformation or fraudulent practices. The closing of Corinthian, ITT Tech, DeVry, and other for-profit colleges adversely affected an estimated 150,000 loan borrowers. It devalued their degrees and made it difficult for them to present documentation of their educational attainments to employers and others. Meanwhile, many of these students owed the federal loan program large sums of money. While the federal government offered them an array of repayment options, the law did not permit them to declare bankruptcy. The Obama administration saw loan cancellation when for-profits failed as a step toward providing some relief.

The for-profit educational sector challenged the legality of the Obama administration's 2016 rule in the federal courts. The Trump administration, which also opposed the Obama rule, used this legal challenge and related factors as a rationale to cease processing the borrowers' cancellation claims. In response, student advocacy groups sued Secretary DeVos for inaction on the BDR. The Department of Education released a statement on June 14, 2017, stating that "due to pending litigation challenging the BDR regulations, the Department is postponing the effective date pursuant to section 705 to the Administrative Procedure Act."[84] Subsequently, the Trump administration sought to delay implementation of the Obama rule until July 1, 2019. Meanwhile, Democratic attorneys general in eighteen states and the District of Columbia sued the Secretary of Education in July 2017 for her suspension of regulations that protected student borrowers from the failures of for-profit colleges.

In response to the lawsuit, Secretary DeVos restarted the rulemaking process introducing several proposed changes, including a formula for partial loan forgiveness based on student income. In their coordinated efforts to demonstrate the extensive financial burdens incurred by former student loan borrowers when the providers committed fraud, some state attorneys general engaged a company to contact pertinent borrowers and assist them in filing claims for loan forgiveness. In October 2018, a federal judge found Secretary DeVos's delays to be an "arbitrary and capricious" violation of the Administrative Procedure Act and ordered immediate implementation of the Obama rule favoring student borrowers.[85] During 2019, three House committees worked together to hold three hearings and issued eleven letters to the Department of Education expressing concerns about the delays in implementing a student loan policy.[86]

Meanwhile, the Department of Education issued new regulations in September 2019 that allowed borrowers to file cancellation claims if they met certain federal standards.[87] However, the new rules created several barriers for student borrowers on loan cancellation. Unlike the Obama-era rules, for instance, student borrowers were generally required to file their claims within three years of graduation. The new rules also weakened the steps that the department could take immediately in fraud cases. They established a formula that limited nearly all applicants to partial, rather than full, relief of their loans.[88] Instead of strengthening oversight of for-profit colleges, the Trump administration placed the burden on student borrowers to rectify matters.

While subject to intense criticism by Democrats, Secretary DeVos vigorously defended her actions at a congressional hearing in December 2019. She asserted that the rule and subsequent decisions to grant only partial or no loan relief to thousands of students who claimed the for-profits had misled them marked a "course correction" from the Obama administration, which had "weaponized" debt relief to undermine for-profit colleges. She affirmed: "I understand that some of you here just want to have blanket forgiveness for anyone who raises their hand and files a claim, but that simply is not right." In turn, Democratic members of the committee used constituent examples to challenge DeVos. For instance, one representative cited a single mother with a sick son who had to take out loans to pay for his medical expenses because she was still saddled with debt from attending a now defunct for-profit institution. While blaming the Obama administration for "encouraging claims to be filed," DeVos acknowledged that her department had a backlog of 600,000 claims to be processed.[89] In a show of bipartisan agreement in March 2020, the Senate voted 53 to 42 to reverse DeVos's attempt to roll back the Obama-era rule. The House had passed a companion rollback in January. As of mid-March, it remained unclear whether President Trump would veto the legislation in an effort to ensure that the DeVos rule would go into effect.[90]

Efforts to Limit Racial Considerations

To encourage racial diversity on campuses, the Obama administration had issued guidance urging colleges and universities to "analyze a number of hypotheticals, and draw conclusions about whether the actions in those hypotheticals would violate the Equal Protection Clause of the Fourteenth Amendment to the Constitution or Title IV or Title VI of the Civil Rights Act of 1964." The Trump administration, which opposed considerations of race in higher education admissions processes, used a Dear Colleague letter in early July 2018 to withdraw this guidance.[91] The Department of Education letter stated that the Obama-era guidance documents advocate "policy preferences and positions beyond the requirements," and "prematurely decide, or appear to decide, whether particular actions violate the Constitution or federal law."

Institutions of higher education responded cautiously to Trump's policy retreat. On July 3, 2018, Harvard responded to the new Department of Education guidance by stating that they "will continue to vigorously defend its rights, and that of all colleges and universities, to consider race as one factor among many in college admissions."[92] The University of Southern California also announced that its admissions process would continue to factor in race.[93] On July 8, 2018, without explicitly stating whether they used race in the admissions process, Northwestern released a statement stating it would not make changes to admissions in response to the Trump guidance.[94]

The Trump administration persisted in its efforts to discourage universities from pursuing diversity practices that took into consideration racial disparity. In August 2018, the Department of Justice filed a Statement of Interest on the side of the plaintiffs who were challenging Harvard's use of race and ethnicity in admissions in a federal district court.[95] The plaintiff, an organization of students and parents, claimed that Harvard's admissions decisions discriminated against Asian American applicants. The Justice Department's Statement of Interest followed its 2017 investigation of Harvard's admissions practices in response to complaints from Asian American organizations. The investigation had reached the conclusion that Harvard had failed to provide sufficient evidence to show that its admissions decisions did not discriminate against Asian Americans. The Justice Department also claimed that Harvard had not seriously looked for alternative ways, beyond using race in its admissions decisions, to diversify its student body. The federal judge heard oral arguments in the lawsuit in February 2019.[96] On October

1, 2019, District Court Judge Allison Burroughs ruled that Harvard's admission policy did not discriminate against Asian Americans. In response, the plaintiffs announced they would file an appeal. On February 25, 2020, the Trump administration took a formal position in support of the plaintiffs. The Department of Justice's Civil Rights Division filed an amicus brief that Harvard's admission policy violated federal civil rights laws. The amicus brief called upon the appellate court to revise the district court ruling.[97]

Reversal in Oversight of Campus Sexual Misconduct

The Obama administration had sought to enhance the rights and more general leverage of students who alleged they were victims of sexual misconduct. In his detailed analysis of the evolving OCR policy on Title IX enforcement, R. Shep Melnick connected Obama administration's adoption of the "new paradigm" to the effective campaign organized by women survivors of sexual violence, the Center for Public Integrity, the National Public Radio's series on inadequate enforcement of Title IX on campus, and congressional advocates.

Melnick described the rationale behind the policy shift: "sexual assault and other forms of harassment were seen not as the work of a few misguided souls, but as the product of a deeply embedded culture that threatens the safety of women."[98] Melnick identified several core features of the OCR's policy that came into full scale during 2011–2014.[99] Among other things, the OCR broadened the definitions of "sexual harassment" and "hostile environment." It urged colleges and universities to discourage cross-examinations of alleged victims and to establish a process to appeal not-guilty findings.

Obama's OCR policy included detailed guidance on adjudicatory procedures for higher education institutions, a policy feature that raised concerns about the OCR's lack of trust in campus administrations. It also inveighed against relying on investigations of criminal conduct by law enforcement authorities. The Obama guidelines endorsed a less demanding standard of proof for validating misconduct accusations.[100] Rather than needing "clear and convincing evidence" to document sexual misconduct, the complainant needed a "preponderance of the evidence."[101]

In a Dear Colleague letter dated September 22, 2017, the Department of Education withdrew this guidance.[102] The letter cited law school faculty at the University of Pennsylvania and Harvard indicating the Obama guidance promoted procedures that "do not afford fundamental fairness" and are "overwhelmingly stacked against the accused."[103] The letter went on to state that "schools face a confusing and counterproductive set of regulatory mandates,"[104] and charged that the guidance was given without notice or opportunity for public comment. The letter referred to documents issued during the George W. Bush administration as offering better guidance on sexual misconduct than those promulgated under Obama.

Legal and legislative reactions were immediate. SurvJustice, Equal Rights Advocates, and the Victim Rights Law Center filed a suit against Secretary of Education Betsy DeVos and Acting Assistant Secretary Candice Jackson accusing them of being motivated "by their discriminatory—and baseless—gender stereotype that many women and girls lack credibility with regard to sexual harassment."[105] On July 25, 2019, SurvJustice filed the motion for summary judgment. At the same time, the chair of the Senate Committee on Health, Education, Labor, and Pension, Senator Lamar Alexander (R-Tennessee), wanted a higher education bill to include Title IX provisions related to gender equity. Senator Patty Murray (D-Washington), the committee's ranking member, insisted that Title IX deal more explicitly with issues of gender equity and sexual misconduct.[106]

Upon assuming office in 2017, Secretary DeVos had promised to end what she called "rule by letter" and to employ formal rulemaking under the Administrative Procedure Act to pursue major policy change.[107] In a sharp departure from the practice of prior presidential administrations, she now applied this approach to sexual misconduct. In November 2018, the Department of Education released a proposed rule targeting the subject. The proposed rule reduced the liability of universities and colleges for investigating cases of sexual misconduct and for protecting the rights of the accused.[108] If finalized, these regulations would allow schools to choose an evidentiary standard in sexual misconduct cases that shifted the burden of proof to the student making the accusation. Opponents argued that this would make it harder for victims to obtain justice. The proposed rule also allowed campuses to reconsider Obama-era policies that had recommended that schools appoint a full-time Title IX coordinator to "ensure sufficient time is available to perform all the role's responsibilities."[109] The proposed rule sparked considerable controversy, with the department receiving over 120,000 public comments on it. Many of these comments, especially those from women's advocacy groups, survivors of sexual assault, and campus leaders, were highly critical. As 2019 closed, the final rule was under review by the Office of Management and Budget. In March 2020, Secretary DeVos indicated that the rule would soon be published and would broaden the opportunity for the accused to challenge those who filed sexual misconduct complaints against them.[110]

While backing away from Obama administration approaches to sexual misconduct, the Department of Education did pursue enforcement actions against universities on a case-by-case basis. For instance, in a high-profile case, it imposed a penalty of $4.5 million on Michigan State University for failing to provide adequate oversight and prevent sexual assaults on scores of female gymnasts, including Olympic medalists, by a physician the university had employed for decades.

In response to the sexual misconduct initiatives of the Trump administration, university officials in several states reaffirmed, at least in general terms, their commitment to the rights of student victims. For instance, the president of the University of California system issued a statement saying the system "remains firmly committed to protecting its students and staff from sexual violence and sexual harassment."[111] In an email to the student body, the UC Berkeley chancellor assured students that the university "remains strongly committed to changing norms and culture to prevent violence and harassment from occurring in the first place and strengthening support for survivors."[112] Officials in other states voiced similar sentiments.

Did Trump's Executive Actions Lead to Major Policy Changes?

At the end of President Trump's second year in office, Secretary DeVos released a very general statement on her accomplishments. She affirmed: "The Secretary challenged department leaders to rethink the way the Department of Education operates so that we can better serve students and use taxpayer funds more wisely. . . . The changes we've undertaken already, and will continue to make into next year, will ultimately lead to the Department becoming more efficient, effective, and accountable."[113] The statement obviously left open the degree to which she had advanced the more specific policy goals of the Trump administrative presidency.

After three years of Trump actions, it remained to be seen whether the administration had substantially modified the federal role in K–12 and higher education, though it clearly has scored some victories. In the case of K–12 education, the Trump administration accelerated the devolution of major decisions to the states, a trend already kindled by ESSA. It revoked Obama-era guidance designed to encourage some responsiveness to federal priorities. By weakening provisions encouraging states to supplement and not supplant, it opened the door further to the diversion of grant funds to program initiatives other than those prioritized in federal education law. It also pulled back further from federally driven, performance-based accountability that had begun to take hold under Ronald Reagan and reached its pinnacle in No Child Left Behind under George W. Bush. In addition, the Trump administration backtracked from federal enforcement of provisions designed to bolster the rights of minorities, women, transgender students, and people with disabilities. Of particular note, it reduced efforts to gather information about state and local practices affecting these groups and significantly reduced civil rights enforcement. It also pushed the envelope in championing school choice, particularly in seeking to make federal aid available to religiously affiliated schools.

The achievements of the Trump administration on these fronts were incremental. State attorneys general and private parties frequently pursued litigation that significantly delayed, and at times blocked, Trump's initiatives. Transgender students, for example, won some court victories affirming their rights to use a bathroom of their choice. And, like his predecessors, Trump faced the reality that states and localities are the principal players shaping who gets what, when, and how in the education arena. Some of these governments went out of their way to disavow the Trump agenda and continue Obama-era practices. In other instances, state education departments and local school districts continued to march to the beat of their own drummers with little attention paid one way or the other to Trump initiatives. However, states and localities that resisted the Obama approach became empowered to pursue their agendas with little risk of federal intervention to thwart them. Without much federal oversight or intervention, variation in the practices of state education departments and local school districts may well grow. For instance, some Republican-dominated states have embraced the Trump administration's school choice initiative by creating scholarship and tax credit programs to boost enrollment in private schools. Other states have shown little interest in such measures.

The Trump administrative presidency also had mixed success in reversing President Obama's policies in higher education. Following the precedent set for Republican presidents by George W. Bush, Trump's political appointees strove to placate the for-profit lobby. This lobby had strongly opposed the GE rule, and the Department of Education responded by rescinding it. The Trump administration also chipped away at the rights of student borrowers, trying to reduce their ability to draw on state law to sue federal service contractors. In addition, the Department of Education moved to increase the administrative burden on borrowers seeking cancellation of their student loans.

As with K–12, issues of equity related to race and gender also preoccupied the Trump administration. For its part, the Justice Department pressed the Trump administration's case that colleges and universities should not factor race into their admission decisions to promote student diversity. Meanwhile, the Department of Education reversed the initiatives of the Obama administration to bolster the procedural rights of students who filed sexual misconduct charges.

As with K–12, court litigation applied the brakes to several Trump initiatives in higher education. For instance, a court of appeals upheld student borrower rights to sue federal loan service contractors under state law. Policymakers in a growing number of states demonstrated interest in affording student borrowers' legal avenues to pursue complaints against for-profit educational institutions and the contractors the federal government employed to service their loans. Democratic state attorneys general at times intervened, as was the case when the Trump administration delayed implementation of the Borrower Defense rule. The courts and resistant state officials did not preclude the Trump administration from making progress on its higher education initiatives but, as with K–12, its victories were relatively modest.

SIX

HOSTILE TAKEOVER, FEDERALISM, AND PUBLIC POLICY

Within the American system of shared power among institutions, the executive branch has played an increasingly prominent policy role relative to Congress since the 1930s. The vast administrative discretion wielded by the executive branch has not signaled the rise of a technocratic state dominated by professionals. Instead, it has elevated the power of the president, especially since the 1970s. A multifaceted, aggressive administrative presidency committed to pursuing partisan policy objectives has risen in lockstep with growing political polarization. Republican and Democratic presidents alike have aggressively employed an array of administrative tools to pursue their policy goals. The administrative assertiveness of presidents does not, however, automatically produce policy triumphs for them or enduring policy achievements for the nation. While the politics and dynamics of the implementation process may derail and thwart congressionally approved legislation, administrative presidency initiatives may be even more vulnerable to them. This possibility seems especially likely when the forces of federalism intervene—when state and local governments play pivotal policy implementation roles and form coalitions designed to challenge or undermine presidential initiatives. Full understanding of the nature and efficacy of the administrative presidency, therefore, requires careful attention to the implementation dynamics that follow a president's decision to shape policy through executive action.

Hostile takeovers provide one dramatic context for studying the policy impact of an administrative presidency. These occur when a new president takes office with highly salient policy goals that depart sharply from the ideologies and objectives that drive an agency and actions taken by the prior presidential administration to promote them. In this context, any implementation difficulties are unlikely to spring from White House inattention and bureaucratic inertia. Instead, they more readily reflect actions linked to a new president's policy agenda and opposition to it. This opposition has in varying ways and degrees been manifested in the three policy spheres at the heart of this book.

This chapter attempts to advance understanding of the administrative presidency through a comparative analysis of the implementation politics that played out in the health care, climate change, and education arenas during the first three years of the Trump presidency. We seek to examine similarities and differences among our three cases.

In the next section, we compare the goals of the Trump White House in these three arenas, assessing the magnitude of the policy changes sought and their orientation toward federalism. We then compare the tools and strategies that characterized executive efforts to reverse course, focusing especially on executive orders, rulemaking, waivers, and legal strategy. The core question of the degree to which the Trump administrative presidency accomplished its goals in these arenas then receives attention. We compare the factors that both enabled and impeded Trump's administrative presidency, devoting special attention to the effects of federalism. We assay the implications of these developments for the ability of Americans to access high quality health care at reasonable cost, experience an environment less threatened by climate change, and engage an effective and equitable educational system.

A final section assesses the implications of these three cases for American democracy. Some see the rise of the administrative presidency as a force for transparency and democratic accountability, while others sharply disagree. The particularly aggressive and often unprecedented executive actions of the Trump administration suggest the need to revisit this debate. We assess whether the checks and balances embedded in American governance, especially the courts and federalism, imposed meaningful constraints on executive branch power and promoted the rule of law.

Objectives

While the Trump administration sought to reverse Obama administration policies, its objectives in the three arenas varied in terms of the magnitude of change sought and the degree to which states and localities would be empowered or constrained relative to the central government. *Magnitude* refers to the degree to which a president through executive action seeks to reorient, undermine, or at the extreme, destroy a program. *Empowerment* implies freeing lower government levels to pursue policy options while sustaining federal funding for them. *Constraint* involves eliminating state and local discretion most directly by preemptive regulation while also undermining their capacity, such as by reducing federal funding.

Magnitude

Trump initiatives with respect to health care and climate change regulation were far more sweeping and precedent-setting than his initiatives in education. The administration's sabotage of Affordable Care Act (ACA) insurance exchanges looms especially large as an example of expansive administrative presidency efforts. Since the rise of the administrative state in the 1930s, no president has approached Trump in efforts toward such massive retrenchment and destruction of a major federal health program via executive action. To an unprecedented degree, the president publicly endorsed measures that would help realize his prediction that the exchanges would explode. In the fashion of death by a thousand cuts, his administration launched a well-coordinated series of incremental measures that, in the aggregate, represented a major assault on the exchanges and on health insurance quality. More recently, the Trump administration has sought to abet the radical destruction of the entire ACA, including its Medicaid expansion, by substantially siding with a Texas federal district court decision voiding the law. By refusing to defend the law's core provisions in court, the administration sought to accomplish the promised ACA repeal that Trump wanted but Congress failed to produce.

Trump also occupies unique climate policy territory. Unlike the ACA, where the Trump administration has sought to sabotage a law recently passed by Congress, it has in the case of climate focused on reversing through administrative action multiple executive initiatives of the prior president. Trump's search and destroy approach to eviscerate every major climate policy initiative taken by Obama has no comparison in the half-century since the advent of the modern American environmental movement and the adoption of far-reaching, durable environmental protection laws. Trump initiatives include attempts to withdraw the United States from international presidential-executive agreements such as the 2015 Paris Agreement on climate change, making it the only nation in the world to do so. This effectively ended a credible American role in international climate negotiation, even though linking U.S. and global efforts would be the only plausible way to reduce climate risks.

The Trump assault also included fundamental attacks on various Obama-era domestic policy provisions. These were designed to extend Clean Air Act (CAA) regulations to carbon dioxide and methane emissions across sectors including transportation, electricity, energy production, and solid waste management. These efforts featured alternative strategies, including waiver withdrawal and regulatory freeze (transportation), regulatory replacement with far more modest alternatives and repeal (electricity and energy production), and regulatory suspension (solid waste). Unlike the ACA case, in climate change there was no new Obama-era statute to confront and no serious consideration of congressional action to alter international or domestic policy. Instead, the Trump team primarily targeted Obama-era reinterpretations of various sections of air quality legislation first adopted in 1967 and sustained in all subsequent revisions. The CAA was a highly durable statute that had demonstrated considerable ability to adapt to changing circumstances across multiple presidencies without further congressional tinkering or extensive court interference.[1] Its transformation into the lead federal climate policy tool was facilitated by a historic 2007 Supreme Court decision, which the Trump administration chose not to challenge directly. Instead, it attempted to maximize prospects for short-term success through sectoral administrative assaults on climate policy alongside international disengagement.

No precedent exists for the range and intensity of his administrative presidency search and destroy mission in climate change or, more broadly, environmental and energy policy.[2] Trump derided climate science on the campaign trail and in office, challenging the premise that federal government efforts to reduce carbon emissions offered any benefits while simultaneously contending that they threatened massive economic disruption unless all other nations matched or surpassed these steps. He routinely disparaged renewable energy sources such as wind, deriding "windmills" as a threat to property values as well as a cancer risk while providing no evidence to support these claims. This created a unique foundation for his assault on multiple policies to reduce greenhouse gas emissions, even in cases like methane from solid waste landfills, over which there was little opposition to Obama regulations.

As a result, Trump administrative efforts moved well beyond other presidents, most notably Ronald Reagan, who had challenged the prevailing environmental policy order. Reagan stocked EPA and other federal agencies with political loyalists charged with seeking deregulatory opportunities while cutting funding and staffing for implementation. He also vetoed clean water legislation in 1987, though it was overridden, and blocked any legislative agreement on sulfur dioxide emissions, which delayed CAA reauthorization until 1990 after his vice president, George H. W. Bush, had succeeded him.

But Reagan never sought all-out repeal or reversal of prior environmental policies. He actually softened his administrative approach after the highly publicized resignations of leading appointees such as Anne Gorsuch Burford at the EPA and James Watt at the Department of the Interior. More moderate leaders followed during latter stages of the administration, and Reagan signed a historic international agreement, the Montreal Protocol, designed to phase out ozone layer–eroding chemicals.[3]

George W. Bush failed in efforts to reauthorize the CAA and initiated steps to undercut climate mitigation strategies launched under Bill Clinton, but these were modest in comparison to Trump's actions.[4] Bush also signed into law a pair of broad energy bills that, in some respects, promoted transition toward renewable energy sources. Consequently, it is impossible to identify another president who matched Trump's aggressive strategy to eviscerate the environmental policy legacy of his predecessor without proposing any serious legislative or administrative alternatives to reduce environmental threats.

The magnitude of the education policy change Trump sought was less dramatic but still significant. The president and his Secretary of Education were outspoken about their intention to reorient the federal elementary and secondary education role. In numerous highly visible speeches, the president advocated shifting federal resources to support school choice, including scholarship programs that would allow parents to send children to private schools, even religiously affiliated ones. The president's second executive order in education issued in 2017 aimed at prohibiting federal intrusion into state and local control of education. Subsequently, federal regulatory guidance ebbed while governors and legislatures, particularly in many states under Republican control, promoted school choice legislation.

The Trump administration did not aspire to dismantle existing federal laws. The bipartisan agreement that yielded the 2015 Every Student Succeeds Act had already devolved considerable discretion to the states, giving Trump a platform for reducing still further the monitoring and direction of state and school district practices. This decline in federal involvement was especially evident in the case of civil rights and regulatory support for students with disabilities. It also found expression in the loosening of regulations on "supplement not supplant," thereby affording states and localities more discretion to divert federal funds from addressing the educational needs of the most disadvantaged students.

In postsecondary education, there was no legislative equivalent of ESSA. Instead, the Trump administration placed a high priority on enhancing the interests of for-profit entities through executive action, such as by rescinding the Obama-era Gainful Employment (GE) rule. The Department of Education also attempted to undercut the rights of student loan recipients in the courts and dragged its feet in providing loan cancellations to borrowers who claimed they had been defrauded. Beyond these initiatives, the Trump administration moved to place greater burdens of proof on campus victims of sexual misconduct and, less directly, to pressure colleges and universities to abandon racial-ethnic considerations in their admissions decisions.

Trump-Style Federalism: State Empowerment or Constraint?

The Trump administration's rhetoric periodically endorsed devolving power to the states but, in practice, this was not a consistent theme across the three policy arenas. Instead, the Trump administration pursued "opportunistic federalism," basing its commitment to empowering or constraining states not on any theory about the appropriate division of labor among levels of government but, rather, on which action would be more likely to serve its substantive policy goals.

Trump initiatives with respect to the ACA reflected that opportunism. Part of the administration's strategic design involved state empowerment. Its regulations with respect to association and short-term health plans provided states with more leeway to promote insurance that did not comply with ACA quality standards. The Trump administration also aggressively used waivers to empower conservative states. The administration's willingness to approve reinsurance waiver requests from more liberal states under ACA Section 1332 most vividly illustrates an exceptional instance where commitment to state empowerment overrode the administration's desire to sabotage the exchanges.

In the case of Medicaid and subsequent decisions with respect to Section 1332 waivers, however, the Trump administration primarily saw waivers as a tool to undermine the ACA. Federal officials understood that more liberal states where Democrats dominated elected offices would spurn its invitation to submit waiver requests that imposed work requirements and other measures to sap enrollments. But many Republican-dominated states would likely apply for Medicaid waivers emphasizing these themes. Their motivation for doing so would be as much about the desire to be part of a vertical partisan coalition to help the party accomplish its national goals as it would be to represent the particular interests of their own states. The trend toward "all politics being national" enhances the value of waiver initiatives for an administrative presidency.[5] It increases variation in the implementation of federal grant programs substantially, though not completely, along predictable partisan lines.

While the Trump administration endorsed several measures to empower states, in other instances it sought to constrain them. The funding cuts to enrollment navigators and insurance companies in the case of the exchanges made it more difficult for states committed to the ACA to achieve their coverage objectives. So, too, centrally imposed changes in rules governing the use of public benefits by noncitizens would decrease Medicaid take-up rates. The Trump administration's refusal to fully defend the constitutionality of key ACA provisions (including the Medicaid expansion) also threatened to vitiate the capacity of states to insure their low-income residents.

The Trump administration expressed considerable sympathy for state empowerment in climate and environmental policy. EPA Administrator Scott Pruitt routinely invoked "cooperative federalism" as a mantra throughout his nineteen-month tenure, embracing maximal state latitude in policy design and implementation. States received considerable regulatory relief in the electricity sector, whether they wanted it or not. More than half had actively opposed the Clean Power Plan for electricity sector carbon emissions. States joining this opposition through litigation and political efforts ranked among the largest producers of coal, oil, and gas and were heavily reliant on fossil fuels for electricity. Consequently, the Obama administration's efforts to transition away from fossil fuels toward greater use of renewable sources threatened them, even though many were already national leaders in the growth of wind and solar production. These opposition states, overwhelmingly led by Republicans, gave Trump some of his largest 2016 victory margins.

They consequently celebrated major shifts in federal climate policy under Trump, particularly when Trump officials eliminated the Clean Power Plan in favor of the Affordable Clean Energy rule. Trump administration reluctance to tackle the endangerment clause necessitated a regulatory replacement process, and the emerging ACE fundamentally differed from its predecessor. Several prominent policy options established under the CPP, including a cap-and-trade system, were prohibited in favor of far narrower efforts to allow states to consider certain operational efficiency measures for coal-burning power plants. These would be very modest and could be phased in at a leisurely pace, creating incentives that could keep coal plants operating longer than planned. As a result, states once oppositional to the Obama regulation became advocates for the Trump repeal-and-replace strategy. The EPA also empowered oil and gas producing states, freeing them from Obama provisions designed to deter methane releases, while also moving to delay implementation of federal requirements on state oversight of methane from solid waste landfills.

Transportation, however, represented a monumental federalism exception, with the Trump administration withdrawing state empowerment in favor of aggressive state constraint. California had used its unique CAA powers for more than a half-century. This involved an unusual waiver specified clearly in statutes that reflected California's acute air quality problems linked to vehicle emissions and the fact that the state took significant policy steps long before other states or the federal government.[6] This waiver was never seriously challenged in court, and federal officials granted nearly 120 waivers between 1968 and 2019, approving California's ongoing requests to set emission standards at a more rigorous level than existing federal ones. This gave California considerable national leverage, especially after the 1977 amendments provided all other states a "bandwagon" option. This allowed them to embrace the California standard once the EPA approved the waivers, which often prompted a comparable federal standard to assure national consistency.

California also set the pace in greenhouse gas emissions through 2002 legislation that triggered a waiver request to reduce carbon releases from vehicles.[7] The Obama administration ultimately approved the waiver in 2009, part of an administrative merger integrating waiver-driven air quality standards with federally preemptive fuel economy provisions, as discussed in chapter 2. The Trump administration, however, attempted to reverse this through the first withdrawal of an approved California waiver in over fifty years and by preempting the state's discretion to set more stringent vehicle emission standards. This constraining action confronted California and over a dozen allied bandwagon states with a major loss of delegated vehicle emission authority and undermined their respective greenhouse gas reduction plans.[8]

This step plunged California and the federal government into high-decibel intergovernmental combat and high-profile litigation. Relations became even more tenuous after California secretly negotiated a pact with four major car manufacturers, a compromise whereby firms agreed to honor much of what California had originally sought through its waiver rather than any revised federal proposal. What was heralded as an innovative breakthrough in Sacramento was condemned by the White House and the EPA as an illegal expansion of state authority in a matter where federal dominance was established. In September 2019, the Trump administration further attempted to constrain any state role through sharply worded letters to California and vehicle manufacturers with whom the state had negotiated, threatening them with investigation of possible antitrust violations for holding private conversations that could allegedly thwart competition. Some observers viewed this less as a serious legal challenge than a politicized effort to discourage vehicle manufacturers from participating in further dialogue with California on any design or emission control issues. The EPA augmented this attack with a withering letter to California later that same month threatening withdrawal of federal highway funds and other sanctions unless the state found ways to better address air and water quality, even though its waiver denial constrained the state's efforts to address air pollution. The Trump administration abandoned its antitrust investigation and did not pursue highway funding withdrawal in early 2020, while remaining unwilling to consider any negotiations with California.

In the education arena, the federalism story is a tale of two policy subsystems. In K–12, as previously discussed, the Trump administration strove to devolve additional authority to states and local school districts nearly across the board. With respect to civil rights, students with disabilities, transgender students, and the implementation of the ESSA, the Trump administration moved to grant states and localities more freedom from federal oversight. To be sure, the Trump administration strongly hoped the states would ramp up their efforts to promote school choice with greater involvement by private schools, but its approach emphasized exhortation and financial incentives rather than federal directives.

In contrast, the Trump administration evinced minimal interest in granting states more authority in the higher education policy subsystem. It struggled to prevent student borrowers from using state antifraud laws to sue the Department of Education's loan service contractors. It took regulatory action in favor of for-profit educational institutions, often at the expense of students who had borrowed significant amounts of money to attend them, Moreover, it adopted assertive rather than deferential postures toward state colleges and universities on issues of sexual misconduct and on the use of racial-ethnic criteria to diversify student bodies.

This is not to say that the Trump administration invariably succeeded in squelching the forces of federalism. When the Department of Education moved to repeal the GE rule, for instance, some states beefed up their regulation of for-profit educational institutions. Students eager to press claims against federal loan processing contractors won, at least temporarily, the right to seek relief in state courts. But overall, the aim of the Trump administration in postsecondary administration constrained rather than empowered states.

Table 6-1 summarizes and illuminates the opportunistic nature of the Trump administration's approach to federalism. Whether with respect to major or more incremental policy changes, Trump officials pursued a mix of state constraining and empowering designs. In considering the division of labor within the federal system, they typically preferred to strengthen whichever level of government would be more likely to advance their policy goals.

Tools and Strategies

The Trump administrative presidency drew on a familiar array of executive tools in reshaping health care, climate, and education policy. These tools were designed and applied by a range of ideologically compatible political appointees in key leadership positions in the Department of Health and Human Services, the Environmental Protection Agency, and the Department of Education. The Trump administration, at times, opted for high-profile, highly partisan figures to staff senior posts while appointing, in other instances, lower-profile individuals with greater technical and legal skill in a policy area.

On the high-profile side, for instance, the White House nominated and won Senate approval for former Oklahoma Attorney General Scott Pruitt to head the EPA, who was accompanied in leadership roles by loyalists from Oklahoma political circles and the oil and gas industry. While Pruitt walled off career staff from major policy development roles, the Trump administration left many positions requiring Senate confirmation vacant for extended periods. Pruitt also made record use of "ad-

TABLE 6-1. *Trump Executive Initiatives: Magnitude of Change Sought by Federalism Design*

Federalism Design	Major Magnitude	Incremental Magnitude
State Constraint	*Sabotage ACA:* Cut funds for exchange enrollments and participating insurance companies; make public charge rules more restrictive; fail to defend the constitutionality of ACA. *Search and Destroy—Climate:* Revoke vehicle emissions control waiver for California and allied states.	*Postsecondary Education:* Reduce regulation of for-profit institutions; weaken state role as avenue for challenging loan service contractors; restrain rights of student loan borrowers; revise procedures for campus handling of sexual misconduct cases; eliminate racial considerations in admissions decisions.
State Empowerment	*Sabotage ACA:* Promote Medicaid waivers to impose work requirements, administrative burdens, and more; encourage certain Section 1332 health reform waivers; provide greater latitude to states to accept non-ACA compliant insurance. *Search and Destroy—Climate:* Replace Clean Power Plan with Affordable Clean Energy rule; replace or eliminate proposed methane standards for oil and gas production and solid waste management.	*K–12 Education:* Reduce federal regulation of ESSA implementation (for example, greater state freedom to adopt alternative systems of student assessment); pursue less oversight of civil rights; reduce intervention on behalf of transgender students; reduce guidance on how to treat students with disabilities.

ministratively determined" special hires as political advisers, although many of these individuals departed with him in mid-2018.

Trump also nominated a high-profile partisan for Secretary of Education, Betsy DeVos. She had been a leading Republican Party activist and donor in Michigan for well over two decades. DeVos was a staunch advocate for school choice, charters, and vouchers for use at private schools, including religiously affiliated ones.

Trump also appointed some individuals with greater technical and legal competence to deliver on key policy shifts. This found reflection in his elevation of Andrew Wheeler as Pruitt's EPA successor, along with numerous associates Wheeler brought into the agency with extensive industry and government experience. The practice also manifested in Seema Verma's appointment as administrator of the Centers for Medicare and Medicaid Services (CMS). Verma had extensive experience in working with Medicaid officials in several Republican states, especially on waiver development.

While recognizing the importance of presidential appointments, we do not focus systematically on them, mindful that other scholars continue to closely study this area.[9] Instead, we have chosen four other Trump administrative presidency tools for more detailed analysis: executive orders, administrative rulemaking, waivers, and formal legal strategy (that is, efforts to affect potential and active federal litigation). Each tool proved particularly pivotal for the Trump administration in carrying out a hostile takeover, albeit with significant differences across policy areas.

Executive Orders

Students of the administrative presidency have devoted considerable attention to executive orders, and the Trump administration employed this tool extensively. Table 6-2 reports the number of Trump executive orders issued through 2019 relative to his five immediate predecessors. In general, the Trump administration was not an outlier in terms of average executive orders issued annually. Though appreciably higher on this metric than the second Bush and Obama administrations, President Trump slightly trailed Reagan and Clinton in his propensity to issue executive orders.

The significance of executive orders as a tool varied by policy sphere. Of President Trump's 136 executive orders through 2019, nine focused on health policy, eight on the environment, and six on education.[10] Like statutes, executive orders vary enormously in their policy significance, so simple counts of them reveal little about their impact. An examination of the content of these orders, however, points to their consider-

TABLE 6-2. *Executive Orders by President Trump and Predecessors, 1981–2019*

President	Number of Executive Orders	Average Executive Orders per Year
Ronald Reagan (1981–1989)	381	47.6
George H. W. Bush (1989–1993)	166	41.5
Bill Clinton (1993–2001)	364	45.5
George W. Bush (2001–2009)	291	36.4
Barack Obama (2009–2017)	276	34.5
Donald Trump (2017–2019)	136	45.3

Source: American Presidency Project, "Executive Orders by President" (www.presidency.ucsb.edu/statistics/data/executive-orders); Trump data from the *Federal Register,* "Executive Orders" (www.federalregister.gov/presidential-documents/executive-orders).

able substantive and symbolic importance. Nowhere is this more evident than in the case of health policy.

The very first executive order President Trump issued reflected the priority he placed on eliminating Obamacare. The January 2017 order titled "Minimizing the Economic Burden of the Patient Protection and Affordable Care Act Pending Repeal" constituted a carte blanche invitation to CMS and other federal agencies to undercut the program. It promised states greater federal flexibility to pursue their health care goals while also signaling to Trump's Republican base that he would honor the party's multiyear commitment to ACA repeal and replacement. Two other executive orders also loomed large in triggering agency actions to vitiate the ACA. The first, issued under the title "Promoting Healthcare Choice and Competition Across the United States," in October 2017, did much to kindle the creation of off-ramps to lower-quality insurance. It directed pertinent cabinet secretaries to consider revisions to guidelines and regulations within sixty days that would promote short-term, limited-duration, and association health plans.

The second notable executive order provided the underpinning for CMS's endorsement of Medicaid waivers featuring work requirements.

Issued in April 2018 under the title "Reducing Poverty in America by Promoting Opportunity and Economic Mobility," the order denounced the tendency of public assistance programs, such as Medicaid, to measure "success by how many people are enrolled in a program rather than by how many have moved from poverty into financial independence."[11] The order endorsed the consideration of work requirements for programs that did not currently require them.

In the case of climate policy, it was the executive order that did not bark that marked Trump's initial period in office. The Trump White House eschewed transition team proposals to issue a sweeping order within hours of inauguration that would have taken a sledgehammer to the entire Obama-era climate agenda in a single step. This proposed order would have withdrawn the United States from the Paris Agreement and reversed the Obama administration's endangerment finding on climate change risks that opened the path to reinterpret the 1990 CAA to address greenhouse gas emissions. It would also have directly attacked key Obama climate regulatory provisions, eliminating them entirely without replacements since climate change would no longer be deemed to pose any endangerment.

Rather than pursue such an all-encompassing strategy, the Trump administration, instead, advanced a search and destroy approach tailored to each policy subarea, issuing executive orders to selectively gut specific Obama regulatory provisions and replace them with far more modest alternatives. Most significantly, a March 2017 executive order focused on promoting "American energy independence" provided a framework for a series of regulatory steps that would prioritize maximum production and use of American fossil fuels over alternative energy sources. This executive order was broadly portrayed initially as focused on increased coal production but, ultimately, had a broader policy reach. It would play a particularly pivotal role in efforts to replace the CPP for the electricity sector in 2019 with a far milder ACE rule. This initiative sought to vitiate the core thrust of Obama's approach while avoiding a massive and legally uncertain endangerment finding assault. If successful, this strategy would leave in place successor regulations that would be far more modest in scope, welcomed by many regulated industries and challenging for any future administration to supplant. While executive orders played a prominent role in reshaping climate policy, other unilateral actions subject to minimal administrative constraints also loomed large, including withdrawal from the Paris Agreement.

The Trump administration also relied on executive orders to shape education policy. An order, "Enhancing Statutory Prohibitions on Federal Control of Education," issued in late April 2017 was particularly important. It affirmed that the federal executive branch was to "protect and preserve state and local control over the curriculum, program of instruction, administration, and personnel of educational institutions, schools, and school systems."[12] The order further directed the Secretary of Education to rescind or revise federal regulations and guidance documents that failed to serve this devolutionary goal. Reinforced by another more general executive order called "Enforcing the Regulatory Reform Agenda," which the president had issued in March 2017, it helped galvanize a flurry of Department of Education initiatives to deregulate K–12 and postsecondary education. The department launched an ongoing, extensive internal review and a few consultative sessions with affected groups, which in October 2017 led to the elimination of 583 guidance documents as well as enumerable Dear Colleague letters, Questions and Answers to Frequently Asked Questions, and Policy memos.[13] For their parts, the department's Office of Postsecondary Education rescinded 398 guidance documents, the Office of Elementary and Secondary Education ninety-seven, and the Office of Special Education and Rehabilitation Services seventy-two.

This deregulation continued in 2018. For example, the Office for Civil Rights eliminated six guidance letters regarding the use of race by educational institutions in July and another six guidance documents on school discipline policy in December.[14] The department's deregulatory efforts targeted not only less formal directives but administrative rules as well. For instance, the department, claiming a cost savings of $7.5 million, issued a final rule that postponed for two years state compliance with a rule designed to provide more protection to students with disabilities.[15] In these and other ways, Trump executive orders sparked a flurry of administrative actions in the Department of Education.

Federal Rulemaking

Presidents can consider an array of less procedurally regulated tools to support a hostile takeover. Executive orders often afford presidents great leeway to make unilateral decisions while also potentially triggering rulemaking, as the ACA and climate change cases illustrate. So, too, do other kinds of directives and signals to agencies. For instance, a president can accomplish substantial regulatory policy alterations by either softening or intensifying enforcement.[16] The Trump administration's arrival prompted a reduction in the Department of Education's enforcement of civil rights provisions. At times, however, a presidential administration cannot accomplish its policy objectives without engaging the process required to change formal administrative rules. Governed by the Administrative Procedure Act of 1946, the formal rulemaking process imposes multiple requirements on the administrative presidency. Agencies generally must promulgate a proposed rule in the *Federal Register*, provide a detailed and reasoned rationale for it, and give the public opportunity to comment. At least formally, agencies may not justify their initiatives on the basis of considerations not explicitly mentioned in the rulemaking records.[17]

When publishing the final rule, agency officials must summarize the comments received and justify their response to them. As two legal experts note, "salient submissions by those who object must be countered by cogent arguments—or at least arguments acceptable to reviewing courts."[18] In this regard, the doctrine of "hard look review" elevates the importance of professional expertise in the rulemaking process. The Administrative Procedure Act authorizes courts to set aside agency actions deemed "arbitrary and capricious." In 1983, the Supreme Court essentially decided that agencies needed to provide expert-driven, technocratic justifications for rule changes rather than resort to the politically driven argument that the changes simply reflected presidential preferences.[19]

These provisions mean that formal rulemaking requires the deployment of substantial administrative resources and typically cannot be done quickly. Health care arena developments illustrate this pattern. The Trump administration pursued three particularly important health policy goals through the rulemaking process, those focused on short-term insurance, association health plans, and public charges. Key characteristics of each of these rules during the first three years of the Trump administration are:

- *association health plans:* proposed rule published on January 5, 2018, and final rule on June 21, 2018; challenged in court, and federal district judge rules against initiative; the Trump administration appeals court ruling

- *short-term health plans:* proposed rule published on February 1, 2018, and final rule on August 3, 2018; challenged in court, and federal district judge sides with Trump administration; decision appealed

- *public charge regulation:* proposed rule published on October 10, 2018, and final rule on August 14, 2019; challenged in various courts, but the Supreme Court in February 2020 allows rule to be implemented while lower courts deliberate

In sum, the Trump administration managed to publish two of the proposed rules about a year after taking office. In each case, it took the administration nearly six months more to promulgate the final rule. The public charge proposal surfaced later and took ten months to finalize. Given court challenges, it remains unclear whether any of these policy changes would be fully in effect before the 2020 elections.

Trump also aggressively used rulemaking to alter climate policy. Each such step followed the general pattern in health care. This routinely consumed considerable amounts of time and featured prolonged delays between an initial announcement of rulemaking process and final rule completion. The administration appeared on track to issue its high-priority rules by the end of its first term. However, determined state opposition, most notably by coalitions of Democratic attorneys general, operated to delay or block rule implementation in multiple instances. Most litigation challenges appear unlikely to be resolved by federal courts prior to 2021 despite Trump administration requests for accelerated review.

In the case of electricity sector emissions, the EPA announced its attempt to eliminate the Obama CPP shortly after Trump's March 2017 executive order on energy dominance. But a proposed rule was not completed until August 2018, and a final version did not emerge until July 2019. Twenty-two Democratic state attorneys general promptly filed suit, attacking administration efforts to implement its alternative ACE rule. In the case of methane emissions from oil and gas production, reversal of Obama regulations coincided initially with the development of a replacement rule. But this initiative also faced unexpected delays, complicated when the EPA attempted to approve several proposed state implementation plans before issuing a final rule. The Trump administration published a proposed rule in August 2018, but a final version was delayed. A coalition of thirteen Democratic state attorneys general announced their intent to litigate once a final rule was issued.

These developments, however, were upstaged in August 2019 by a more far-reaching Trump administration proposed rule designed to eliminate entirely direct federal regulation of methane emissions from oil and gas drilling. This rule would subdivide the entire production and distribution supply chain of oil and gas into smaller units, arguing that no single component of that chain produced sufficient emissions to warrant regulation. The EPA argued that the CAA could indirectly cover methane through regulatory provisions for volatile organic compounds, although these would not encompass all geographic areas, segments of the energy supply chain, and instances where such compounds had been removed from methane. This proposal divided oil and gas producing industries, with larger firms generally opposed given their considerable investments in methane abatement technology while smaller firms, lacking sufficient resources for rigorous monitoring and mitigation, welcomed the proposal. Divides also surfaced among states, with many energy production states supporting this proposed regulatory relief, while counterparts from many energy importing states expressed strong concerns.

In education, the Trump administration often employed more informal means, such as the withdrawal of guidance documents and Dear Colleague letters, to reverse policies. On several occasions, however, it used rulemaking to pursue new policy directions. In July 2019, for instance, it formally rescinded the Obama administration's GE rule, which required certain career and technical education programs to demonstrate that their graduates had achieved employment outcomes that would enable them to repay their federal loans. In September 2019, the Department of Education published a final rule designed to resolve the controversy and litigation surrounding the borrower defense rule. Among other things, the new rule redefined the procedures under which former borrowers could obtain reductions or cancellations of their student loans.

The Department of Education sharply broke with the practice of prior presidential administrations by proposing a formal rule in November 2018 dealing with sexual misconduct complaints and other matters of gender discrimination. The last time the federal government issued a regulation interpreting Title IX was 1975, and that rule did not address sexual harassment as a form of gender discrimination. Prior administrations had tended to rely on informal processes and tools to provide civil rights guidance and directives, a practice that had kindled scholarly criticism on procedural grounds.[20] It deserves note that the exacting demands of the federal rulemaking process delayed rule-based policy changes in education until well into Trump's third year in office.

While the rulemaking process slows down and at times thwarts the administrative presidency, it rewards a president who successfully pursues change through this venue. Once in place, any attempt to modify the new rules must navigate the same protracted process. A modest exception to this arduous procedural requirement exists thanks to the 1996 Congressional Review Act. This law allows Congress to disapprove a regulation within sixty legislative days of its issuance. So long as the president concurs with its action, the agency, going forward, cannot issue another rule in substantially the same form. The law provided the Trump administration and a Republican Congress a brief window of opportunity to strike down rules promulgated by the Obama administration during its final months in office.

Used only once before under President George W. Bush, the Trump administration, in concert with Congress, aggressively employed the act to eradicate sixteen Obama-era regulations by mid-May 2017.[21] These disapprovals did not play a significant role in the health care and climate arenas. In education, however, Congress used the act in 2017 to strike down Accountability State Plan regulations promulgated late in the Obama administration, which had sought to shape state ESSA implementation.

Waivers

Decisions concerning waivers can also advance administrative presidency goals. The utility of this tool to a president seeking to encourage new initiatives depends on states or localities responding favorably to the proposed waiver themes. In cases where a presidential administration is trying to negate the practices of its predecessor, a decision not to renew or phase out an existing waiver may serve its policy goals.

Formal procedural requirements similar to those of federal rulemaking do not uniformly apply to waivers in different substantive areas. In the health arena, however, Congress, through the ACA, formalized the process surrounding the granting of Section 1115 Medicaid demonstration waivers to bolster transparency and due process. This decision reflected the growing importance of this tool, with about one-third of federal Medicaid expenditures supporting waiver activities.[22]

The Obama administration issued new regulations interpreting the ACA provision in 2012. This assured that there would be at least a thirty-day opportunity for public comment on the waiver proposal at the state level prior to its CMS submission. Once CMS had conducted a review of the waiver request and decided to move forward, it would also solicit comments for thirty days. (Similar public comment periods apply to processes for approving state innovation waivers under ACA Section 1332.) Both state and federal governments had to summarize the comments received and indicate their response. These requirements and others, such as the need for demonstrations to be budget neutral and formally evaluated, impose some constraints on a presidential administration. They make it harder to move quickly to grant waivers to states interested in promoting an administration's policy goals.

At the same time, the various waiver requirements need not thwart a president. The Trump administration approved several waivers even when public comments on them at the state and federal levels were overwhelmingly negative. Presidential administrations eager to endorse a waiver on substantive grounds can typically find ways to skirt certain procedural requirements. In the case of Medicaid demonstration waivers, for instance, federal officials have occasionally accepted optimistic, unrealistic estimates of its budget neutrality and downplayed having the waiver rigorously evaluated by an independent agent.[23]

A broader issue, which has surged to the fore under the Trump administration, is whether a waiver goes so far as to violate a statute's purposes.[24] In general, Medicaid demonstration waivers during the Clinton, second Bush, and Obama years did not move so dramatically in this direction as to trigger successful court challenges to them. Approved waivers that sponsored major departures from the regular Medicaid program generally sought to expand insurance coverage. Perhaps most notably, this includes the high-profile Massachusetts waiver promoted by then Governor Mitt Romney and approved in 2006 before becoming an ACA template. The Trump administration's approval of waivers featuring work requirements and other measures likely to reduce Medicaid enrollments sharply departs from this pattern. As of late 2019, a federal district judge had ruled that enrolling eligible people in Medicaid is an overriding statutory goal, and that the Trump waivers impermissibly had the opposite effect. The Trump administration appealed this ruling, and if it prevails in the higher courts it will have forged a considerable expansion of executive discretion and heightened the allure of waivers as a tool.

The Trump administration's efforts to push the envelope also extends to ACA Section 1332 state innovation waivers. It invited states to use these waivers to create additional off-ramps to cheaper, lower-quality insurance. Legal developments here will constitute yet another test of the degree to which waivers can shift power from Congress to the executive branch.

Waivers can take many forms. In the area of air quality, a highly structured waiver process designed to give one state access to expansive regulatory authority has endured for more than half a century. California acquired unique status spelled out initially in 1967 legislation and sustained in subsequent legislation and amendments approved in 1970, 1977, and 1990. Every governor from Pat Brown to Jerry Brown requested at least one waiver under this provision to set vehicle emission standards more stringent than national ones. This reflected the state's acute environmental challenges linked to smog from vehicles and to their extensive regulatory program launched long before comparable federal policy. In turn, every president from Lyndon Johnson to Barack Obama had approved one or more waiver requests, with 117 approvals overall before Trump took office. Indeed, Ronald Reagan occupied the unique position of requesting multiple waivers during his two terms as governor of California and later approving many of them from his successors during his two terms as president.

This waiver process is fundamentally different from those in health care and education. The statute specifies in unusually clear terms when California could request such a waiver and the three exact criteria the federal government would employ to evaluate these requests. Once approved, as noted, the California waiver can trigger a bandwagon mechanism allowing other states to adopt its standard rather than the national one. Historically, this fueled a state policy diffusion process and a form of "iterative federalism" whereby the federal government came to embrace state-led policy.[25] The entire process involves a set of formal requests and responses by both parties that are public and maintained on an EPA website.

The Obama-era effort to merge this waiver program under the CAA with a federally preempted program for national vehicle fuel economy without recourse to Congress in 2009 yielded bold emission-reduction targets, which the administration subsequently extended through the mid-2020s. It required a new managerial partnership between the EPA and the Department of Transportation. The Trump administration did not attempt to eliminate this cross-agency arrangement or the core thrust of the merged emission and fuel economy program. It made no request to Congress that it amend the CAA to alter its waiver policy. Instead, it took the unprecedented steps of revoking a waiver that California had already received from the EPA while contending that federal fuel economy standards preempted any air quality waiver. It then pursued a plan to freeze fuel economy standards through 2026, although hinting in early 2020 that its final rule might allow some modest adjustments during that period.

If successful, this policy shift would limit further decreases in allowable vehicle emissions or fuel economy increases beyond any second

Trump term. It would likely weaken the political and legal standing of the state that had routinely led the opposition to Trump administration efforts in climate change and other policy areas while undermining any credible chance that California would attain its climate mitigation and air quality goals. The policy shift also had significant consequences beyond California, because thirteen bandwagon states had already adopted its standards for vehicle emissions and two others expressed interest in doing so. This waiver controversy drifted steadily toward protracted intergovernmental combat and litigation in 2019 and early 2020, potentially generating a landmark case on administrative presidency powers under regulatory federalism.

While waivers loomed large as a Trump administrative presidency tool in health care and climate policy, they were not as central to its education initiatives. The Obama administration had aggressively used waivers to circumvent the ambitious performance goals of the No Child Left Behind legislation approved under George W. Bush. But 2015 ESSA passage gave states considerably greater flexibility, and the Trump White House saw little need to employ waivers to galvanize broad policy shifts. However, the administration did endorse waivers as vehicles for incremental steps toward greater devolution. In particular, Secretary DeVos encouraged states to use waivers to develop innovative approaches to assess student achievement. ESSA limits to 1 percent in a given subject the proportion of students (for example, those with intellectual disabilities) who may take an alternative assessment to the one a state has generally chosen. In response to DeVos's signals of federal flexibility, dozens of states requested waivers of the 1 percent cap. However, procedural issues related to the proposed timing of waiver implementation led the Department of Education to reject, at least temporarily, many of these requests. In other cases, the denials appeared more substantive. For instance, the Trump administration rejected proposals from Michigan and New York to exclude recently arrived English learners from the state accountability system.

Formal Legal Strategy

Formal legal strategy includes actions at the top levels of a presidential administration to shape potential and active federal litigation. Among other things, it involves decisions concerning the appropriate interpretation of law and how to respond to suits challenging the administrative presidency. A comprehensive review of the Trump administration's formal legal strategy would require a book in itself. Instead, we note two major elements of his legal strategy, both having considerable relevance to understanding the dynamics of an aggressive administrative presidency.

First, the Trump administration nominated judges believed to be sympathetic to the president and his policy positions. In doing so, Trump relied heavily on vetting and lists provided by the Heritage Foundation, a conservative think tank, and the Federalist Society, a professional organization that promotes conservative legal interpretations. In addition to appointing two Supreme Court Justices during his first three years in office, Trump has attempted to shape the partisan composition of district and appellate courts. As of January 2018, the circuit courts were about evenly split between Republican and Democratic judges, while Democrats controlled nearly 60 percent of the district court appointments.[26] Vacancies and expected retirements may well allow Trump to fill an estimated 38 percent of district and appellate court positions in a single term, a higher proportion than any of his predecessors dating back to Reagan.[27] These appointments may not only help Trump leave his mark on the judiciary over the long term but help his policies prevail in key court decisions during his time in office or beyond.

Second, the Trump administrative presidency rejected an approach to law rooted in a model of legalism or formalism. This model stresses the role of lawyers and judges as independent experts in reaching impartial decisions about what the law means and how it should be applied. It envisions legal assessments generally and judicial opinions more specifically as derived from "an intellectual system—a methodology—adopted on politically neutral grounds to generate objective decisions."[28] Within the federal government, it implies substantial presidential deference to the views of the Attorney General and the Office of Legal Counsel within the Justice Department.

This formal, legalistic model had its heyday under President Jimmy Carter as he attempted to rebuild federal government credibility after the Watergate scandal.[29] Carter extended the efforts of his predecessor, Gerald Ford, who was troubled by the growing Justice Department politicization he had observed over time and reached extremes under Richard Nixon. One of Ford's key steps in promoting a strong, independent voice in the Justice Department was selecting University of Chicago President Edward Levi as Attorney General.[30] In turn, Carter had campaigned on the position that the Justice Department ought to be a "neutral zone" free from political influence. Once in office, he substantially deferred to his Attorney General Griffin Bell and the Office of Legal Counsel to determine the legality of actions he wished to take. This model quickly faded in the post-Carter era as presidents became more assertive about seeking legal advice that would support their policy preferences. Legal power increasingly diffused to federal agencies and the office of White House Counsel. This decentralization enabled presidents to engage in a kind of "forum shopping" within the executive branch, seeking out legal advice most supportive of their policy objectives. Meanwhile, congressional gridlock fueled by partisan polarization more readily tempted presidents to act on novel, expansive legal interpretations.

The Trump administration has persistently sought to make the institutions of executive branch legalism subservient to its policy goals. On a personal level, the president has asserted that the Attorney General and the law enforcement establishment work for him with scant regard for their professional independence and, often, their advice. The Trump administration's decision to support the district court finding that the ACA was unconstitutional vividly illustrates the triumph of partisan policy commitments over the formal, legalistic model. In ordering this change, Trump reportedly accepted the advice of his highly conservative Acting Chief of Staff and the chair of his Domestic Policy Council, overriding concerns and reservations expressed by the White House Counsel and Attorney General, among others.[31]

Highly expansive interpretations of law also mark the climate and education arenas. As just discussed, the Trump administration pushed the legal envelope considerably when it threatened California with possible investigations or sanctions under multiple statutes if it persisted in challenging federal authority over vehicle emissions. In education, the Trump administration expansively interpreted a 2017 Supreme Court ruling to affirm that it would be unconstitutional for the Department of Education to enforce Elementary and Secondary Education Act provisions assuring that service providers be independent of religious organizations. In these and myriad other ways, the Trump administrative presidency aggressively stretched the limits in its legal strategy.

The Administrative Presidency Triumphant?

To what degree did the Trump administrative presidency accomplish its policy goals during its first three years? No major health care, climate, or education legislation was adopted during this period. Through executive action, however, the Trump administration laid the groundwork for significant and possibly radical policy shifts in the health and climate arenas. It also set the stage for possible significant policy modifications in education. To be sure, these policy changes remained largely, though not completely, unrealized as Trump concluded his third year, reflecting administrative delays and legal challenges in finalizing new regulations, linked in large part to a series of challenges brought by coalitions of opposing states.

In the health care arena, two scenarios concerning Trump's policy accomplishments joust for attention. The first involves possible court ratification of the ACA nuclear option, which would mean an unprecedented victory for the Trump administrative presidency. A court decision to throw out the entire ACA or severely wound it by destroying one or several of its key components (for example, protections for those with preexisting conditions) would signal a dramatic policy achievement. Moreover, from the perspective of executive branch action, the victory would be durable. The only federal remedy for opponents would be statutory—with Congress passing replacement legislation that a president would sign. To a far greater degree than his other initiatives, Trump would be riding, in such a case, on the coattails of Republican attorneys general and an increasingly conservative and aggressive judiciary in achieving his policy goal. But the White House decision to substantially aid and abet partisan advocates for the nuclear option would also be a likely contributing factor.

The second scenario assumes that efforts to destroy or severely wound the ACA via the courts fail. Political scientist Paul Pierson has argued that social policy retrenchment need not take the form of major legislative (or in this case, court) action but can, instead, be "invisible at the surface" and akin to "termites working on a foundation."[32] The effect of the "termites" the Trump administration has unleashed through its various initiatives above all manifests itself in declining Medicaid and exchange enrollments. More generally, it finds expression in the growing number of Americans without health insurance of high quality. Ultimately, the degree of impact will heavily depend on judicial rulings in the several cases discussed in chapter 3. At least during Trump's first term, however, it is unlikely that the ACA's edifice would be massively or irreparably altered. Should a Democrat win White House control in 2020, he or she could take meaningful executive actions to repair the ACA's foundation and prospects, even if Congress did not engage. This could include reversals on Trump's waiver policies, moves to close various off-ramps to lower-quality insurance, restoration of funds for insurers and outreach, as well as other measures. If President Trump wins a second term, the degree of damage to ACA enrollments would continue to depend on whether the courts approve his initiatives. It would also hinge on the president's willingness to launch new sabotage initiatives, such as eliminating silver loading or approving waivers to block grant Medicaid. State policy responses would also matter. If Republicans fare well at the state level in the 2020 election, the threat to the ACA posed by the Trump administration's sabotage initiatives would grow.

Any current or future successes of the Trump administration in promoting the president's health care agenda bodes poorly for those who believe that all Americans should have access to quality care. This is not because the ACA is an elixir, as Democratic supporters of Medicare for All assert. Even if vigorously implemented, the ACA has limits as a vehicle for achieving a better balance among access, quality, and cost in the health care system, as well as for promoting better health outcomes. Still, the accomplishments of the ACA should not be slighted. Among other things, it appreciably reduced the ranks of the uninsured and improved the quality of coverage experienced by many Americans. In all probability, it had a positive effect on health outcomes for the Medicaid expansion population and others. From these and other perspectives, the ACA was far more likely to improve health outcomes than the legislation congressional Republicans proposed to replace it. These proposals would have led, without exception, fewer Americans to have quality health insurance. For his part, President Trump at no point proposed a detailed health care plan that would come close to achieving the insurance coverage provide by Obamacare.

Viewed historically, Republican behavior reflects the rise of polarization in the health care arena. As Paul Starr observes, for much of the period since the 1960s, "Republicans had accepted the legitimacy of universal coverage as a national objective. That is no longer true; the earlier moral consensus has disappeared."[33] One would be hard pressed to come up with a more vivid example of this development than the actions of the Trump administrative presidency to sabotage the ACA.

In the climate policy arena, the accomplishments of the Trump administrative presidency will depend heavily on court responses to state-led litigation and future election outcomes. At one level, the Trump administration has achieved considerable success by avoiding an assault on the endangerment finding, though thereby tacitly acknowledging that the CAA can be interpreted to reduce greenhouse gas emissions. This set the stage for Trump's search and destroy approach to every aspect of President Obama's climate strategy, drawing on executive orders, the weakening of regulations, waiver withdrawals, and implementation delays. But many Trump initiatives proceeded very slowly, encountered serious setbacks in initial court reviews, and faced aggressive legal challenges led by Democratic state attorneys general. States also retained considerable authority to design their own policies to reduce emissions commensurate with Obama-era targets, with many new initiatives proposed or adopted between 2018 and early 2020.[34] They could also join political and legal forces behind California in confronting the historic waiver withdrawal and state preemption under fuel economy standards. The administration also faced potential challenges from industry divides. Vehicle manufacturers began to sort out their federal versus state loyalties in ways the Trump administration found threatening, with growing evidence in early 2020 that at least four would continue to pursue direct collaboration with Sacramento rather than D.C. in setting emission standards. Similar industry splintering was evident among electric utilities and oil and gas producing firms in response to proposed weakening of federal regulations in those sectors.

The fate of Trump's climate initiatives was unlikely to be resolved by the end of his fourth year. Even formal withdrawal from the Paris Agreement would not occur until the eleventh hour of those four years. Nor would one expect major changes in annual greenhouse gas emissions during Trump's initial term. These emissions began to decline during the Obama presidency, most markedly in the electricity sector. It was not, however, likely that many of these reductions could be linked to Obama policies, many of which were only beginning to take effect when he left office, though full implementation of his policies would have likely placed continued downward pressure on emissions. The first full year of the Trump administration, 2017, featured continued emissions decline, for which the administration claimed credit. However, emissions climbed by 3.1 percent in 2018, the largest increase since 2010, before declining 2.1 percent in 2019, due almost exclusively to continued phaseout of coal plants. Longer-term, sustained implementation of Trump policies would likely place American greenhouse gas (and conventional air contaminant) emissions considerably above where they would have stood with Obama policies. This was perhaps most notable for methane emissions from oil and gas production as federal regulatory oversight was withdrawn amid dramatically expanded output from two massive shale reservoirs in states with industry-accommodating regulatory policies.[35]

All this underscores the question of whether a Trump second term would enable him to consolidate his administrative presidency and prevail over time in legal and political battles. There are enormous questions about climate policy durability after Trump exits the presidency, whether that occurs in 2021 or 2025. A second full term would allow Trump to veto any climate legislation that might emerge, maintain pressure on agencies to see various steps through to implementation, and continue to appoint judges inclined to endorse his policies. This could do much to secure his legacy as a president who derided climate science, withdrew from international climate agreements, and took far-reaching administrative steps to prevent use of the CAA to reduce greenhouse gas emissions, arguing that any economic benefits from inaction trumped any environmental costs.

Such policies could be further insulated by a federal judiciary increasingly dominated by Trump appointees. Jeff Holmstead, former EPA air quality head under George W. Bush, noted in June 2019 that there was "no way" a recently reconfigured Supreme Court would have accepted the CPP as an appropriate interpretation of CAA authority and that "I'm pretty confident we have at least five justices—and maybe seven—who will agree that EPA's authority is limited."[36]

However, much of the Trump effort would likely be reversible if Democrats regain the presidency in 2021. Presidential-executive agreements such as the Paris Agreement could be rapidly restored and even expanded with future pledges. Regulatory repeal-and-replacement policies also could be reversed, particularly in cases where these remained works in progress as 2021 dawned. One inevitable question surrounding a possible Democratic presidential win would be whether there might be sufficient bipartisan support in Congress to address climate change, possibly through a market-based approach such as a carbon tax.[37] No serious congressional consideration of CAA amendments has occurred since 1990, and this law does not specifically address greenhouse gases, thereby creating a complex set of challenges in extending various provisions to carbon dioxide or methane through administrative presidency tools.

The shift of much of the Republican Party in the 2010s away from its earlier receptivity to carbon pricing and other climate policy options bodes poorly for prospects that Congress would approve bipartisan legislation more explicitly focused on reducing greenhouse gas emissions. Even with Democratic majorities, congressional votes in support of consequential climate policies are highly uncertain, as Bill Clinton and Barack Obama learned early in their respective presidencies when climate legislation floundered amid Democratic control. The uncertainty of future congressional engagement on this issue makes it likely that climate policy will continue to feature back-and-forth shifting driven by the administrative presidency and respective state coalitions, as discussed in chapter 4. The Trump administration has taken its search and destroy mission of Obama-era policies to unprecedented lengths, yet its handiwork is not necessarily any more durable than that of his three predecessors. Numerous 2020 Democratic presidential aspirants listed administrative restoration of multiple Obama-era policies, usually beginning with Paris but often addressing new areas, such as prohibiting drilling through fracking techniques, halting energy production on federal lands, or declaring a climate emergency to legitimize the launch of new policies as among the very first steps that they would take upon entering the Oval Office. Their platforms, however, said very little about how they would pursue these goals if elected and what statutory or constitutional authority they might use.

Of course, any future Democratic president considering executive approaches to climate mitigation could count on at least one aggressive form of political opposition: the large coalition of Republican-led states, especially attorneys general, that repeatedly challenged the Obama administration on climate change. These partisans shifted into a far quieter mode during the Trump presidency. But any future effort to reverse Trump climate policies by a Democratic administration would rekindle their opposition. One reality of the ongoing administrative presidency in climate change involves shifting state coalitions in active opposition to or support of each president. One could argue that blue states got the best climate deal during the Obama administration, shifting into opposition mode only in 2017. And red states emerged as big winners under his successor, pivoting from opposition to Obama toward support of Trump.

In education, the Trump administrative presidency could rely on more incremental measures to advance its goals rather than attempts at massive policy transformation as was the case with the ACA and climate policy. A bipartisan congressional agreement in elementary and secondary education embodied in the 2015 ESSA had already devolved substantial policy discretion to the states. Nonetheless, the Trump administration took additional executive actions to weaken federal oversight and direction. It curbed Obama-era guidance to states on ESSA implementation and found avenues to support school choice, including state and local efforts to subsidize student enrollment in religious schools. It sought to undercut targeting of federal funds to the most disadvantaged students by relaxing federal requirements that such monies supplement and supplant school district support for this cohort. The Trump administration also took significant steps to weaken civil rights enforcement. The Department of Education's Office for Civil Rights reduced its reporting requirements and its enforcement activities appreciably. It withdrew Obama-era guidelines designed to reduce racial and other discrimination in the implementation of school disciplinary actions.

Responding to social conservatives in the Republican Party, the Trump administration went out of its way to distance itself from, if not stigmatize, transgender students. In a Dear Colleague letter, the Department of Education reduced its commitment to investigating transgender complaints. It supported an investigation of Connecticut, which had allowed transgender students to compete in school athletic contests based on their chosen sexual identity. The Trump administration also weakened federal guidance designed to assure that states and school districts provided required services to students with disabilities. On balance, Trump initiatives meant that who got what, when, and how from K–12 education would depend more heavily on the politics and policy dynamics of the fifty states and thousands of local school districts.

In postsecondary education, the Trump administration initiatives primarily played out in three spheres: campus sexual misconduct cases, student borrower protection, and regulation of for-profit institutions. The Department of Education took steps to reverse Obama-era guidelines that had increased the procedural rights of students who claimed they had been sexually abused. The department initiative had the effect of placing a greater burden of proof on those filing complaints. The Trump administration also sought to restrict the ability of student borrowers to sue loan service contractors under state law. It strove to delay cancellation or reduction of student loan payments for those who had attended for-profit institutions that went out of business. So, too, the Trump administration rescinded Obama-promulgated regulations to penalize for-profit vocational schools that had failed to attain employment targets for their graduates.

As in the ACA and climate arenas, Trump administration initiatives encountered considerable resistance from Democratic (and occasionally Republican) state officials. Some passed laws directly opposed to Trump initiatives. For their part, Democratic state attorneys general filed suits to delay or block several measures. Private individuals, such as student borrowers or advocates for transgender students, also took their cases to court, often with some success. Many universities, states, and school districts remained committed to Obama-era policies despite Trump administrative initiatives to undermine them.

All this is not to gainsay the potential impact of the Trump administration's executive actions on education. State and local school officials that had resisted the Obama goals could now engage in a wide range of practices with little concern of federal intervention. Private for-profit institutions knew they had a White House ally averse to new regulations who had engaged in a protracted, successful effort to rescind the GE rule. As in other areas, the durability of Trump's achievements rest heavily on the 2020 election. A second term could foster new initiatives and efforts to overcome resistance to ones already instigated. If a Democrat enters the White House, most of the Trump initiatives would be reversible through executive action.

In sum, a review of health care, climate, and education policy arenas after Trump's first three years points to considerable uncertainty over the impact of his administrative presidency, given political and legal uncertainties. In addition, the forces of federalism loom large. As political scientist John Kincaid has noted, federalism offers a "consolation prize" to parties that do not control the presidency but can confront it from statehouses where they do have control.[38] In many respects, these state forces act more like the formal political opposition to a president than do members of Congress from the other party. This may be an enduring feature in each of our policy arenas for future presidencies, assuming Congress remains on the policy sidelines.

Implications for American Democracy

Beyond these policy ramifications, what are the implications of the Trump administrative presidency for American democracy, especially checks and balances and the rule of law? Several prominent students of the administrative presidency have cast it as favorable for democracy. For instance, in his seminal work in the early 1980s, political scientist Richard P. Nathan argued that the administrative presidency could enhance "popular control, given the tendency of industrialized states to become increasingly controlled from bureaucratic and technocratic power centers." Nathan concluded that "properly reflective of legal and constitutional requirements," the administrative presidency "is fully consistent with democratic values."[39]

Writing in the *Harvard Law Review* about two decades later, Elena Kagan (later a Supreme Court Justice) developed a more detailed defense of "presidential administration" and its role in serving democratic accountability. She argued that "in comparison with other forms of control," an assertive administrative presidency "renders the bureaucratic sphere more transparent and responsive to the public while also promoting important kinds of regulatory competence and dynamism." In Kagan's view, a vigorous administrative presidency "enhances transparency, enabling the public to comprehend more accurately the sources and nature of bureaucratic power," thereby establishing an "electoral link between the public and the bureaucracy."[40] Kagan acknowledges that presidents "tend to push the envelope when interpreting statutes," thereby raising the threat of "presidential lawlessness." But she believes that judicial review of administrative actions substantially ameliorates this threat.[41] By the same token, however, she argues for considerable court deference to the president. Since presidential administration is by and large "a salutary development," courts should "through their articulation of administrative law . . . recognize and promote this kind of control over agency policymaking." In the face of statutory ambiguity, courts should have "an additional reason to defer to administrative decisions in which the President has played a role." This "would reduce the frequency with which the courts reverse administrative action."[42]

Not surprising, views about the sanguine implications of the administrative presidency have sparked strong criticism, with some seeing it as a fundamental threat to the rule of law and democratic accountability.[43] Among other things, they express skepticism that the administrative presidency necessarily fosters greater transparency, noting how hyperpartisan media outlets devote sporadic, highly biased, and often misinformed attention to presidential action. They further observe that, to the degree that executive action does not proceed through notice and comment provisions of the Administrative Procedure Act, transparency may be minimal.[44] In an era of intense partisan polarization, they question whether presidential executive action will be responsive to dominant public opinion.[45]

Donald Trump's ascent has reinforced earlier concerns about the implications of a muscular administrative presidency for democracy. Numerous political scientists have noted the general threat to democratic norms and practices that the Trump presidency poses. One group of these scholars notes: "Trump openly derides core institutions of democratic governance: the independent press, the judiciary, the bureaucracy, the validity of elections, the legitimacy of democratic contestation, and the centrality of facts to political discourse."[46] Others emphasize

Trump's corrosive effect on norms of mutual toleration and forbearance, which have long fortified the U.S. constitutional system.[47] Summing up more broadly, two other political scientists observe: "The election of Donald Trump has challenged the widespread assumption that rich, liberal democracies are invulnerable to subversion by autocrats who come to power through electoral means."[48]

The impeachment process initiated in September 2019 further fueled impressions of legal impropriety by President Trump. Hence, the robust features of democracy that proponents of the administrative presidency have relied on to counter executive "lawlessness" and excess have been called into question. The issue of whether forces embedded in American politics and governance can check an excessive administrative presidency becomes ever more central.

A general assessment of competing views about the administrative presidency role in fostering or undermining democratic accountability lies beyond the scope of this book. Instead, we seek to make a more modest contribution to this discussion based on our three policy cases. It remains to be seen whether the Trump administration will suffer at the ballot box for its positions on health, climate change, and education—whether transparency and public opinion will in some sense foster accountability. But we can, at least, offer a preliminary assessment of the degree to which key institutions—especially the courts and federalism—have curbed the Trump administrative presidency in its first three years.

The Courts: Partisans in Robes?

Administrative presidency supporters have tended to rely on the courts to check its possible excesses. The nature and magnitude of any such check depend, however, on what motivates judicial behavior. One explanatory lens rooted in research emphasizing "legal realism" tends to portray federal judges as "politicians in robes."[49] In this view, policy preferences anchored in the partisan ideology of judges weigh heavily in their decisions, especially in the Supreme Court but also in lower federal courts.[50]

Hence, recent presidents have paid increasing attention to the ideology of judges in nominating them for court appointments. As with executive branch appointments, the president often expects judicial nominees to be partisan supporters. To the degree that judges, in fact, behave as loyal allies, the fortunes of a given administrative presidency heavily depend on the partisan composition of the judiciary, namely the extent to which they were nominated by a Republican or Democratic president. Under this model, a partisan tilt would influence the judiciary's willingness to check the administrative initiatives of a given president.

To be sure, forum shopping opportunities counter the weight of sheer numbers of Republican and Democratic judges. Those opposing an executive initiative can bring the case to judges they expect will be sympathetic to their policy views. Hence, the current Republican-appointed Supreme Court majority looms large since many pivotal cases will reach it on appeal. If this partisan model prevails, the administrative presidencies of Republicans will likely face fewer court checks than those of their Democratic counterparts for the foreseeable future.

While noting the rise of partisan ideology in shaping judicial decisions, scholars have also stressed that judges are only partly politicians in robes.[51] In doing so, they have identified multiple factors that inhibit partisan behavior by judges. These include: a commitment to various legal methodologies for interpreting the law, norms of collegiality, the desire to be respected within professional legal circles, interest in preserving court legitimacy under the separation of powers system, personal ambition (for example, desire for promotion to a higher court), and more. To the degree these factors shape judicial decisions, Republican and Democratic presidents may have more similar fates in the courts. This prospect comports more closely with the view that courts should be an independent, politically neutral umpire in the American governmental system.

In assessing the degree to which the federal courts checked the Trump administrative presidency, we face two major uncertainties. First, the outcomes of court challenges to Trump initiatives were unclear after three years. Second, we have no way of knowing the degree to which the anticipated reactions of courts played a role in inhibiting the White House from launching certain initiatives. Did CMS officials refrain from approving certain Medicaid waiver proposals because they anticipated that the courts would invalidate them? Did the EPA recoil from an endangerment finding challenge for fear it would lose in court and then face more difficult challenges advancing other components of its strategy? The court role in deterring potential initiatives of an administrative presidency may be a major source of judicial power, albeit very difficult to calibrate.

While acknowledging uncertainties, our three cases provide preliminary evidence of court influence and the role of partisanship. Clearly, court challenges appreciably delayed any administrative presidency impact. Final resolution of significant court cases was unlikely to emerge until the last year of Trump's first term, if then. Too, the Trump administration experienced mixed success in the courts. In the health care arena, the White House suffered court defeats over its sponsorship of association health plans and Medicaid work waivers. But a district court ruled in favor of the Trump administration's proposal to expand the availability of short-term health plans. Of even greater importance, a Texas district court called for terminating the entire ACA, and an appellate court reaffirmed its fundamental finding. (If the Supreme Court upholds the Texas decision, it would raise other issues of democracy, primarily whether the court had overstepped its proper role in the separation-of-powers system by destroying a congressionally approved program already providing benefits to millions of Americans.)

Very preliminary evidence from the health arena suggests some partisan tilt in court decisions. For instance, the same Democratic judge ruled against the Trump administration on three separate suits challenging Medicaid work waivers. Prior to intervention by the Supreme Court, three different Democratic judges respectively issued injunctions blocking implementation of the public charge rule. In turn, Republican judges substantially upheld Trump administration preferences with respect to short-term health plans. Republican judges were also united in finding the individual mandate without the tax penalty unconstitutional. In addition to the Fort Worth district judge, the two Fifth Circuit judges who adopted this view had been appointed by Republican presidents. The dissenting appellate court judge was a Carter appointee. However, a Republican judge sided with the Democratic state attorneys general challenging the Trump initiative on association health plans. And the appellate court judge who wrote the unanimous opinion invalidating Arkansas's work requirement waiver was a Reagan appointee.

In climate policy, the partisan affiliation of judges did not appear to have any bearing on four significant lower court rulings. In each case, the court rebuked the Trump administration regardless of whether the judge had been appointed by a Democratic or Republican president, behavior generally consistent with a broader pattern of court responses in other environmental cases.[52] In July 2017, a D.C. Circuit Court judge appointed by a Democrat vacated the EPA's efforts to delay an Obama-era rule intensifying monitoring for methane leaks from oil and gas drilling operations. In April 2018, a Second Circuit Court ruling issued by a Republican appointee held that the National Highway Transportation Safety Administration had exceeded its authority in suspending monetary penalties applied to vehicle manufacturers that violated fuel-economy standards. In May 2019, Judge Haywood Gilliam Jr., a Democratic appointee to the court for the Northern District of California, rejected the EPA's proposals to delay implementation of Obama-era requirements to limit methane releases from sanitary landfills. Gilliam dismissed the EPA's claim that states lacked legal standing to file suit against the agency, noting that "just as Congress afforded Massachusetts a right to challenge EPA's decision not to regulate greenhouse-gas emissions, Congress afforded the State Plaintiffs here the right to challenge EPA's failure to perform its discretionary duty."[53] In March 2020, Senior Judge William Shubb for the U.S. District Court for the Eastern District of California, a George W. Bush appointee, rejected the Trump administration's claim that California's cap-and-trade agreement with Québec violated constitutional provisions on treaties with foreign powers.

Republican and Democratic judges have, to a degree, also checked the initiatives of the Trump administrative presidency in the education arena. In the case of higher education, for instance, two former students at a for-profit college sued the Department of Education over its delay in implementing a 2016 Obama administration rule restricting this educational sector and bolstering the rights of student borrowers. Judge Randolph Moss, a Democratic appointee on the D.C. federal district court, sided with the plaintiffs in October 2018, ordering rule implementation, even though a for-profit group still had a suit pending that challenged it.[54]

Another higher education case involved the Great Lakes Educational Loan Services organization, an entity under contract with the Department of Education to service student loans (for example, receive payments, negotiate new payment schedules). In March 2018, the Trump administration published an official *Federal Register* "interpretation" that state laws were preempted and did not offer an avenue of relief for student borrowers who believed loan service contractors had misled or defrauded them.[55] Whether this view would prevail came to a head when borrower Nicole Nelson sued the contractor, Great Lakes Educational Loan Services, on grounds that it had provided her with deceptive information that harmed her financially. She pursued the litigation under an Illinois law forbidding misrepresentation and fraud. Nelson lost in a federal district court presided over by a judge whom President Obama had nominated. She then appealed this decision to the Seventh Circuit Court of Appeals, where a three-judge panel (one Democrat and two

Republicans) reversed the district court's support of federal preemption and remanded the case to it for further deliberation.[56]

The Forces of Federalism

In a system built on federalism, states and localities may check or facilitate the power of an administrative presidency. The three policy cases in this book point to two major pathways in this regard. The first stresses the increasingly central role of coalitions of state attorneys general in rallying the courts to strike down presidential initiatives. The second focuses on the role of top state government policymakers, including governors, state agency heads, and legislators. The influence of these policymakers substantially, though not completely, depends on their role as major implementing agents of federal programs. Partisan polarization strongly shapes the nature and degree to which the two pathways check or facilitate the power of the administrative presidency.

Chapter 1 highlighted the growing influence of state attorneys general in American politics and governance over the last three decades. This development partly stems from court willingness to grant them standing and the legal doctrine that a single district court ruling may apply to the entire country rather than just the geographic area in which the court has jurisdiction. It also reflects the realization of private interests that it makes sense to support and cooperate with these attorneys general to advance their policy goals.

From the perspective of democracy, federalism, and the administrative presidency, the activities of state attorneys general have special status. The cases they bring to court typically assert that presidential executive actions violate the law, constitutional or otherwise. "Legal realism" devotees may portray their litigation as yet another manifestation of one set of partisans appealing to a likeminded set of "politicians in robes." But, as discussed, other evidence holds out more hope that nonpartisan interpretations of law may prevail and more genuinely serve democratic values. It is, of course, important to remember that state attorneys general are not alone in using the courts to advance their concepts of law. Private parties have filed suit to block initiatives of the administrative presidency in all three of the policy arenas assessed in this book.

In our three policy cases, state attorneys general actively sought to shape policy outcomes via court litigation. In the health care arena, coalitions of Democratic attorneys general sued to block the Trump administration's public charge and association health plan initiatives. Even more dramatically, they became substitutes for the White House–dominated Justice Department in defending federal law and executive branch discretion. When the Trump administration refused to defend the executive branch's right to make cost sharing reduction payments to insurers and, more important, ACA constitutionality, Democratic state attorneys general stepped in to support federal law and executive discretion. In turn, Republican state attorneys general have substantially served Trump administration preferences by seeking to destroy the entire ACA through court litigation.[57]

Democratic state attorneys general have also vigorously challenged Trump initiatives to weaken Obama climate policies. In the electricity sector, Democratic attorneys general from twenty-two states and lawyers from the Democratic-led District of Columbia and six major cities announced plans in August 2019 to combat the Trump administration's ACE rule in court. They argued that the administration was violating CAA provisions requiring use of the "best system" of emissions reduction.[58] "Without significant course correction, we are careening towards a climate disaster," said New York Attorney General Letitia James. "Rather than staying the course with policies aimed at fixing the problem and protecting people's health, safety, and the environment, the Trump Administration repealed the Clean Power Plan and replaced it with this 'Dirty Power' rule."[59]

In the transportation sector, California Attorney General Xavier Becerra led other Democratic attorneys general in early 2019 challenging the Trump administration's proposed initiative to withdraw the state's emission control waiver. This opening salvo preceded the Trump administration's September 2019 issuance of a final rule that preempted California and revoked its waiver. This action triggered a subsequent suit in D.C. federal district court from Becerra, twenty-two other Democratic state attorneys general, and lawyers for the District of Columbia. In *California v. Chao*, the plaintiffs declared the Trump action was "unlawful" and "contravenes Congressional intent," further contending that "the California standards at issue in this case are longstanding and fundamental parts of many State Plaintiffs' effort to protect public health and welfare in their states, to meet state goals for the reduction of harmful air pollution including greenhouse gases, and to attain or maintain federal air quality standards."[60]

State attorneys general also played a significant albeit less dramatic role in the education arena. In an amicus brief filed in the Eleventh Circuit Court of Appeals, twenty Democratic state attorneys general supported the rights of a Florida transgender student to use the boys' bathroom at school. Likewise, when the Trump administration stopped processing cancellation claims primarily from students who had attended for-profit institutions of postsecondary education in early 2017, eighteen Democratic state attorneys general along with the District of Columbia sued the Department of Education. The federal district court sided with the states, finding the actions of the department to be "arbitrary and capricious" under the Administrative Procedure Act.

While state attorneys general may serve democratic values by substantially checking an overweening administrative presidency and promoting the rule of law, their growing activism over the last three decades has prompted concern. A leading expert on this development, Paul Nolette, observes that the litigation advanced by these attorneys general proceeds in highly technical, complex "venues largely shielded from normal democratic process. Unlike policymaking in legislatures or administrative agencies . . . policymaking is largely conducted behind closed doors."[61] He further notes that litigation may undermine the "healthy dialogue" associated with the "ordinary politics" of the policy process dominated by governors and state legislatures. Litigation as a form of "state policymaking limits dialogue more than it promotes it." The "end goal is not negotiation and compromise" but to promote "one particular vision" of sound policy rooted in "the winner-take-all nature of active litigation."[62] Such court action may yield policy impacts far different than those that ordinary politics would produce, including more active engagement from Congress in adopting and revising legislation. Concerns such as these warrant serious consideration, even though others might bemoan that intense partisan polarization in many states yields an ordinary politics featuring very little healthy dialogue and negotiation.[63] Regardless, from the perspective of checking an administrative presidency pursuing initiatives that threaten the rule of law, the potentially sanguine role of state attorneys general (typically from the opposing political party) deserves emphasis. They may be especially significant in offering a partisan alternative to the presidential party, particularly during prolonged periods of congressional inertia.

As indicated throughout this book, the actions of governors, legislators, and other state officials engaged in "ordinary politics" may check or facilitate the administrative presidency. With politics increasingly becoming "national," a president can usually count on state policymakers from his own party to promote his agenda and those from the opposing party to undermine it. For instance, the climate policy sphere features a "tale of two climate nations" among states, with deep divides among them generally following partisan divisions. State policymakers may deter implementation of the president's policy initiatives while awaiting court decisions on their legality. For instance, the great majority of states (especially, but not exclusively, those controlled by Democrats) did not propose Medicaid work requirement waivers in the period prior to the lower court ruling invalidating them. To be sure, state policymakers from both parties at times provide few if any safeguards from the perspective of advancing the rule of law. They often prefer permissive interpretations of federal statutes that push the envelope in terms of enhancing their discretion to implement federal programs. They, at times, cooperate with the administrative presidency to reshape and even violate federal law.[64] On other occasions, they drag their feet or refuse to implement perfectly lawful federal initiatives. On balance, however, state elected officials from the opposition party to the president often apply brakes to extreme executive decisions that are, or border on being, lawless. In this respect, they serve the values of democracy in an era of aggressive administrative presidencies prone to expansive interpretations of the law amid general congressional drift.

Conclusion

This book has explored the potential and limitations of the administrative presidency as a vehicle for policy transformation under conditions of hostile takeover where the forces of federalism loom large. In two policy arenas, health care and climate, the Trump administration pursued radical, unprecedented actions to destroy the policies of its predecessor. In a third, education, it took more incremental measures to reverse certain Obama-era policies. On balance, the Trump administration scored some victories, but oppositional states and the courts had done much by the end of its third year to delay and block its policy reversal efforts. To be sure, the Trump administration may ultimately win decisively. Legal dynamics it has facilitated may foster Supreme Court decisions that destroy the ACA and cripple EPA capacity to reduce greenhouse gas emissions under the CAA. Reversing such decisions would require congressional legislation rather than executive actions by a subsequent president.

Elections, of course, matter. A second Trump term would provide him additional opportunities to launch new initiatives to realize his policy goals. Of paramount importance, he would continue to shape the partisan composition of the federal judiciary. To the degree that his appointees behave as partisans in robes, the impact of his administrative presidency on health care, climate, and education could become substantial. If the Democrats win the White House in 2020, the achievements of the Trump administrative presidency would likely be much more modest. While it would take time and effort to reverse Trump administrative rules and other measures, a Democratic president would have the executive tools needed to attempt to do so. Barring major court defeats, a Democratic president could take steps to revitalize the ACA, enlist the EPA to fight greenhouse gas emissions, and strengthen the federal role in education to curb abuses by for-profit colleges, promote student rights, and advance other Obama-era goals.

Beyond the policy consequences of the Trump administrative presidency are issues of democracy. Under Trump, Frederick C. Mosher's concern, introduced in chapter 1, about agency professionals being on top rather than on tap has morphed into concern about how to keep the administrative presidency safe for democracy. Mosher's view conforms to traditional political science concerns that the core problem is one of assuring that administrative agents are responsive to their elected political principals. In this vein, the rise of the aggressive, partisan, multifaceted administrative presidency was seen by some as serving democratic accountability. But the Trump administrative presidency vividly illustrates how political principals, rather than administrative agents, can threaten democracy.[65]

Going forward, chief executives regardless of party are likely to pursue assertive administrative presidencies, particularly if Congresses led by either party continue to struggle to provide clear and timely direction on key policy issues through legislation. If so, one can hope that the forces of federalism and the courts remain important checks on presidential power. Even more fundamentally, we can hope that future presidents possess a deep and abiding commitment to the norms of forbearance and mutual toleration needed to sustain American democracy.

Notes

Chapter 1

1. Robert Pear, "Health Chief Hears It from Democrats on Benefits," *New York Times*, June 13, 2018, p. A14.

2. Maggie Haberman and Robert Pear, "Fiery Meeting Swayed Trump in Health Fight," *New York Times*, March 28, 2019, p. A1.

3. Benjamin J. Hulac, "John Dingell's Towering and Complicated Environmental Legacy," *Roll Call*, February 8, 2019.

4. Lisa Friedman, "Trump Wants to Repeal Obama's Climate Plan," *New York Times,* September 28, 2017 (www.nytimes.com/2017/09/28/climate/clean-power-plan.html).

5. Executive Order 13791 *Enforcing Statutory Prohibitions on Federal Control of Education,* April 26, 2017.

6. Joy Resmovits, "What Does Trump's Executive Order in Education Do? Not Much," *Los Angeles Times*, April 26, 2017.

7. Clyde Wayne Crews Jr., "New Trump Executive Orders Spotlight Interior and Education 'Regulatory Dark Matter,'" *Forbes*, April 27, 2017.

8. Francis E. Lee, *Insecure Majorities* (University of Chicago Press, 2016); Thomas E. Mann and Norman Ornstein, *It's Even Worse Than It Looks* (New York: Basic Books, 2012).

9. Philip Wallach, "Congress Indispensable," *National Affairs* (Winter 2018), pp. 19–32.

10. Suzanne Mettler, "The Policyscape and the Challenges of Contemporary Politics to Policy Maintenance," *Perspectives on Politics* 14, no. 2 (June 2016), pp. 369–90 (doi.org/10.1017/S1537592716000074).

11. See David Epstein and Sharon O'Halloran, *Delegating Powers* (Cambridge University Press, 1999); Eric A. Posner and Adrian Vermuele, *The Executive Unbound* (Oxford University Press, 2010).

12. Frederick C. Mosher, *Democracy and the Public Service* (Oxford University Press, 1968).

13. Evan Osnos, "Trump vs. the 'Deep State'," *New Yorker*, May 21, 2018, p. 3 (www.newyorker.com/magazine/2018/05/21/trump-vs-the-deep-state).

14. For a discussion of agency ideologies, see, for instance, David Lewis, Patricia Bernhard, and Emily You, "President Trump as Manager: Reflections on the First Year," *Presidential Studies Quarterly* 48, no. 3 (2018), pp. 480–501.

15. Given this definition, a newly elected Democratic president replacing a Republican counterpart would likely not meet our criteria for engaging in a hostile takeover, at least in our three policy spheres. While she would strive to mitigate and reverse the executive actions of her Republican predecessor, she would be sympathetic to the core ideologies and objectives of the agency or program. In a sense, the takeover would be "restorative," although it would also entail aggressive uses of executive power.

16. Sidney M. Milkis and Nicholas Jacobs, "'I Alone Can Fix It' Donald Trump, the Administrative Presidency. And Hazards of Executive-Centered Partisanship," *The Forum* 15, no. 3 (2017), pp. 587–88 (doi.org/10.1515/for-2017-0037).

17. Richard P Nathan, *The Administrative Presidency* (New York: Macmillan, 1983).

18. Elena Kagan, "Presidential Administration," *Harvard Law Review* 114 (2001), p. 2277.

19. Robert F. Durant, *The Administrative Presidency Revisited* (State University of New York Press, 1992), p. 4.

20. Various scholars have focused on these tools of the administrative presidency. See, for instance, Nathan, *The Administrative Presidency*; Richard Waterman, *Presidential Influence and the Administrative State* (University of Tennessee Press, 1989); Durant, *The Administrative Presidency Revisited*; David Lewis, *The Politics of Presidential Appointments* (Princeton University Press, 2008).

21. William Howell, *Power Without Persuasion* (Princeton University Press, 2003), p. 175; see also, Phillip J. Cooper, *By Order of the President* (University Press of Kansas, 2003).

22. William G. Resh, *Rethinking the Administrative Presidency* (Johns Hopkins University Press, 2015), p. 27.

23. Kagan, "Presidential Administration," p. 2248.

24. Ibid., pp. 2281, 2293.

25. Frank J. Thompson, *Medicaid Politics: Federalism, Policy Durability, and Health Reform* (Georgetown University Press, 2012), chapter 5.

26. Resh, *Rethinking the Administrative Presidency*, p. 31.

27. William G. Howell, "Unilateral Powers: A Brief Overview," *Presidential Studies Quarterly* 35, no. 3 (2005), pp. 434–35.

28. Richard W. Waterman, "The Administrative Presidency, Unilateral Power, and the Unitary Executive Theory," *Presidential Studies Quarterly* 39, no. 1 (2009), pp. 5–9.

29. Milkis and Jacobs, "'I Alone Can Fix It'," p. 609; see, also, Louis Fisher, *President Obama: Constitutional Aspirations and Executive Actions* (University Press of Kansas, 2018).

30. Andrew Rudalevige, "The Obama Administration Presidency: Some Late-Term Patterns," *Presidential Studies Quarterly* 46, no. 4 (June 2016), p. 870 (doi.org/10.1111/psq.12323).

31. Jerry Mashaw and David Berke, "Presidential Administration in a Regime of Separated Powers," *Yale Journal of Regulation* 35 (2018), p. 594.

32. Kagan, "Presidential Administration," p. 2321.

33. Mashaw and Berke, "Presidential Administration," pp. 577, 593, 608.

34. John Hudak, *Presidential Pork* (Brookings Institution Press, 2014); Douglas L. Kriner and Andrew Reeves, *The Particularistic President* (Cambridge University Press, 2015).

35. Kenneth Wong, "Federal ESEA Waivers as Reform Leverage: Politics and Variation in State Implementation," *Publius: The Journal of Federalism* 45, no. 3 (2015), pp. 405–26.

36. Frank J. Thompson and Michael K. Gusmano, "The Administrative Presidency and Fractious Federalism: The Case of Obamacare," *Publius: The Journal of Federalism* 44, no. 3 (2014), pp. 369–98 (doi.org/10.1093/publius/pju011).

37. Thomas Gais and James Fossett. "Federalism and the Executive Branch," in *The Executive Branch,* edited by Joel D. Aberbach and Mark A. Peterson (Oxford University Press, 2005), pp. 486–524.

38. Barry Rabe, "Environmental Policy and the Bush Era: The Collision between the Administrative Presidency and State Experimentation," *Publius: The Journal of Federalism* 27, no. 3 (2007), pp. 413–31 (doi.org/10.1093/publius/pjm007).

39. Some states that declined to run the insurance exchanges authorized by the ACA passed laws that made it difficult for federally supported navigators to assist those seeking to enroll on the exchanges.

40. Paul Nolette, "The Dual Role of State Attorneys General in American Federalism: Conflict and Cooperation in an Era of Partisan Polarization," *Publius: The Journal of Federalism* 47, no. 3 (2017), pp. 342–77 (doi.org/10.1093/publius/pjx036).

41. Nolette ("The Dual Role," pp. 364–70) notes this pattern of "cooperative federalism" on such matters as criminal law, fraud by the pharmaceutical industry, and abuses by for-profit educational institutions.

42. Nolette, "The Dual Role," pp. 344–45, 355; see also, Samuel Bray, "Multiple Chancellors: Reforming the National Injunction," *Harvard Law Review* 131, no. 2 (2017), pp. 417–82.

43. Durant, *The Administrative Presidency Revisited.*

44. See, for instance, Joshua B. Kennedy, "The Limits of Presidential Influence: Two Environmental Directives and What They Mean for Executive Power," *Journal of Policy History* 30, no. 1 (2018), pp. 1–24.

45. For instance, Kennedy ("The Limits to Presidential Influence") focuses on the implementation of two environmental executive orders, one issued during the last year of the Reagan administration concerning property takings and the other issued during the second year of the George W. Bush administration promoting cooperative conservation. See also, William F. West, "The Administrative Presidency as Supervised Collaboration: The Case of Ocean and Coastal Zone Management," *Congress & the Presidency* 44, no. 1 (2017), pp. 1–28 (doi.org/10.1080/07343469.2016.1259276).

46. Eric Patashnik, *Reforms at Risk: What Happens after Major Policy Changes Are Elected* (Princeton University Press, 2008).

47. This figure includes New Jersey, which switched from divided government to Democratic control after a 2017 election; the numbers do not include the District of Columbia (https://ballotpedia.org/Attorneys_General_(state_executive_office)).

48. Michael Lewis, *The Fifth Risk* (New York: W. W. Norton, 2018).

49. David Frum, *Trumpocracy* (New York: HarperCollins, 2018), p. 78.

50. Kathryn Dunn Tenpas, "White House Staff Turnover in Year One of the Trump Administration: Context, Consequences, and Implications for Governing," *Presidential Studies Quarterly* 48, no. 3 (2018), pp. 502–16.

51. Frum, *Trumpocracy*, pp. 78, 99.

52. Michael Nelson, *Trump's First Year* (University of Virginia Press, 2018), p. 149.

53. Lewis and others, "President Trump as Manager," p. 496.

54. The remaining categories of appointments included 680 noncareer positions of the Senior Executive Service, 1,400 lower-level Schedule C jobs, and 350 higher-level posts (primarily in the White House) that did not require Senate confirmation. Zach Parker, "Help Wanted: 4,000 Presidential Appointees," March 16, 2016 (http://presidentialtransition.org/blog/posts/160 316_help-wanted-4000-appointees.php).

55. Nelson, *Trump's First Year*, p. 47.

56. Kathryn Watson, "Report: Office Responsible for Vetting Trump Appointees Plagued by Personnel Problems," March 30, 2018 (www.cbsnews.

com/news/report-office-responsible-for-vetting-trump-appointees-plagued-by -personnel-problems-report/).

57. Lewis and others, "President Trump as Manager."

58. "Tracking How Many Key Positions Trump Has Filled So Far," *Washington Post*, June 28, 2018 (www.washingtonpost.com/graphics/politics/trump -administration-appointee-tracker/database/).

59. Mashaw and Berke, "Presidential Administration," p. 605.

60. Nelson, *Trump's First Year*, p. 30.

61. Mashaw and Berke, "Presidential Administration," pp. 551, 607.

62. Nelson, *Trump's First Year*, p. 42.

63. Mashaw and Berke, "Presidential Administration," p. 603.

64. Our collaboration on this volume rested on three practicalities. First, the three of us had enjoyed collegial relations for decades, fortifying our sense that we would have a productive partnership as coauthors. Second, each coauthor had studied and written about policy evolution in one of the three arenas over an extended period—Thompson on health care, Rabe on climate, and Wong on education. None of us had studied immigration policy. Third, we believed, as did our publisher, that a shorter book would more likely reach a larger audience. We invite other scholars to consider using our framework to study Trump-era policies for immigration and other areas not examined in these pages.

65. Annie Correal, " 'Sanctuary' Can Be Reason To Block Grants, A Court Rules," *New York Times*, February 27, 2020, p. A21.

66. Zolan Kanno-Youngs, "ICE Arrests Away From Border Decline 10%," *New York Times*, December 12, 2019, p. A17.

67. Gary Reich, "Hitting a Wall? The Trump Administration Meets Immigration Federalism," *Publius: The Journal of Federalism* 48, no. 3 (2018), pp. 372–95 (doi.org/10.1093/publius/pjy013).

68. Kirk Semple, "Violence Drives Surge in Mexican Migrants at U.S. Border," *New York Times*, December 8, 2019, p. A8.

69. Ibid.

Chapter 2

1. The ACA requires large employers to offer full-time employees and their families a health insurance plan that provides certain essential coverage. Firms can require employees to contribute to their premium costs, but the amount cannot exceed just under 10 percent of their household incomes. Employers that fail to comply will typically be subject to a financial penalty.

2. For an overview, see Nicholas Bagley, "Legal Limits and the Implementation of the Affordable Care Act," *University of Pennsylvania Law Review* 164 (2016), pp. 1715–52.

3. Frank J. Thompson, *Medicaid Politics: Federalism, Policy Durability, and Health Reform* (Georgetown University Press, 2012), pp. 101–66.

4. The following description draws heavily on Frank J. Thompson, Michael K. Gusmano, and Shugo Shinohara, "Trump and the Affordable Care Act: Congressional Repeal Efforts, Executive Federalism, and Program Durability," *Publius: The Journal of Federalism* 48, no. 3 (2018), pp. 396–424.

5. Waiver states often feature practices consistent with both themes but tend to stress one or the other.

6. Another variant of this approach, which has affected fewer enrollees, uses Medicaid monies to subsidize an enrollee's employer-sponsored insurance.

7. A newly elected Democratic governor terminated the waiver in 2015.

8. In addition to approving market-oriented waivers, the Obama administration used the waiver renewal process to motivate resistant states to expand Medicaid. In particular, it strove to phase out waivers that allowed states to divert Medicaid monies into subsidies for hospitals rather than insurance for individuals. The Obama administration saw no need to continue these subsidies when states could address problems of uncompensated care by expanding Medicaid.

9. Frank J. Thompson and Michael K. Gusmano, "The Administrative Presidency and Fractious Federalism: The Case of Obamacare," *Publius: The Journal of Federalism* 44, no. 3 (2014), pp. 439–40.

10. Five of these states relied on the federal enrollment platform.

11. Michael A. Morrisey, Alice M. Rivlin, Richard P. Nathan, and Mark A. Hall, *Five-State Study of ACA Marketplace Competition* (Brookings Center for Health Policy, 2017). Each state has rating areas (typically counties or clusters of counties). Insurance company participation and the premiums they charged varied considerably from one rating area to the next.

12. *United States House of Representatives v. Sylvia Matthews Burwell*, Opinion in the U.S. District Court for the District of Columbia, Civil Action No. 14-1967 (RMC), May 12, 2016.

13. Daniel Béland, Philip Rocco, and Alex Waddan, *Obamacare Wars* (University Press of Kansas, 2016), p. 124.

14. Steven Brill, *America's Bitter Pill* (New York: Random House, 2015), p. 366.

15. Charles Gaba, "How Many Grandfathered or Transitional Plans Are Still Around Anyway?" February 24, 2016 (http://acasignups.net/16/03/24/how-many-grandfathered-or-transitional-plans-are-still-around-anyway); "Consumers Can Keep 'Grandfathered' Plans for One More Year, CMS Says," February 27, 2017 (www.advisory.com/daily-briefing/2017/02/27/grandfathered).

16. U.S. Census Bureau, *Income, Poverty, and Health Insurance Coverage in the United States: 2010* (Washington, D.C., 2011); *Health Insurance Coverage in the United States: 2016* (Washington, D.C., 2017).

17. Some scholars contend that this reflected a strategic decision to down-

play climate change to boost his re-election prospects, thereby increasing the risk that his subsequent administrative reforms would face a shortened time window for completion during his lame-duck term. Bethany Davis Noll and Richard Revesz, "Regulation in Transition," *University of Minnesota Law Review* 104, no. 1 (November 2019), p. 48.

18. Barack Obama, Second Inaugural Address, January 21, 2013.

19. Norma Riccucci, *Policy Drift: Shared Powers and the Making of U.S. Law and Policy* (New York University Press, 2018), pp. 170–72.

20. David G. Victor, *The Collapse of the Kyoto Protocol and the Struggle to Slow Global Warming* (Princeton University Press, 2001).

21. Barry G. Rabe, "The Aversion to Direct Cost Imposition: Selecting Climate Policy Tools in the United States," *Governance: An International Journal of Policy, Administration, and Institutions* 23, no. 4 (October 2010), pp. 583–608.

22. John D. Graham, *Obama on the Home Front: Domestic Policy Triumphs and Setbacks* (Indiana University Press, 2016).

23. Ann Carlson and Dallas Burtraw, editors, *Lessons from the Clean Air Act: Building Durability and Adaptability into U.S. Climate and Energy Policy* (Cambridge University Press, 2019); Richard E. Cohen, *Washington at Work: Back Rooms and Clean Air* (Boston: Allyn and Bacon, 1992).

24. Charles O. Jones, *Clean Air: Policies and Politics of Pollution Control* (University of Pittsburgh Press, 1975); William R. Lowry, *The Dimensions of Federalism: State Governments and Pollution Control Policies* (Duke University Press, 1992).

25. Barry G. Rabe, "Leveraged Federalism and the Clean Air Act," in *Lessons from the Clean Air Act,* chapter 4.

26. Rabe, "Leveraged Federalism and the Clean Air Act"; Emily Upton and Thomas Van Heeke, "Federalism and California's Role in Light-Duty and Heavy-Duty Vehicle Emission Standards," *Issues in Energy and Environmental Policy,* no. 36 (July 2018), pp. 1–22 (http://closup.umich.edu/files/ieep-20 18-california-emissions.pdf).

27. *Massachusetts et al. v. Environmental Protection Agency et al.,* 594 U.S. 497 (2007).

28. Ibid.

29. Norman J. Vig, "Presidential Powers and Environmental Policy," in *Environmental Policy: New Directions for the Twenty-First Century*, edited by Vig and Michael E. Kraft (Washington, D.C.: SAGE/CQ Press, 2019), p. 102.

30. On the political evolution of this program and its profound differences from the CAA, see Pietro Nivola, "The Long and Winding Road: Automotive Fuel Economy and American Politics," in *Greenhouse Governance: Addressing Climate Change in America*, edited by Barry G. Rabe (Brooking Institution Press, 2010), pp. 260–85.

31. *Green Mountain Chrysler Plymouth Dodge Jeep v. Crombie,* 508 F. Supp. 2d 295 (D. Vt. 2007).

32. Rabe, "Leveraged Federalism and the Clean Air Act," pp. 139–40.

33. Official miles per gallon routinely exceed actual driving experience. Federal measures are linked to testing under laboratory conditions, whereas actual driving includes use of air conditioning, speeds exceeding official limits, idling during traffic delays, and numerous other behaviors that reduce fuel efficiency. Official standards of fifty-five miles per gallon were expected to translate into the mid-thirties range of actual experience given these differences.

34. Twenty-three states adopted carbon cap-and-trade programs between 2002 and 2009, concentrated in three regions. However, thirteen repealed their commitments between 2010 and 2012, leaving only California and nine Northeastern states still committed to electricity sector reductions through this policy at the point that the CPP was introduced. New Jersey joined the Northeastern effort in 2019, making it the eleventh state with cap-and-trade. Democratic governors in Pennsylvania and Virginia expressed support for taking such a step but faced considerable opposition in their legislatures in 2019. Barry G. Rabe, *Can We Price Carbon?* (MIT Press, 2018).

35. Paul Manna, *Collision Course: Federal Education Policy Meets State and Local Realities* (Washington, D.C.: CQ Press, 2010).

36. Frederick Hess and Michael Petrilli, *No Child Left Behind Primer* (New York: Peter Lang Publishing, 2006); *No Remedy Left Behind*, edited by Frederick Hess and Chester Finn Jr. (Washington, D.C.: American Enterprise Institute Press, 2007); David Cohen and Susan Moffitt, *The Ordeal of Equality* (Harvard University Press, 2009).

37. Kenneth K. Wong and Anna Nicotera, *Successful Schools and Educational Accountability* (Boston: Pearson Education, 2007).

38. Cynthia Brown and others, *State Education Agencies as Agents of Change* (Washington, D.C.: Center for American Progress, 2011).

39. James Kim and Gail Sunderman, "Measuring Academic Proficiency under No Child Left Behind: Implications for Educational Equity," *Educational Researcher* 34, no. 8 (2005), pp. 3–13.

40. The two entities are similar to the Australian Curriculum Assessment and Reporting Authority.

41. U.S. Department of Education, *Non-Regulatory Guidance on Title I, Part A Waivers* (Washington, D.C., 2009).

42. C. J. Bowling and J. M. Pickerill, "Fragmented Federalism: The State of American Federalism 2012–13," *Publius: The Journal of Federalism* 43, no. 3 (2013), pp. 315–46.

43. S. Gramkhar and J. M. Pickerill, "The State of American Federalism 2011–2012: A Fend for Yourself and Activist Form of Bottom-Up Federalism," *Publius: The Journal of Federalism* 42, no. 3 (2013), pp. 357–86.

44. Center on Education Policy, *States' Perspectives on Waivers: Relief from NCLB, Concern about Long-Term Solutions* (Washington, D.C., 2013).

45. Wayne Riddle, *Major Accountability Themes of Initial State Applications for NCLB Waivers* (Washington, D.C.: Center on Education Policy, 2011).

46. Sean Whaley, "Feds Approve Nevada Waiver from No Child Left Behind," *Record Courier*, August 8, 2012 (www.recordcourier.com/article /20120808/NEWS/120809916/1062&ParentProfile=1049).

47. Kenneth K. Wong and Meaghan Reilly, "Education Waivers as Reform Leverage in the Obama Administration: State Implementation of ESEA Flexibility Waiver Request," Paper delivered at the annual meeting of the American Political Science Association, 2014.

48. Andrew Saultz, Lance D. Fusarelli, and Andrew McEachin, "The Every Student Succeeds Act, the Decline of the Federal Role in Education Policy, and the Curbing of Executive Authority," *Publius: The Journal of Federalism* 47, no. 3 (2017), pp. 426–44.

49. Approved in 1972, Title IX prohibits discrimination based on sex in any federally funded education program or activity.

50. Helene Cooper, "Obama Aims at Disparity in Education," *New York Times* (New York edition), April 7, 2011, p. A16.

51. U.S. Department of Interior, American Indian Education Study Group, "Proposal to Redesign the U.S. Department of Interior's Bureau of Indian Education: Findings and Recommendations" (Washington, D.C., June 6, 2014).

52. Ibid.

53. Doug Lederman and Paul Fain, "The Higher Education President," *Inside Higher Ed,* January 19, 2017 (www.insidehighered.com/news/2017 /01/19/assessing-president-obamas-far-reaching-impact-higher-education).

54. Suzanne Mettler, *Degrees of Inequality* (New York: Basic Books, 2014), p. 146.

55. Ibid., pp. 147, 156–57.

56. Under Obama, the Department of Education's Office of Civil Rights issued thirty-four Dear Colleague letters, more than all prior presidential administrations combined. R. Shep Melnick, *The Transformation of Title IX: Regulating Gender Equality in Education* (Washington, D.C.: Brookings Institution Press, 2018), p. 73.

57. Ibid.

58. Ibid., p. 215.

59. Mettler, *Degrees of Inequality*, p. 95.

60. Ibid., pp. 1, 29.

61. Ibid., p. 98.

62. Ibid., pp. 104–06.

63. Jesse Naranjo and Michelle Hackman, "Lawmakers Eye Loophole on For-Profit Colleges' Funding," *Wall Street Journal*, August 19, 2019, p. A3.

64. Quoted in James Ottavio Castagnera, "The Decline in For-Profit Higher Education during the Obama Administration and Its Prospects in the Trump Presidency," *Industry & Higher Education* 31, no. 4 (2017), p. 244.

65. Robin Howarth and Lisa Stifler, *The Failings of Online for-Profit Colleges: Findings from Student Borrower Focus Groups* (report), Brookings Institution, March 28, 2019.

Chapter 3

1. *City of Columbus et al. v. Donald J. Trump et al.* In the United States District Court for the District of Maryland, Case No. 18-CV-2364, filed August 2, 2018, p. 4.

2. Article 4, Section 3 of the Constitution.

3. Frank J. Thompson, Michael K. Gusmano, and Shugo Shinohara, "Trump and the Affordable Care Act: Congressional Repeal Efforts, Executive Federalism, and Program Durability," *Publius: The Journal of Federalism* 48, no. 3 (2018), pp. 396–424.

4. For instance, Democrats in the House of Representatives introduced a bill called the Undo Sabotage and Expand Affordability of Health Insurance Act of 2018. Ariel Cohen, "E&C to Examine Bills to Fix ACA via Reinsurance, More Exchange Funds," March 4, 2019 (https://insidehealthpolicy.com/daily-news/ec-examine-bills-fix-aca-reinsurance-more).

5. *Merriam-Webster Dictionary* (www.merriam-webster.com/dictionary/sabotage).

6. This section draws heavily on Thompson and others, "Trump and the Affordable Care Act," pp. 400–02.

7. The limit would derive from computing the average cost of five categories of Medicaid enrollees (for example, the elderly).

8. Congressional Budget Office, *The American Health Care Act* (Washington, D.C., 2017).

9. Ibid.

10. Congressional Budget Office, *H.R. 1628, Better Care Reconciliation of 2017* (Washington, D.C., 2017).

11. Rachel Garfield, Larry Levitt, Robin Rudowitz, and Gary Claxton, *State-by-State Estimates of Changes in Federal Spending on Health Care under the Graham Cassidy Bill* (Washington, D.C.: Kaiser Family Foundation, 2017).

12. Congressional Budget Office, *Preliminary Analysis of Legislation That Would Replace Subsidies for Health Care with Block Grants* (Washington, D.C., 2017).

13. Congressional Budget Office, *Repealing the Individual Health Insurance Mandate: An Updated Estimate* (Washington, D.C., 2017).

14. Tax effort equals total state and local revenues per capita from their

own resources divided by total taxable resources per capita with adjustments for federal tax write-offs or credits.

15. Congressional Joint Committee on Taxation, "Macroeconomic Analysis of the 'Tax Cut and Jobs Act' as Ordered by the Senate Committee on Finance on November 16, 2017" (Washington, D.C., 2017).

16. Jacob S. Hacker and Paul Pierson, "The Dog That Almost Barked: What the ACA Repeal Fight Says about the Resilience of the American Welfare State," *Journal of Health Politics, Policy, and Law* 43, no. 4 (2018), pp. 557, 558, 573.

17. Timothy Jost, "Trump Executive Order on ACA: What It Won't Do, What It Might Do, and When," *Health Affairs Blog*, January 20, 2017 (www.healthaffairs.org/do/10.1377/hblog20170121/..058405/full/).

18. Thompson and others, "Trump and the Affordable Care Act," p. 408.

19. Amy Lotven, "Nearly 200 Patient Groups Urge CMS To Restore Navigator Funding," July 24, 2018 (https://insidehealthpolicy.com/daily-news/nearly-200-patient-groups).

20. Amy Lotven, "Verma Dismisses California's Push for CMS to Boost Exchange Advertising," May 3, 2018 (https://insidehealthpolicy.com/daily-news/verma-dismisses-californias-push).

21. Amy Lotven, "Consumer Advocates Worried as CMS Relaxes ACA Navigator Standards," April 11, 2018 (https://insidehealthpolicy.com?daily-news/consumer-advocates-worried-cms-).

22. Thompson and others, "Trump and the Affordable Care Act," p. 408.

23. Robert Pear, "Late Surge in Insurance Enrollment Shows Health Law 'Far from Dead'," *New York Times*, December 20, 2018, p. A18.

24. Department of Health and Human Services, "Patient Protection and Affordable Care Act: Market Stabilization, Final Rule," *Federal Register* 83, no. 4 (April 18, 2017), pp. 18346–82.

25. Ibid., p. 18346.

26. Cynthia Cox, Ashley Semanskee, Gary Claxton, and Larry Levitt, *Explaining Health Care Reform: Risk Adjustment, Reinsurance, and Risk Corridors* (Washington, D.C.: Kaiser Family Foundation, 2016).

27. Rather than purchase health coverage for their employees from insurance companies, many large employers self-insure, setting aside their own funds to pay these medical expenses.

28. Amy Lotven, "Insurers Score Big Win in SCOTUS Risk Corridors Case," April 27, 2020 (https://insidehealthpolicy.com/daily-news/insurers-scorer-big-win-scotus-risk-corridors-case).

29. On December 31, 2019, a federal appeals court upheld the federal government's methodology for risk adjustment. Katie Keith, "Tenth Circuit Upholds HHS Risk Adjustment Methodology," *Health Affairs Blog*, January 1, 2020 (doi: 10.1377/hblog20191231.739669).

30. Timothy Jost, "California, New York Lead Group of States Seeking to Intervene in Legislation Over Cost-Sharing Reduction Payments, *Health Affairs Blog*, May 8, 2017 (http://healthaffirs.org/blog/2017/05/18/California-newyork-).

31. Ariel Cohen, "Left-Leaning Policy Groups Urge Congress to Tread Carefully on CSRs to Avoid Hiking Consumer Costs," March 12, 2018 (https://insidehealthpolicy.com/daily-news/left-leaning-policy-groups-urge-congress).

32. More specifically, the federal subsidy is linked to the premium cost of the second lowest priced silver plan offered on the exchanges.

33. The ACA provides this subsidized cohort with further protection from premium increases by imposing an upper limit on the percentage of a family's income it must spend on benchmark insurance premiums.

34. However, enrollees (those between 100 percent and 250 percent of poverty) can access CSR subsidies only if they opt for a silver plan. David Anderson and Adrianna McIntyre, "Policy Implications of Utah's Proposed Limited Medicaid Expansion," *Health Affairs Blog*, February 12, 2019 (doi: 10.1377/hblog20190212.230279).

35. Stan Dorn, "Silver Lining for Silver Loading," *Health Affairs Blog*, June 3, 2019 (doi: 10.1377/hblog20190530.156427).

36. Ariel Cohen, "CBO Adds Silver Loading to Baseline, Says Not Funding CSRs Would Increase Costs," April 10, 2018 (https://insidehealthpolicy.com/daily-news/cbo-adds-silver-loading-baseline-says).

37. Cohen, "Left-Leaning Policy Groups."

38. Amy Lotven, "CA Court Dismisses CSR Case; States Can Refile If CMS Scraps Silver-Loading," July 18, 2018 (https://insidehealthpolicy.com/daily-news/ca-court-dismisses-csr-case-).

39. This court hears monetary claims against the federal government based on the Constitution, statutes, executive regulations, and contracts.

40. Amy Lotven, "Florida Issuers Sue Over CSRs, Judge Seeks Comments on Stay," November 30, 2018 (https://insidehealthpolicy,com/daily-news/florida-issuers-sue-over-csrs-judge-).

41. Ariel Cohen, "Verma Noncommittal As Stakeholders Worry CMS May Ban Silver-Loading," November 27, 2018 (https://insidehealthpolicy.com/daily-news/verma-noncommittal-stakeholders-worry).

42. While these indicators of health insurance quality are particularly important, we make no claim that they comprise an exhaustive list. Other pertinent indicators would, for instance, include such factors as the scope and adequacy of an insurance plan's provider networks.

43. Executive Order 13813, *Federal Register* (October 17, 2017), p. 22677.

44. Departments of the Treasury, Labor, and Health and Human Services, "Short-Term, Limited Duration Insurance; Final Rule," *Federal Register* 83, no. 150 (August 3, 2018), pp. 38212–43.

45. Larry Levitt, Rachel Fehr, Gary Claxton, Cynthia Cox, and Karen

Pollitz, *Why Do Short-Term-Health Insurance Plans Have Lower Premiums than Plans that Comply with the ACA?* (Washington, D.C.: Kaiser Family Foundation, 2018).

46. *Association for Community Affiliated Plans et al. v. United States Department of the Treasury et al.* In the United States District Court for the District of Columbia, Civil Action 18-2133, filed September 14, 2018.

47. Ariel Cohen, "Judge Upholds Short-Term Plan Rule, Stakeholders to Appeal Ruling," July 19, 2019 (https://insidehealthpolicy.com/daily-news/judge-upholds-short-term-plan-rule-stakeholders).

48. The ACA had sought to incentivize small business to purchase ACA-compliant coverage for their employees by establishing a tax credit that absorbed half the cost to the employer of providing insurance. However, unlike large employers, small businesses face no federal penalty for failure to provide coverage. John E. McDonough, *Inside National Health Reform* (University of California Press, 2011), p. 115.

49. Katie Keith, "Final Rule Rapidly Eases Restrictions on Non-ACA-Compliant Association Health Plans," *Health Affairs Blog*, June 21, 2018 (www.healthaffairs.org/do/10.1377/hblog20180621.671483/full/), pp. 6–7.

50. Department of Labor, "Definition of 'Employer' Under Section 3(5) of ERISA–Association Health Plans," *Federal Register* 83, no. 20 (June 21, 2018), p. 28912–64.

51. Ibid., p. 28922.

52. Ibid, "Definition of Employer," pp. 28950–51.

53. *State of New York et al. v. U.S. Department of Labor.* In the U.S. District Court for the District of Columbia, Case 1:18-cv01747, filed July 26, 2018.

54. Ibid., p. 49.

55. Thomas E. Price, Letter to State Governors, Washington, D.C.: Office of the Secretary for Health and Human Services, March 2017.

56. Ariel Cohen, "CMS Shifts Focus of 1332 Waivers to Bolster Non-ACA Coverage," October 22, 2018 (https://insidehealthpolicy.com/daily-news/CMS.shifts.focus.of.1332.waivers).

57. Jennifer Tolbert and Karen Pollitz, *New Rules for Section 1332 Waivers: Changes and Implications* (Washington, D.C.: Kaiser Family Foundation, 2018). The authors also review other highly technical changes that would make it easier for states to win waiver approval.

58. Cohen, "CMS Shifts Focus of 1332 Waivers."

59. Robert Pear, "Policy Change Lets States Skirt Health-Act Basics," *New York Times*, October 23, 2018, p. A10.

60. Amy Lotven, "CMS RFI Seeks to Spur State Interest in Eased 1332 Waiver Criteria," May 1, 2019 (https://insidehealthpolicy.com/daily-news/cms-rfi-seeks-spur-states/).

61. Adam Liptak, "How Judge-Shopping in Texas Led to Ruling Against Health Law," *New York Times*, December 25, 2018, p. A17.

62. *Texas et al. v. United States of America, and California et al.* Federal Defendants' Memorandum in Response to Plaintiffs' Application in the U.S. District Court of the Northern District of Texas, Fort Worth Division, Case 4:18-CV-00167-0, June 7, 2018.

63. *Texas et al. v. United States,* Intervenor-Defendants' Brief in Opposition to Plaintiffs Application, pp. 1, 25.

64. Ibid., Intervenor Defendants, p. 3.

65. Jan Hoffman, Robert Pear, and Adam Liptak, "Scholars Say Ruling on Health Law Rests on Shaky Ground," *New York Times*, December 16, 2018, p. A16.

66. Maggie Haberman and Robert Pear, "Fiery Meeting Swayed Trump in Health Fight," *New York Times*, March 28, 2019, p. A1.

67. Brief for the Federal Defendants. *State of Texas et al. v. United States et al.* In the United States Court of Appeals for the Fifth Circuit. Case: 19-10011, Document: 00514939490, filed May 1, 2019, pp. 28, 37.

68. In the wake of the 2018 election, the number of plaintiff states had declined by two. Twenty-one states had by late 2019 intervened to uphold the ACA. Katie Keith, *"Texas v. United States*: Where Are We Now and What Could Happen Next," *Health Affairs Blog*, July 9, 2019 (doi: 10.11377/hblog20190709.772192), p. 5.

69. *Texas et al. v. United States et al., with California et al., as Intervenor Defendants*. In the United States Court of Appeals for the Fifth Circuit. Case: 19-10011, Document 00515242592, filed December 18, 2019.

70. Even if limited to the plaintiff states, a court ruling throwing out the ACA would presumably terminate ongoing Medicaid expansions in six states: Arkansas, Arizona, Indiana, Louisiana, North Dakota, and West Virginia.

71. Frank J. Thompson, *Medicaid Politics: Federalism, Policy Durability, and Health Reform* (Georgetown University Press, 2012).

72. Donald Moynihan, Pamela Herd, and Hope Harvey, "Administrative Burden: Learning, Psychological, and Compliance Costs in Citizen-State Interactions," *Journal of Public Administration Research and Theory* 25, no. 1 (2015), pp. 43–70.

73. Marybeth Musumeci, *Medicaid and Work Requirements* (Washington, D.C.: Kaiser Family Foundation, 2017).

74. Take-up rates equal the number of Medicaid enrollees divided by those in a population who could meet the eligibility criteria.

75. Speech: Remarks by Administrator Seema Verma at the National Association of Medicaid Directors (NAMD) 2017 Fall Conference, November 7, 2017 (www.cms.gov/Newsroom/MediaReleaseDatabase/Fact- sheets/2017).

76. Ibid.

77. Ariel Cohen, "CMS No Longer Lists Expanding Coverage as a Goal of 1115 Waivers," November 9, 2017 (https://insidehealthpolicy.com/daily-news/cms-no-longer-lists-expanding).

78. Centers for Medicare and Medicaid Services, "Opportunities to Promote Work and Community Engagement among Medicaid Beneficiaries," Letter to State Medicaid Directors, January 11, 2018.

79. Waiver requests from Alabama, Idaho, Mississippi, Montana, Oklahoma, South Dakota, Tennessee, and Virginia were pending at that time.

80. Kaiser Family Foundation, June 2017 (www.kff.org/health-reform-poll-finding/kaiser-health-tracking-poll-june-2017).

81. James Romoser, "Verma Signals Caution on Medicaid Work Requirements in Non-Expansion States," May 2, 2018 (https://insidehealth policy.com/daily-news/verma-signals-caution-medicaid-work-requirements).

82. Government Accountability Office, *Medicaid Demonstrations: Actions Need to Address Weaknesses in Oversight of Costs to Administer Work Requirements* (Washington, D.C., GAO-20-149, 2019).

83. *Gresham et al. v. Azar et al., Complaint for Declaratory and Injunctive Relief.* In the U.S. District Court for the District of Columbia, Case 1:18-cv-01900, filed August 14, 2018, pp. 18–19.

84. Robin Rudowitz, MaryBeth Musumeci, and Cornelia Hall, *A Look at November State Data for Medicaid Work Requirements in Arkansas* (Washington, D.C.: Kaiser Family Foundation, 2018).

85. Medicaid managed care organizations under contract with the state would bill for and collect the premiums.

86. *Stewart et al. v. Hargan et al., Class Action Complaint for Declaratory Injunctive Relief.* In the U.S. District Court for the District of Columbia Case 1:18-cv-00152, filed January 24, 2018, p. 26.

87. Government Accountability Office, *Medicaid Demonstrations: Actions Needed*, p. 38.

88. *Stewart et al. v. Hargan et al.*, pp. 1, 4.

89. Other targeted waiver provisions included cutting back on the statutory obligation to provide nonemergency transportation services for enrollees, the imposition of monetary penalties for enrollees seeking "non-urgent" care from hospital emergency rooms, and the denial of three-month retroactive coverage to the newly enrolled.

90. James Romoser, "Kentucky Joins DC Lawsuit Over Work Requirements; Reiterates Threat to End Its Medicaid Expansion," March 30, 2018 (https://insidehealthpolicy.com/daily-news/kentucky-joins-dc-lawsuit-over-work-).

91. *Ronnie Maurice Stewart et al. v. Alex M Azar et al., Memorandum Opinion.* In the United State District Court for the District of Columbia, Civil Action No. 18-152 (JEB), June 29, 2018, pp. 3, 32, 38.

92. James Romoser, "Kentucky Cuts Dental and Vision for a Half-Million Medicaid Beneficiaries," July 2, 2018 (https://insidehealthpolicy.com/daily-news/kentucky-cuts-dental-and-vision-half-million).

93. *Gresham et al. v. Azar et al.* In the U.S. District Court for the District of Columbia. Case 1:18-cv-01900, filed August 14, 2018.

94. CHIP stands for Children's Health Insurance Program, which provides federal grants to the states to insure children in families with incomes above the Medicaid eligibility threshold.

95. A bipartisan oversight and advisory body created by the ACA.

96. James Romoser, "MACPAC Alarmed by Initial Data on Arkansas Medicaid Work Requirements," September 14, 2018 (https://insidehealthpolicy. com/daily-news/macpac-alarmed-initial-data-arkansas).

97. James Romoser, "More Than 4,000 Arkansans Lose Medicaid Coverage in First Round of Disenrollments Due to Work Requirements," September 13, 2018 (https://insidehealthpolicy.com/daily-news/more-4000-arkansans-lose-medicaid).

98. James Romoser, "Verma, Responding Forcefully to Critics, Calls Medicaid Work Requirements Compassionate," September 27, 2018 (https:// insidehealthpolicy.com/daily-news/verma-responding-forcefully-critics-calls).

99. Rudowitz and others, *A Look at November State Data*.

100. Sara Rosenbaum, " 'We Have All Seen This Movie Before': Once Again, a Federal Court Vacates HHS Approval of a Medicaid Work Experiment," *Health Affairs Blog*, August 2, 2019 (doi:10.1377/hblog20190801.892432).

101. Department of Homeland Security, "Inadmissibility on Public Charge Grounds," Proposed Rule, *Federal Register* 83, no. 196 (October 10, 2018), pp. 51114–19.

102. Department of Homeland Security, "Inadmissibility on Public Charge Grounds," Final Rule, *Federal Register* 84, no. 157 (August 14, 2019), p. 41304.

103. Samantha Artiga, Rachel Garfield, and Anthony Damico, *Estimated Impacts of the Final Public Charge Inadmissibility Rule on Immigrants and Medicaid Coverage* (Washington, D.C.: Kaiser Family Foundation, September 2019).

104. James Romoser, "State Health Groups File Two More Lawsuits Over Public Charge Rule," August 20, 2019 (https://insidehealthpolicy.com/daily-news/state-health-groups-file-two-more-lawsuits).

105. Amy Lotven, "Subsidized ACA Plans Not Acceptable for Lawful Immigrant Entry," October 7, 2019 (https://insidehealthpolicy.com/daily-news/subsidized-aca-plans-not acceptable).

106. Annie Karni, "Plan to Alter How Poverty Is Calculated by Census," *New York Times*, May 8, 2019, p. A18.

107. Abby Goodnough, "Shift Allows States to Restrict Medicaid Benefits for Millions of People," *New York Times*, January 31, 2020, p. A21.

108. Michelle M. Stein, "CMS Plans Reg Overhaul of Medicaid Eligibility in Light of Improper Pay," November 22, 2019 (https://insidehealthpolicy. com/daily-news/cms-plans-reg-overhaul-medicaid-eligibility).

109. One estimate indicates that overturning the ACA would cause 17 million to lose coverage immediately. It may also set in play the erosion of

coverage for others, especially those with preexisting conditions. Lilliard E. Richardson Jr., "Medicaid Expansion during the Trump Presidency: The Role of Executive Waivers, State Ballot Measures, and Attorney General Lawsuits in Shaping Intergovernmental Relations," *Publius: The Journal of Federalism* 49, no. 3 (2019), p. 454.

110. Government Accountability Office, *Health Insurance Exchanges: Claims Costs and Federal and State Policies Drove Issuer Participation, Premiums, and Plan Design* (Washington, D.C., 2019), p. 25.

111. Rachel Fehr, Rabah Kamal, and Cynthia Cox, *Insurance Participation on ACA Marketplaces, 2014–2020* (Washington, D.C.: Kaiser Family Foundation, 2019).

112. Office of the Assistant Secretary for Planning and Evaluation, Department of Health and Human Services, *Health Plan Choices and Premiums in the 2018 Federal Health Insurance Exchange* (Washington, D.C., 2018), p. 8.

113. Rabah Kamal, Cynthia Cox, Rachel Fehr, Marco Ramirez, Katherine Horstman, and Larry Levitt, *How Repeal of the Individual Mandate and Expansion of Loosely Regulated Plans are Affecting 2019 Premiums* (Washington, D.C.: Kaiser Family Foundation, 2018).

114. Abby Goodnough, "Cheaper Plans and More Options as A.C.A. Stabilizes From Onslaught," *New York Times*, October 23, 2019, p. A17.

115. Kaiser Family Foundation, *Marketplace Enrollment, 2014–2019* (database) (www.kff.org/health-reform/state-indicator/marketplace-enrollment/).

116. Amy Lotven, "Healthcare.gov Enrollment Steady With 8.3M As Of Dec. 17," December 20, 2019 (https://insidehealthpolicy.com/daily-news/healthcaregov-enrollment-steady).

117. Kaiser Family Foundation, *Marketplace Enrollment.*

118. Thompson and others, "Trump and the Affordable Care Act," p. 418.

119. Heifi Wen, Brendan Saloner, and Janet R. Cummings, "Behavioral Health and Other Chronic Conditions among Adult Medicaid Enrollees: Implications for Work Requirements," *Health Affairs* 38, no. 4 (2019), pp. 660–67.

120. Leighton Ku and Erin Brantley, "Medicaid Work Requirements in Nine States Could Cause 600,000 to 800,000 Adults to Lose Medicaid Coverage," June 21, 2019 (www.commonwealthfund.org/blog/2019/Medicaid-work-requirement-could-cause).

121. Kaiser Family Foundation, *Total Monthly Medicaid and CHIP Enrollment* (database) (www.kff.org/health-reform/state-indicator/total-monthly-medicaid-and-chip).

122. In Montana, voters rejected a 2018 ballot measure that would have made its expansion permanent with financing to come from higher cigarette taxes. In 2019, state policymakers approved continuation of the expansion to be accompanied by a waiver request.

123. Edward R. Berchick, Emily Hood, and Jessica C. Barnett, *Health Insurance Coverage in the United States: 2017* (Washington, D.C.: U.S. Census Bureau, 2018), p. 1; Edward C. Berchick, Jessica C. Barnett, and Rachel D. Upton, *Health Insurance Coverage in the United States: 2018* (Washington, D.C.: U.S. Census Bureau, 2019), pp 1–2, 19.

124. *Key Facts about the Uninsured Population* (Washington, D.C.: Kaiser Family Foundation, 2018), pp. 1, 7.

125. Amy Goodnough and Margot Sanger-Katz, "After '16, a 400,000 Increase in Children Without Insurance," *New York Times,* October 23, 2019, p. A1.

126. Dan Witters, "U.S. Uninsured Rate Rises to Four-Year High," January 28, 2019 (https://new.gallup.com/poll/246135/uninsured-rate-rises-four-year-high.aspx). Gallup uses a "point-in-time" approach asking a sample whether they have health insurance currently.

Chapter 4

1. Leslie H. Gelb and Richard K. Betts, *The Irony of Vietnam: The System Worked* (Washington, D.C.: Brookings Institution Press, 1979), chapter 4; Jeffrey Race, *War Comes to Long An* (University of California Press, 1972).

2. Charles J. Finocchiaro, "Interbranch Relations and the Struggle for Power," *Extensions* (Winter 2019), pp. 2–3.

3. Katie Reilly, "President Trump Discusses Climate Change with Prince Charles and Blames Other Countries for Inaction, Despite U.S. Emissions Surge," *Time,* June 6, 2019 (https://time.com/5601169/donald-trump-prince-charles-climate-change/).

4. Philip A. Wallach and Nicholas W. Zeppos, "How Powerful Is the Congressional Review Act?" April 4, 2017 (brookings.edu/research/how-powerful-is-the-congressional-review-act/).

5. Ibid.

6. David M. Konisky and Neal D. Woods, "Environmental Federalism and the Trump Presidency: A Preliminary Assessment," *Publius: The Journal of Federalism* (April 20, 2018), pp. 351–52 (doi.org/10.1093/publius/pjy009).

7. Bethany A. Davis Noll and Richard L. Revesz, "Regulation in Transition," *University of Minnesota Law Review* 104, no. 1 (November 2019).

8. Geof Kass, "Energy Incentives May Be Back on the Table," *E&E News,* March 1, 2018 (www.eenews.net/stories/1060075115).

9. Prime examples include the Competitive Enterprise Institute and the Heartland Institute.

10. Keith B. Belton and John D. Graham, "Trump's Deregulatory Agenda: An Assessment at the Two-Year Mark" (American Council for Capital Formation, 2019), pp. 32–36.

11. Richard N. L. Andrews, "The Trump Agenda," in *Managing the En-*

vironment, Managing Ourselves: A History of American Environmental Policy,* revised edition (Yale University Press, 2020), chapter 17.

12. Kimberly A. Strassel, "A Back-to-Basics Agenda for the EPA," *Wall Street Journal* (February 18–19, 2017), p. A11.

13. Kevin Bogardus, "Faced with Budget Cuts, Pruitt Emphasizes States' Role," *E&E News,* April 3, 2017 (www.eenews.net/eedaily/2017/04/03/stor ies/1060052479).

14. On the governance risks of neglecting these relationships in an admin-istration, see Belton and Graham, "Trump's Deregulatory Agenda," p. 40; William G. Resh, *Rethinking the Administrative Presidency* (Johns Hopkins University Press, 2015).

15. Michael D. Shear, "Trump Will Withdraw U.S. from Paris Climate Agreement," *New York Times,* June 1, 2017.

16. Norma M. Riccucci, *Policy Drift: Shared Powers and the Making of U.S. Law and Policy* (New York University Press, 2018), p. 171.

17. Ibid.

18. Manjana Milkoreit, "The Paris Agreement on Climate Change—Made in USA?" *Perspectives in Politics* 17, no. 4 (December 2019), 1019–37 (doi. org/10.1017/S1537592719000951).

19. Jane Leggett, *Political Implications of U.S. Withdrawal from the Paris Agreement on Climate Change* (Washington, D.C.: Congressional Research Service, 2019).

20. Quoted in Konisky and Woods, "Environmental Federalism and the Trump Presidency," p. 345.

21. Timothy J. Conlan, "The Changing Politics of American Federalism," *State and Local Government Review* 49, no. 3 (September 2017), p. 177.

22. U.S. Climate Alliance, *Alliance States Take the Lead: 2017 Annual Report.*

23. Exceptions include Maryland Governor Larry Hogan, Massachusetts Governor Charles Baker, and Vermont Governor Phil Scott.

24. Philanthropist and former New York City mayor Michael Bloomberg founded America's Pledge in 2017, a group supporting and celebrating state climate policy development, and added former California governor Jerry Brown as cochair after he completed his final term in office in 2019. See *Ac-celerating America's Pledge* (Bloomberg Philanthropies, 2019).

25. Brad Plumer, "How Can U.S. States Fight Climate Change If Trump Quits the Paris Accord?" *New York Times,* September 25, 2017.

26. Annie Sneed, "Why Automakers Keep Beating Government Standards," *Scientific American,* December 1, 2016 (www.scientificamerican.com/article /why-automakers-keep-beating-government-standards/?utm_source=feed burner&utm_medium=feed&utm_campaign=Feed%3A+sciam%2Ftechnol ogy+%28Topic%3A+Technology%29).

27. Portions of this section draw heavily on Barry G. Rabe, "Leveraged Federalism and the Clean Air Act: The Case of Vehicle Emissions Control," in *Lessons from the Clean Air Act*, edited by Ann Carlson and Dallas Burtraw (Cambridge University Press, 2019), pp. 113–58.

28. Camille von Kaenel, "Calif., Pruitt Set for Collision over Vehicle Standards," *E&E News*, January 19, 2017.

29. Doug Obey and Lee Logan, "EPA's Reopening of Vehicle GHG Decision Opens Door for Industry Pitch," *Inside EPA/Climate*, March 15, 2017.

30. In water policy, for example, the EPA and the Army Corps of Engineers have been at loggerheads for decades to reconcile differences between respective guiding statutes as they have addressed the regulatory role of states and possible paths toward delegating permitting authority to them. *Final Report of the Assumable Water Subcommittee*, U.S. Environmental Protection Agency (May 2017).

31. Maxine Joselow, "EPA Wanted Its Logo Removed from Controversial Rollback," *E&E News*, August 16, 2018 (www.eenews.net/climatewire/stories/1060094235/).

32. Camille von Kaenel, "Pruitt Did It: Here's Why He's Loosening the Car Rules," *E&E News*, April 3, 2018 (www.eenews.net/stories/1060077987).

33. Maxine Joselow, "Carmakers Boost Fuel Economy Despite Rollback—EPA Report," *E&E News*, March 6, 2019 (www.eenews.net/greenwire/stories/1060123311).

34. Coral Davenport, "Automakers Tell Trump His Pollution Rules Could Mean 'Untenable' Instability and Lower Profits," *New York Times*, June 6, 2019.

35. Doug Obey, "Wheeler Draws Democrats' Fire on Vehicle GHG Preemption, GHG Claims," *Inside EPA/Climate* (April 9, 2019).

36. Lee Logan and Doug Obey, "EPA, California Engage in Sharp War of Words Over Vehicle GHG Rollback," *Inside EPA/Climate* (June 20, 2019).

37. Letter from Andrew R. Wheeler to the Honorable Cathy McMorris Rodgers and the Honorable John Shimkus. In discussing Nichols, Wheeler added that "her irresponsible testimony about conspiracy theories that 'the oil industry drove this action' and that it is being done by 'the former oil and coal industry lobbyists and lawyers who now work in leadership at the Agency' is beneath the responsibilities of the substantial position she holds."

38. Benjamin Storrow, "Wheeler Same as Pruitt on Car Rules—Calif. Official," *E&E News*, July 18, 2018 (www.eenews.net/climatewire/stories/1060089467/).

39. The original bandwagon states included Connecticut, Delaware, Maine, Maryland, Massachusetts, New Jersey, New York, Oregon, Pennsylvania, Rhode Island, Vermont, and Washington.

40. U.S. Climate Alliance, "U.S. Climate Alliance Governors Issue the 'Nation's Clean Car Promise,'" July 9, 2019.

41. Timothy Cana, "Trump Officials Defend Plan to Revoke Calif. Waiver," *E&E News*, September 19, 2019 (www.eenews.net/stories/1061139 351/).

42. *Central Valley Chrysler Jeep Inc. v. Goldstone; Green Mountain Chrysler Plymouth Dodge Jeep v. Crombie.* For further background on the statutory and legislative histories in these cases, see Greg Dotson, "State Authority to Regulate Mobile Source Greenhouse Gas Emissions, Part I: History and Current Challenge," *Environmental Law Reporter* 46 (2019), p. 11037; Dotson, "State Authority to Regulate Mobile Source Greenhouse Gas Emissions, Part 2: A Legislative and Statutory History Assessment," *Georgetown Environmental Law Review* (forthcoming).

43. Lee Logan and Doug Obey, "Targeting Venue, States Quickly Sue over California Auto GHG Preemption," *Inside EPA/Climate* (September 30, 2019).

44. Coral Davenport, "California Sues the Trump Administration in its Escalating War over Auto Emissions," *New York Times* (September 20, 2019).

45. Letter from Andrew R. Wheeler to Mary D. Nichols, September 24, 2019.

46. Coral Davenport, "A 'Chilling Message': Trump Critics See a Deeper Agenda in California Feud," *New York Times* (October 3, 2019).

47. Letter from Donald S. Welsh to Andrew R. Wheeler, September 26, 2019. ECOS concerns were shared by the National Association of Clean Air Agencies, which noted no awareness of any comparable letter ever sent by an EPA administrator to any state or local air quality official in the history of the CAA.

48. "California Has Treated the Auto Industry Very Poorly for Many Years, Harming Workers and Consumers. We are Fixing this Problem!" wrote Trump on October 30, via Twitter, October 30, 2019 (https://twitter.com/realdonaldtrump/status/1189592785311223815?lang=en).

49. Jennifer Hijazi, "Trump Gains Allies in His Fight with Calif.," *E&E News*, November 27, 2019 (www.eenews.net/stories/1061655673/).

50. Coral Davenport and Katie Rogers, "His White House Engulfed, Trump Keeps California in the Cross Hairs," *New York Times* (November 22, 2019).

51. Kirsten H. Engel, "EPA's Clean Power Plan: An Emerging New Cooperative Federalism?" *Publius: The Journal of Federalism* 45, no. 3 (June 4, 2015), pp. 452–74 (doi.org/10.1093/publius/pjv025).

52. Steven Levitsky and Daniel Ziblatt, *How Democracies Die* (New York: Crown, 2018), p. 164.

53. Bethany Davis Noll and Richard Revesz contend that use of court abeyance requests represents a major extension of administrative presidency approaches during the Trump presidency. Noll and Revesz, "Regulation in Transition," *University of Minnesota Law Review* 104, no. 1 (November 2019).

54. Quoted in Gilbert Metcalf, *Paying for Pollution* (Oxford University Press, 2019), p. 118.

55. Zack Colman and Robin Bravender, "Trump Stops Short of Killing Climate Rule. Here's His Pitch," *E&E News*, August 21, 2018 (www.eenews. net/climatewire/2018/08/21/stories/1060094803).

56. Lisa Friedman and Brad Plumer, "E.P.A. Announces Repeal of Major Obama-Era Carbon Emissions Rule," *New York Times* (October 9, 2017).

57. Lisa Friedman, "Trump Wants to Repeal Obama's Climate Plan," *New York Times,* September 28, 2017 (www.nytimes.com/2017/09/28/ climate/clean-power-plan.html).

58. Georgetown Climate Center, *Final Rule Raises State Concerns,* July 2, 2019.

59. As one environmental agency head of a state involved in litigation against the CPP noted in one off-record meeting of state officials in Washington, D.C., "We knew that Clean Power Plan compliance was not a big deal for us, especially given all of the wind power we are bringing on. But we had to oppose it for political reasons."

60. Maxine Joselow, "Lawyer Who Fought Clean Power Plan on 'Battle Royal'," *E&E News*, June 14, 2019 (www.eenews.net/greenwire/2019/06/14/ stories/1060580849).

61. Amelia Keyes, Kathleen F. Lambert, Dallas Burtraw, Jonathan J. Buonocore, Jonathan I. Levy, and Charles T. Driscoll, "The Affordable Clean Energy Rule and the Impact of Emissions Rebound on Carbon Dioxide and Criteria Air Pollutant Emissions," *Environmental Research Letters,* April 9, 2019 (doi.org/10.1088/1748-9326/aafe25).

62. Seth Feaster, "Record Drop in U.S. Coal-Fired Capacity Likely in 2018," *Institute for Energy Economics & Financial Analysis* (October 24, 2018).

63. Neil Craik, Isabel Studer, and Debora VanNijnatten, editors, *Climate Change Policy in North America: Designing Integration in a Regional System* (University of Toronto Press, 2013).

64. Barry G. Rabe, *Can We Price Carbon?* (MIT Press, 2018).

65. Pamela King, "Trump Sues Calif. over Cap-and-Trade Agreement," *E&E News,* October 23, 2019 (www.eenews.net/stories/1061356795).

66. Barry G. Rabe, "Shale Play Politics: The Intergovernmental Odyssey of American Shale Governance," *Environmental Science & Technology* 48, no. 15 (August 2014), pp. 8369–75 (doi.org/10.1021/es4051132).

67. Tony Addison, "Climate Change and the Extractives Sector," in *Extractive Industries* (Oxford University Press, 2018), pp. 460–82.

68. State Energy & Environmental Impact Center, *Climate & Health Showdown in the Courts* (2019).

69. Lee Logan, "Some Oil & Gas States Urge EPA to Limit Rollback of Methane Rule," *Inside EPA/Climate* (December 31, 2018).

70. Jenny Mandel and Niina H. Farrah, "EPA Chief Floats Change to Methane Oversight," *E&E News,* May 24, 2019 (www.eenews.net/stories /1060387889).

71. Barry G. Rabe, Isabel Englehart, and Claire Kaliban, "Taxing Flaring: The Politics of Extending State Severance Taxes to Methane," *Review of Policy Research* 37, no. 1, January 13, 2020 (doi.org/10.1111/ropr.12369).

72. Federal lands constitute a major amount of drilling territory in states like Alaska and New Mexico but very small amounts in states like North Dakota and Pennsylvania.

73. State Energy and Environmental Impact Center, *Climate and Health Showdown in the Courts,* pp. 30–32.

74. *State of California et al. v. U.S. Department of Interior et al.* See Dawn Reeves, "Court Scraps DOI Royalty Rule Repeal, Signaling Warning for EPA Rollbacks," *Inside EPA/Climate* (April 16, 2019).

75. Donald Jacobs, *BP Blowout: Inside the Gulf Oil Disaster* (Brookings Institution Press, 2016); Ted Mann, "Warnings on Oil-Drilling Rule Deleted," *Wall Street Journal,* February 27, 2020, p. A2.

76. Roger Karapin, *Political Opportunities for Climate Policy: California, New York, and the Federal Government* (Cambridge University Press, 2016), pp. 29, 207.

77. According to Bethany Davis Noll and Richard Revesz, "In contrast to recent administrations, the Trump administration revived many of the strategies that the Reagan administration had used: more aggressively using suspensions to delay rules that were already effective but still had compliance dates in the future, and using suspensions to delay rules for lengthy and sometimes indefinite periods of time." They note EPA use of this approach as well as other federal agencies, such as the Department of Energy, Department of Transportation, and Department of Interior. Noll and Revesz, "Regulation in Transition," *University of Minnesota Law Review* 104, no. 1 (November 2019), p. 37.

78. Dawn Reeves, "States, Environmentalists Urge EPA to Drop Landfill Methane Extension Plan," *Inside EPA/Climate* (January 7, 2019).

79. Ibid.

80. Dawn Reeves, "District Court Sets Tight Deadlines for EPA on Landfill Methane Standards," *Inside EPA/Climate* (May 7, 2019).

81. Keith Belton and John Graham have noted the Trump administration's poor showings compared to prior presidencies in tackling legal challenges to their regulatory interpretations with judges appointed by presidents of both parties. "An overarching legal vulnerability for Trump's deregulatory initiatives is insufficient attention to the construction of an administrative record with factual findings that can support deregulation. Weaknesses in the administrative record may be particularly serious in some of the deregulatory rulemakings related to energy and the environment. So far, themes of the

Trump administration's judicial setbacks have been (1) unlawful delay of effective dates, (2) failure to supply formal analyses required to support a deregulatory action, and (3) failure to consider the foregone benefits of a regulation." Belton and Graham, *Trump's Deregulatory Agenda,* pp. 27–29.

Chapter 5

1. *The Economist,* February 4, 2017.

2. Juliet Eilperin and Darla Cameron, "How Trump Is Rolling Back Obama's Legacy," *Washington Post,* January 20, 2018.

3. *Federal Register* 72, no. 16 (January 25, 2007), Notices: pp. 3432–40.

4. Ibid.

5. U.S. Department of Education, "Program Integrity: Gainful Employment," *Federal Register* 84, no. 126 (July 1, 2019), p. 31394.

6. Suzanne Mettler, *Degrees of Inequality* (New York: Basic Books, 2014), p. 95.

7. U.S. Department of Education, Office of Elementary and Secondary Education, "A State's Guide to the U.S. Department of Education's Assessment Peer Review Process, September 24, 2018 (www2.ed.gov/admins/lead/account/saa/assessmentpeerreview.pdf).

8. Ibid.

9. U.S. Department of Education, letter to chief state school officers signed by Education Secretary Betsy DeVos, February 10, 2017 (/www2.ed.gov/documents/press-releases/02102017-essa-letter.pdf).

10. Mettler, *Degrees of Inequality,* pp. 120–21.

11. Alyson Klein and Andrew Ujifusa, "Democrats Press Betsy DeVos on Privatization, ESSA, and LGBT Rights," *Education Week, Politics K–12* (blog), January 17, 2017 (http://blogs.edweek.org/edweek/campaign-k-12/2017/01/betsy_devos_senate_confirmation_hearing.html).

12. Albert Cheng, Michael B. Henderson, Paul E. Peterson, and Marty R. West, "Public Support Climbs for Teacher Pay, School Expenditures, Charter Schools, and Universal Vouchers," *Education Next* 19, no. 1 (Winter 2019).

13. *Federal Register,* "Proclamation 9571 of January 25, 2017—National School Choice Week, 2017" (www.federalregister.gov/documents/2017/01/30/2017-02092/national-school-choice-week-2017); *Federal Register,* "Proclamation 9692 of January 22, 2018—National School Choice Week, 2018" (www.federalregister.gov/documents/2018/01/25/2018-01620/national-school-choice-week-2018); *Federal Register,* "Proclamation 9837 of January 18, 2019—National School Choice Week, 2019" (www.federalregister.gov/documents/2019/01/25/2019-00220/national-school-choice-week-2019).

14. *Federal Register,* "Proclamation 9692 of January 22, 2018—National School Choice Week, 2018" (www.federalregister.gov/documents/2018/05/11/2018-10275/national-charter-schools-week-2018).

15. Government Accountability Office, *Private School Choice: Account-*

ability in State Tax Credit Scholarship Programs (Washington, D.C.: GAO-19-664, 2019).

16. Bayliss Fiddiman and Jessica Yin, *The Danger Private School Vouchers Pose to Civil Rights* (Washington, D.C.: Center for American Progress, 2019).

17. Associated Press, "Trump Administration to Renew School-Choice Push with $5 Billion Federal-Tax-Credits Proposal," February 28, 2019 (www.marketwatch.com/story/trump-administration-to-renew-school-choice-push-with-5-billion-federal-tax-credits-proposal-2019-02-28).

18. U.S. Department of Education, "Key Policy Letters Signed by the Education Secretary or Deputy Secretary," March 13, 2017 (www2.ed.gov/policy/elsec/guid/secletter/170313.html).

19. Ibid.

20. Erica Green, "After Demanding Local Control, DeVos Finds that It Limits Her Influence," *New York Times,* March 9, 2018 (www.nytimes.com/2018/03/09/us/politics/betsy-devos-education-reform-states.html).

21. U.S. Department of Education, letter to chief state school officers signed by Education Secretary Betsy DeVos.

22. Council for American Private Education, "Secretary DeVos Announces Equitable Services with State CAPE Leaders," *CAPE Outlook*, no. 4444, April 2019 (www.capenet.org/pdf/Outlook444.pdf).

23. U.S. Department of Education, "Key Policy Letters Signed by the Education Secretary or Deputy Secretary," March 11, 2019 (www2.ed.gov/policy/elsec/guid/secletter/190311.html).

24. Lauren Camera, "Supreme Court to Hear School Choice Case," *US News,* June 28, 2019 (www.usnews.com/news/education-news/articles/2019-06-28/supreme-court-to-hear-school-choice-case).

25. Mark Walsh, "Justice Department Backs Religious School Choice in Case of Maine Tuition Program," *Education Week, School Law* (blog), June 12, 2019 (blogs.edweek.org/edweek/school_law/2019/06/trump_administration_backs_rel.html).

26. *United States's Statement of Interest in Support of Plaintiffs' Motion for Summary Judgment filed in the United State District Court for the District of Maine,* case no. 1:18-cv-00327 DBH, p. 2.

27. Matt Bryne and Megan Gray, "Fight over State Funding for Religious Schools Heads to Federal Appeals Court," *Portland Press Herald,* June 27, 2019 (www.pressherald.com/2019/06/26/federal-judge-bars-state-funding-to-pay-for-religious-schools/).

28. See Erica L. Green, "Betsy DeVos Backs $5 Billion in Tax Credits for School Choice," *New York Times,* February 28, 2019 (www.nytimes.com/2019/02/28/us/politics/devos-tax-credit-school-choice.html); see also Clare Lombardo, "DeVos Announces Support for Proposed School Choice Tax Credit," *NPR,* February 28, 2019 (www.npr.org/2019/02/28/698686759/devos-announces-support-for-proposed-school-choice-tax-credit).

29. Betsy DeVos, Ted Cruz, and Bradley Bryne, "America's Students Deserve Freedom to Choose Their Education Options: DeVos, Cruz, Bryne," *USA Today,* February 28, 2019 (www.usatoday.com/story/opinion/2019/02/28/trump-school-choice-students-education-options-scholarships-tax-credits-column/3002868002/).

30. Dana Goldstein, "Obama Education Rules Are Undone by Congress," *New York Times,* March 10, 2017, p. A22.

31. Paul Peterson, Barry Rabe, and Kenneth Wong, *When Federalism Works* (Washington, D.C.: Brookings Institution Press, 1986).

32. U.S. Department of Education, "Secretary DeVos: Final 'Supplement, not Supplant' Guidance Helps Promote Effective Spending, Flexibility," USDOE Press Office, June 20, 2019.

33. Laura Jimenez and Antoinette Flores, *3 Ways DeVos has Put Students at Risk by Deregulating Education* (Washington, D.C.: Center for American Progress, 2019).

34. Michael Katz, "Letting Federal Data Drive State and Local Policy Under Secretary DeVos," *Urban Wire,* February 27, 2017.

35. Erica L. Green, "Education Dept. Says It Will Scale Back Civil Rights Investigations." *New York Times,* June 17, 2017, p. A19.

36. Benjamin Wermund, "DeVos Closes Civil Rights Complaints at Faster Clip than Predecessor," *Politico,* August 10, 2017 (www.politico.com/story/2017/08/10/devos-closes-civil-rights-complaints-at-faster-clip-than-prede cessors-241483).

37. U.S. Department of Education, "New Data Show Secretary DeVos' Reforms to the Office for Civil Rights are Driving Better Results for Students," USDOE Press Office, July 10, 2019 (www.ed.gov/news/press-releases/new-data -show-secretary-devos-reforms-office-civil-rights-are-driving-better-results -students).

38. Laura Meckler, "Betsy DeVos's Civil Rights Office Closes More Cases than Predecessor," *Washington Post,* July 10, 2019 (www.washingtonpost.com /local/education/betsy-devoss-civil-rights-office-closes-more-cases-than-prede cessor/2019/07/10/5710449e-a345-11e9-bd56-eac6bb02d01d_story.html).

39. Laura Meckler, "Trump Administration Revokes Effort to Reduce Racial Bias in School Discipline," *Washington Post,* December 21, 2018.

40. U.S. Department of Education, " 'Dear Colleague' letter."

41. Ibid.

42. Erica L. Green, "Chicago Public Schools Ordered to Toughen Sexual Misconduct Policies," *New York Times,* September 12, 2019, p. A24.

43. Resolution Agreement Chicago Public Schools District 299 OCR Complaint Nos. 05-15-1178 and 05-17-1062, September 11, 2019.

44. Ali Vitale, Peter Williams, and Mary Emily O'Hara, "White House Rolls Back Obama-Era Transgender Bathroom Protections," NBC News, February 22, 2017.

45. U.S. Department of Justice and U.S. Department of Education, "Dear Colleague Letter," February 22, 2017 (www2.ed.gov/about/offices/list/ocr/letters/colleague-201702-title-ix.pdf).

46. Jeremy W. Peters, Jo Becker, and Julie Hirschfeld Davis, "Trump Rescinds Rules on Bathrooms for Transgender Students," *New York Times,* February 22, 2017 (www.nytimes.com/2017/02/22/us/politics/devos-sessions -transgender-students-rights.html).

47. Sheryl Gay Stolberg, "Bathroom Case Puts Transgender Student on National Stage" *New York Times*, February 23, 2017 (www.nytimes.com /2017/02/23/us/gavin-grimm-transgender-rights-bathroom.html).

48. See Mark Walsh, "Federal Judge Issues Injunction for Gavin Grimm in Transgender Rights Case," *Education Week, School Law* (blog), August 11, 2019 (http://blogs.edweek.org/edweek/school_law/2019/08/federal_judge_issues _injunctio.html).

49. For example, see Iowa Department of Education, "Equality for Transgender Students," October 2017 (https://educateiowa.gov/resources/legal-re sources/legal-lessons/equality-transgender-students).

50. New Jersey School Boards Association, "NJSBA Issues New Guidance on Rights of Transgender Students," *School Board Notes*, October 2, 2018 (www.njsba.org/news-publications/school-board-notes/october-2-2018-vol -xlii-no-10/new-guidance-issued-by-njdoe-on-rights-of-transgender-stud ents/).

51. Colorado General Assembly, 72nd General Session, 2nd Regular Session, HB19-1039 co-sponsored by Daneyar Esgar and DominickMoreno, "Identity Documents for Transgender Persons," Colorado General Assembly, May 31, 2019.

52. See MJ Okma, "One Year After Trump Revoked Federal Non-Discrimination Guidance Protect Transgender Students, States Are Emboldened to Target Trans Youth," GLAAD, February 22, 2018 (www.glaad.org/blog/one-year-after-trump-revoked-federal-non-discrimination-guidance-pro tect-transgender-students).

53. Rewire.News, "Missouri Bill Requiring Gender-Divided Restrooms (HB 1755)," February 4, 2019 (https://rewire.news/legislative-tracker/law/missouri-bill-requiring-gender-divided-restrooms-hb-1755/).

54. The Supreme Court initially accepted but ultimately vacated Gavin Grimm's case over transgender access to bathrooms in a Virginia public high school.

55. Megan Trimble, "20 States, D.C. Back Transgender Student in Lawsuit over Bathroom Policy," *USNews*, March 1, 2019.

56. State of New York Attorney General Letitia James, *Brief for the States of New York, Washington, California, Connecticut, Delaware, Hawaii, Illinois, Iowa, Maine, Maryland, Massachusetts, Michigan, Minnesota, New Jersey, New Mexico, Oregon, Pennsylvania, Rhode Island, Vermont, and*

Virginia, and the District of Columbia, as Amici Curiae in support of Appellee, Drew Adams, Plaintiff-Appellee, v. The School Board of St. Johns Count, Florida, Defendant-Appellant. On Appeal from the United States District Court for the Middle District of Florida, United States Court of Appeals for the Fifth Circuit, February 28, 2019, Number 18-13592.

57. New York State Attorney General Press Office, "Attorney General James Leads Coalition of 21 Attorneys General in Filing Amicus Brief in Support of Transgender Student Discriminated Against by School New York State Attorney General," March 1, 2019.

58. Carolyn Phenicie, "Supreme Court Could Hear Arguments from Students Claiming that School Policies Protecting Transgender Rights Violate Their 'Bodily Privacy,' " *The 74*, March 19, 2019.

59. Pat Eaton-Robb, "Civil Rights Probe Opened into Transgender Athlete Policy," Associated Press, August 8, 2019 (https://apnews.com/f553f2367f9 64462aab8cabdae38622e?utm_source=newsletter&utm_medium=email &utm_campaign=cb_bureau_national).

60. Moriah Balingit, "DeVos Rescinds 72 Guidance Documents Outlining Rights for Disabled Students," *Washington Post*, October 21, 2017.

61. Ibid.

62. Ibid.

63. Abigail Abrams, "How Donald Trump Sparked a New Disability Rights Movement," *Time,* February 26, 2018.

64. See Ann Schimke, "Douglas County District Pays $1.3 Million to Settle Landmark Special Education Case *Endrew F. v. Douglas County School District*," *Chalkbeat,* June 20, 2018 (https://chalkbeat.org/posts/co/ 2018/06/20/douglas-county-district-pays-1-3-million-to-settle-landmark-special-education-case/).

65. See Lawrence R. Jones, "Autism and the Law, Part 1," *New Jersey Law Journal,* April 5, 2019 (www.law.com/njlawjournal/2019/04/05/autism-and-the-law-part-1-how-endrew-can-improve-future-educational-prospects/?slret urn=20200208184551).

66. See Edwin Rios, "A New Lawsuit Alleges Trump's Education Department Is Failing Students of Color with Disabilities," *Mother Jones,* July 12, 2018; Denise Marshall, "COPAA Victorious in Lawsuit Against Secretary DeVos, ED—Council of Parent Attorneys and Advocates," Maryland Council of Parent Attorneys and Advocates, March 7, 2019 (www.copaa .org/news/441156/COPAA-victorious-in-lawsuit-against-Secretary-DeVos -ED.htm).

67. U.S. Department of Education, *Individuals with Disabilities Education Act: Notice of Appeal in COPAA v. DeVos* (Washington, D.C., May 24, 2019).

68. John Fensterwald, "Gov. Newsom Proposes Tighter Rules on Charter School Enrollment," *EdSource,* March 23, 2019.

69. Manuel Buenrostro and Carlos Machado, "Uncharted Waters: Recommendations for Prioritizing Student Achievement and Effective Governance in California's Charter Schools" (California School Boards Association, 2018).

70. For example, see Holly Ramer, "Senate Considers Bill to Address Discrimination in Schools," Associated Press, March 4, 2019; and Holly Ramer, "NH House Advances School Anti-Discrimination Bill," Associated Press, May 8, 2019.

71. Rent seeking occurs when organizations pursue material gains from government at the expense of their competitors without contributing to the overall well-being of the sector. It entails attempts to influence government to extract more profits from their goods and services than they would otherwise obtain. See Mettler, *Degrees of Inequality*, p. 15.

72. Robin Howarth and Lisa Stifler, *The Failing of Online For-Profit Colleges: Findings from Student Borrower Focus Groups* (Washington, D.C.: Brookings Institution Press, 2019).

73. Joselynn Hawkins Fountain, "The Effect of the Gainful Employment Regulatory Uncertainty on Student Enrollment at For-Profit Institutions of Higher Education," *Research in Higher Education*, July 26, 2017.

74. See U.S. Department of Education Press Office, "Secretary DeVos Announces Regulatory Reset to Protect Students, Taxpayers, Higher Ed Institutions," June 14, 2017 (www.ed.gov/news/press-releases/secretary-devos-announces-regulatory-reset-protect-students-taxpayers-higher-ed-institutions).

75. Department of Education, "Program Integrity: Gainful Employment," pp. 31392–93, 31397.

76. Speaker of the House Nancy Pelosi Newsroom, "Pelosi's Statement on Trump Administration's Repeal of Gainful Employment Rule," U. S. Congress, June 29, 2019 (www.speaker.gov/newsroom/62819-4/).

77. Ashley A. Smith, "States Seeks Tighter Regulations of For-Profits," *Inside HigherEd,* March 14, 2019.

78. Andrew Kreighbaum, "States Put Stamp on Student Loan Oversight," *Inside HigherEd,* July 19, 2019 (www.insidehighered.com/news/2019/07/19/states-pass-flurry-bills-targeting-loan-servicers).

79. Education Secretary Betsy DeVos, "Memo to James W. Runcie, Chief Operating Officer, Federal Student Aid: Student Loan Servicer Recompete," U.S. Department of Education, April 11, 2017 (www2.ed.gov/documents/press-releases/student-loan-servicer-recompete.pdf).

80. Kreighbaum, "States Put Stamp on Student Loan Oversight."

81. Ben Barrett, "States Should and Can Hold Federal Student Loan Servicers Accountable," *New America, Education Policy* (blog), August 24, 2017 (www.newamerica.org/education-policy/edcentral/states-can-and-should-hold-federal-student-loan-servicers-accountable/).

82. Kreighbaum, "States Put Stamp on Student Loan Oversight."

83. Spiros Protopsaltis and Libby Masiuk, *Protecting Students and Taxpayers: Why the Trump Administration Should Heed History of Bipartisan Efforts* (Washington, D.C.: Center on Budget and Policy Priorities, December 1, 2017).

84. U.S. Department of Education Press Office, "Secretary DeVos Announces Regulatory Reset to Protect Students, Taxpayers, Higher Ed Institutions," June 14, 2017 (www.ed.gov/news/press-releases/secretary-devos-announces-regulatory-reset-protect-students-taxpayers-higher-ed-institutions).

85. Katie Lobosco, "Judge Unblocks Obama Rule on Student Debt Relief after Delays by DeVos," *CNN Politics,* October 16, 2018 (www.cnn.com/2018/10/16/politics/devos-borrower-defense-lawsuit/index.html).

86. Jackson Gode and Lily Gong, "Congress's Oversight Mandate Goes beyond Impeachment," *FixGov* (blog), Brookings Institution, November 22, 2019.

87. U.S. Department of Education, "Student Assistance General Provisions, Federal Family Education Loan Program, and William D. Ford Federal Direct Loan Program, Final Rule," *Federal Register* 8, no. 184 (September 23, 2019), p. 49788.

88. American Council on Education, "Education Department Releases Final Borrower Defense Rules," September 6, 2019 (www.acenet.edu/News-Room/Pages/Education-Department-Releases-Final-Borrower-Defense-Rules.aspx).

89. Erica L. Green, "DeVos Defends Limiting Debt Relief for Bilked Students," *New York Times,* December 13, 2019, p. A22.

90. Erica L. Green and Stacy Cowley, "Senate Rejects Devos Rule Restricting Debt Relief for Bilked Students," *New York Times,* March 11, 2020 (www.nytimes.com/2020/03/11/us/politics/student-debt-relief-senate-devos.html?action=click&module=News&pgtype=Homepage).

91. U.S. Department of Education, Office for Civil Rights, and U.S. Department of Justice, Civil Rights Division, "Dear Colleague Letter," signed by Assistant Secretary for Civil Rights and Acting Assistant Attorney General, July 3, 2018 (www2.ed.gov/about/offices/list/ocr/letters/colleague-title-vi-201807.pdf).

92. Harvard University, "Harvard Response to Departments of Education and Justice Letter," July 3, 2018 (https://admissionscase.harvard.edu/news/response-departments-education-and-justice-letter).

93. Lucas Daprile, "Despite Trump's Guidance on Using Race in Admissions, USC Plans to Keep Current Policy," *The State,* July 16, 2018 (www.thestate.com/news/local/education/article214759980.html).

94. Alan Perez, "Northwestern Says It Won't Make Changes to Admissions after Trump Administration Rescinds Obama-Era Guidance," *The Daily Northwestern,* July 8, 2018 (https://dailynorthwestern.com/2018/07/08/cam

pus/northwestern-says-it-wont-make-changes-to-admissions-after-trump-administration-rescinds-obama-era-guidance/).

95. U.S. Department of Justice, *United States Statement of Interest in Opposition to Defendant's Motion for Summary Judgement, in the United States District Court for the District of Massachusetts Boston Division, Students for Fair Admissions, Inc., Plaintiff, v. President and Fellows of Harvard College (Harvard Corporation), Defendant*, case 1:14-cv-14176-ADB, document 497, filed August 3, 2018.

96. Joan Biskupic, "Judge Hears Final Argument in Harvard Case that Could Decide Future of Affirmative Action," *CNN Politics*, February 13, 2019 (www.cnn.com/2019/02/13/politics/harvard-asian-americans-affirmative-action-hearing/index.html).

97. U.S. Department of Justice, Civil Rights Division, *Brief for the United States as Amicus Curiae Supporting Appellant and Urging Reversal, Students for Fair Admissions, Inc., Plaintiff-Appellant v. President and Fellows of Harvard College, Defendant-Appellee, on Appeal from the United States District Court for the District of Massachusetts*, case 19-2005, document: 00117556565, February 25, 2020.

98. R. Shep Melnick, *The Transformation of Title IX: Regulating Gender Equality in Education* (Washington, D.C.: Brookings Institution Press, 2018), p. 222.

99. Melnick, *The Transformation of Title IX*, chapter 11.

100. U.S. Department of Education, "Department of Education Issues New Interim Guidance on Campus Sexual Misconduct," USDOE Press Office, September 22, 2017.

101. Stephanie Saul and Kate Taylor, "Betsy DeVos Reverses Obama-Era Policy on Campus Sexual Assault Investigations," *New York Times*, September 22, 2017 (https://www.nytimes.com/2017/09/22/us/devos-colleges-sex-assault.html).

102. U.S. Department of Education, Office for Civil Rights, "Dear Colleague Letter," signed by Acting Assistant Secretary for Civil Rights Candice Jackson, September 22, 2017 (www.cmu.edu/title-ix/colleague-title-ix-201709 pdf).

103. Ibid.

104. Ibid.

105. *SURVJUSTICE, Inc., v. Betsy DeVos Complaint for Injunctive Relief—Demand for Jury Trial, United States District Court Northern District of California San Francisco Division*, case 3:18-cv-00535, document 1, filed January 25, 2018 (www.documentcloud.org/documents/4359855-SurvJustice-v-Devos.html).

106. Andrew Kreighbaum, "Title IX a Sticking Point in Talks Over Higher Ed Law," *Inside HigherEd*, August 6, 2019 (www.devoss-plan-to-overhaul-rules-on-sexual-assault-probes/2019/01/30/).

107. Melnick, *The Transformation of Title IX,* p. 21.

108. Erica L. Green, "Sex Assault Rules under DeVos Bolster Defendants' Rights and Ease College Liability," *New York Times,* November 16, 2018 (www.nytimes.com/2018/11/16/us/politics/betsy-devos-title-ix.html).

109. Anna North, "Students Trusted Her with Sexual Assault Complaints. Then She Lost Her Job," *Chronicle of Higher Education,* June 28, 2018.

110. See Laura Meckler, "Betsy DeVos Poised to Issue Sweeping Rules Governing Campus Sexual Assault," *Washington Post,* November 25, 2019 (www.washingtonpost.com/local/education/betsy-devos-poised-to-issue). See also Juan Perez Jr. and Bianca Quilantan, "How the New Devos Rules on Sexual Assault Will Shock Schools—And Students," *Politico*, March 6, 2020 (www.politico.com/news/2020/03/06/betsy-devos-school-sexual-assault-rules-122401).

111. University of California Berkeley, Communications and Public Affairs, "Campus, UC Respond to Trump Administration's Title IX Changes," September 7, 2017.

112. Ibid.

113. Valerie Strauss, "Betsy DeVos Gets Bad Reviews from Employees as Morale at Education Department Plummets, Survey Finds," *Washington Post*, December 12, 2018.

Chapter 6

1. Ann Carlson and Dallas Burtraw, editors, *Lessons from the Clean Air Act* (Oxford University Press, 2019).

2. Richard N. L. Andrews, *Managing the Environment, Managing Ourselves: A History of American Environmental Policy,* 3rd edition (Yale University Press, 2020).

3. Lou Cannon, *President Reagan: The Role of a Lifetime* (New York: Public Affairs, 2000), pp. 467–71.

4. Barry G. Rabe, "Environmental Policy and the Bush Era: The Collision between the Administrative Presidency and State Experimentation," *Publius: The Journal of Federalism* 37, no. 3 (Summer 2007), pp. 413–32.

5. See Daniel J. Hopkins, *The Increasingly United States* (University of Chicago Press, 2018). Two developments undergird the "nationalization" of politics. First, "voters use the same criteria to choose candidates across the federal system." Second, "voters are engaged with and knowledgeable about national politics to the exclusion of state and local politics" (p. 3).

6. Charles O. Jones, *Clean Air: The Policies and Politics of Pollution Control* (University of Pittsburgh Press, 1975); David Vogel, *California Greenin': How the Golden State Became an Environmental Leader* (Princeton University Press, 2018).

7. Barry G. Rabe, *Statehouse and Greenhouse: The Emerging Politics of*

American Climate Change Policy (Washington, D.C.: Brookings Institution Press, 2004), chapter 4.

8. Coral Davenport, "A 'Chilling Message': Trump Critics See a Deeper Agenda in California Feud," *New York Times,* October 3, 2019.

9. For instance, David Lewis, *The Power of Presidential Appointments* (Princeton University Press, 2008).

10. We defined "environment" broadly to include not just activities of the EPA but also efforts to promote energy development that could impose environmental risks. Our categorization also included environmental orders not directly linked to climate, including water policy.

11. Executive Order 13828, *Federal Register* 83, no. 72 (April 10, 2018), p. 15941.

12. Executive Order 13791, *Federal Register* 82, no. 82 (May 1, 2017).

13. U.S. Department of Education, *Regulatory Task Force Status Report,* October 2017.

14. Ibid., December 2018.

15. Ibid.

16. For example, B. Dan Wood and Richard W. Waterman, "The Dynamics of Political Control of the Bureaucracy," *American Political Science Review* 85, no. 3 (1991), pp. 801–28.

17. Jerry L. Mashaw and David Berke, "Presidential Administration in a Regime of Separated Powers: An Analysis of Recent American Experience," *Yale Journal on Regulation* 39 (2018), p. 611.

18. Ibid., p. 612.

19. *Motor Vehicle Manufacturers Association v. State Farm Mutual Auto Insurance Company* 463 U.S. 29 (1983); see also, Lisa Marshall Manheim and Kathryn A. Watts, "Reviewing Presidential Orders," *University of Chicago Law Review* 86, no. 7 (2019), pp. 1743–824.

20. See, for instance, R. Shep Melnick, *The Transformation of Title IX: Regulating Gender Equality in Education* (Washington, D.C.: Brookings Institution Press, 2018).

21. Keith B. Belton and John D. Graham, *Trump's Deregulatory Record: An Assessment at the Two-Year Mark* (Washington, D.C.: American Council for Capital Formation, 2019), pp. 21–22.

22. Government Accountability Office, *Medicaid Demonstrations: Approvals of Major Changes Need Increased Transparency* (Washington, D.C.: GAO-19-315, 2019), p. 1.

23. Frank J. Thompson, *Medicaid Politic: Federalism, Policy Durability, and Health Reform* (Georgetown University Press, 2012), pp. 135–36, 163; Government Accountability Office, *Medicaid Demonstrations: Evaluations Yielded Limited Results, Underscoring Need for Changes to Federal Policies and Procedures* (Washington, D.C.: GAO-18-220, 2018).

24. David J. Barron and Todd D. Rakoff, "In Defense of Big Waiver," *Columbia Law Review* 113, no. 2 (2013), pp. 332, 340.

25. Ann Carlson, "Iterative Federalism and Climate Change," *Northwestern University Law Review* 103, no. 3 (2019), pp. 1097–161.

26. Belton and Graham, *Trump's Deregulatory Record*, p. 28.

27. Robert R. Kaufman and Stephan Haggard, "Democratic Decline in the United States: What Can We Learn from Middle-Income Backsliding?" *Perspectives on Politics* 17, no. 2 (2019), p. 426.

28. Lee Epstein, William M. Landis, and Richard A. Posner, *The Behavior of Federal Judges* (Harvard University Press, 2013), p. 2.

29. Daphna Renan, "The Law Presidents Make," *Virginia Law Review* 103 (2017), pp. 805–904.

30. James Cannon, *Gerald R. Ford: An Honorable Life* (University of Michigan Press, 2013), chapter 18.

31. Maggie Haberman and Robert Pear, "Fiery Meeting Swayed Trump in Health Fight," *New York Times*, March 28, 2019, p. A1.

32. Paul E. Pierson, "The Rise of Activist Government," in *The Transformation of American Politics*, edited by Paul Pierson and Theda Skocpol (Princeton University Press, 2007), p. 33.

33. Paul Starr, *Remedy and Reaction* (Yale University Press, 2013), p. 297.

34. America's Pledge Initiative on Climate Change, *Accelerating America's Pledge: Going All-In to Build a Prosperous, Low-Carbon Economy for the United States* (New York: Bloomberg Philanthropies, 2019).

35. These included the Permian Basin in Texas and New Mexico and the Bakken Basin in North Dakota and Montana, both of which reported enormous increases in methane flaring in 2018 and 2019.

36. Dawn Reeves, "Experts Spar Over Whether ACE Litigation Will Resolve EPA GHG Authority," *Inside EPA/Climate* (June 28, 2019).

37. Barry G. Rabe, *Can We Price Carbon?* (MIT Press, 2018).

38. John Kincaid, "The Trump Interlude and the States of American Federalism," *State and Local Government Review* 49, no. 3 (September 2017), p. 165.

39. Richard P. Nathan, *The Administrative Presidency* (New York: Macmillan 1983), p. 93.

40. Elena Kagan, "Presidential Administration," *Harvard Law Review* 114 (2001), pp. 2252, 2331–32.

41. Ibid., pp. 2349–50,

42. Ibid., pp. 2363, 2382.

43. Peter M. Shane, *Madison's Nightmare: How Executive Power Threatens American Democracy* (University of Chicago Press, 2009), pp. 158–61.

44. Mashaw and Berke, "Presidential Administration," pp. 579, 611–12.

45. Shane, *Madison's Nightma*re, pp. 160–61; see also Martin Gilens

and Benjamin I. Page, "Testing Theories of American Politics: Elites, Interest Groups, and Average Citizens," *Perspectives on Politics* 12, no. 3 (2014), pp. 564–81.

46. Robert C. Lieberman, Suzanne Mettler, Thomas P. Pepinsky, Kenneth M. Roberts, and Richard Valelly, "The Trump Presidency and American Democracy: A Historical and Comparative Analysis," *Perspectives on Politics* 17, no. 2 (2019), p. 470.

47. Steven Levitsky and Daniel Ziblatt, *How Democracies Die* (New York: Crown Publishing Group, 2018); they define forbearance as "avoiding actions that, while respecting the letter of the law, obviously violate its spirit" (p. 106). See also Shane, *Madison's Nightmare*.

48. Kaufman and Haggard, "Democratic Decline in the United States," p. 417.

49. Epstein and others, *The Behavior of Federal Judges*, p. 3.

50. Ibid. See also Neal Devins and Lawrence Baum, *The Company They Keep* (Oxford University Press, 2019). Partisan proclivities may arise not only from the policy preferences of judges but their methods of legal interpretation, such as originalism and textualism in the case of conservative judges.

51. Devins and Baum, *The Company They Keep.*

52. Belton and Graham, *Trump's Deregulatory Record*, p. 28.

53. Dawn Reeves, "EPA Failure on Standing Claim in Landfill Suite Boosts Massachusetts' Role," *Inside EPA/Climate* (May 10, 2019).

54. Harvard Law School Legal Services Center organizes the project on predatory student lending, where Harvard law students and clinical faculty engage in partnership with community-based organizations to support and monitor litigation activities. See Harvard Law School Legal Services Center, "Court Ruling Clears the Way for 2016 Borrower Defense Rule to Take Effect," press release, October 16, 2018 (https://predatorystudentlending.org/new/press-releases/court-clears-way-borrower-defense).

55. U.S. Department of Education, "Federal Preemption and State Regulation of the Department of Education's Federal Student Loan Programs and Federal Student Loan Services—Interpretation," *Federal Register* 83, no. 48 (March 12, 2018), pp. 10619–22.

56. United States Court of Appeals for the Seventh Circuit, *Nicole D. Nelson v. Great Lakes Educational Loan Services, Inc., et al.,* no. 18-1531, June 27, 2019.

57. Ben Merriman, *Conservative Innovators: How States Are Challenging Federal Power* (University of Chicago Press, 2019).

58. Timothy Puko, "Suit Contests Eased Climate Rules," *Wall Street Journal*, August 14, 2019.

59. Pamela King, "Blue States Urge Court to Take Down Trump Carbon Rule," *E&E News,* August 13, 2019.

60. Lee Logan and Doug Obey, "Targeting Venue, States Quickly Sue Over California Auto GHG Preemption," *Inside EPA/Climate,* September 20, 2019.

61. Ibid., p. 5.

62. Paul Nolette, *Federalism on Trial* (University Press of Kansas, 2015), pp. 205–06.

63. Moreover, some evidence raises doubts that state policy processes are responsive to public opinion. See, for instance, Jeffrey R. Lax and Justin H. Phillips, "The Democratic Deficit in the States," *American Journal of Political Science* 56, no. 1 (2011), pp. 148–66.

64. Jessica Bulman-Pozen and Gillian E. Metzger, "The President and the States: Patterns of Contestation and Collaboration under Obama," *Publius: The Journal of Federalism* 46, no. 3 (2016), p. 328.

65. See, especially, Gary J. Miller and Andrew B. Whitford, *Above Politics* (Cambridge University Press, 2016).

Index

www.ingramcontent.com/pod-product-compliance
Lightning Source LLC
Chambersburg PA
CBHW031126270326
41929CB00011B/1508